harper ✦ torchbooks

† The New American Nation Series, edited by Henry Steele Commager and Richard B. Morris.
‡ American Perspectives series, edited by Bernard Wishy and William E. Leuchtenburg.
* The Rise of Modern Europe series, edited by William L. Langer.
** History of Europe series, edited by J. H. Plumb.
¶ Researches in the Social, Cultural, and Behavioral Sciences, edited
§ The Library of Religion and Culture, edited by Benjamin Nelson.
Σ Harper Modern Science Series, edited by James R. Newman.
° Not for sale in Canada.
△ Not for sale in the U. K.

History: Ancient

History: Medieval

History: Renaissance & Reformation

History: Modern European

HEBREW ORIGINS

THEOPHILE JAMES MEEK

HARPER TORCHBOOKS / The Cloister Library

HARPER & ROW, PUBLISHERS

New York, Evanston, and London

EDWARD MINER GALLAUDET MEMORIAL LIBRARY
GALLAUDET COLLEGE
WASHINGTON, D. C.

To My Wife

60-3551

HEBREW ORIGINS

Copyright © *1936, 1950, 1960 by Harper & Row, Publishers, Incorporated*
Printed in the United States of America
All rights in this book are reserved.
No part of the book may be used or reproduced
in any manner whatsoever without written per-
mission except in the case of brief quotations
embodied in critical articles and reviews. For
information address:
Harper & Row, Publishers, Incorporated,
49 East 33rd Street, New York 16, N. Y.

This book was first published in 1936.
A revised edition appeared in 1950.

First HARPER TORCHBOOK edition published 1960

933
M49h
1960

direct 1.96

CONTENTS

108348

PREFACE TO
THE TORCHBOOK EDITION

I HAVE taken the opportunity provided by this book's reappearance in the Torchbook series to make certain corrections in the text and some changes. The latter have to do largely with the chronology of Egypt, where I have followed that of the acknowledged authority in the field, Richard A. Parker, in his privately distributed typescript of April, 1955.

Scholars have been so busy in recent years with the Dead Sea Scrolls that comparatively little has been written in the field covered by my book, and nothing has appeared to cause me to alter my views in any significant respect. I still feel that my interpretation of the biblical and archaeological data best presents the course of history as it evolved. Some of my reviewers have accused me of separating the Joseph tribes entirely from any sojourn in Egypt, but that is not at all the case. It is true that I do not find them in Egypt during the time of Moses, but rather during the Hyksos period, and all the evidence, as I indicate on pages 17 f., would seem to support that view. It was manifestly with the Hyksos that the Jacob-Joseph tribes (personified as patriarchs) went to Egypt, and it was with them that they left Egypt, when the Hyksos were overthrown and driven out of the country *ca.* 1560 B.C. The only certain evidence that we have for the existence of Hebrews in Egypt in the later period is the occurrence of Egyptian personal names with the Levites, indicating that they at least must have lived for some time in Egypt, and the evidence indicates that they were there in the time of Moses, as I show on pages 31-33.

Since my book was published in 1950 the site of Jericho has undergone another series of excavations, this time by Kathleen M. Kenyon, and after a very thorough exploration of the ground over several years she has come to the conclusion that no exact date can be established for the capture of Jericho by Joshua, but what evidence there is points to a date in the third quarter of the fourteenth century B.C.; see her *Digging Up Jericho* (1957), Chapter Eleven. Later than that there seems to have been little at Jericho for Joshua to conquer, at most a small, insignificant fort. The excavations show that Canaanite Jericho was captured and destroyed *ca.* 1550 B.C. (apparently by the Egyptians in driving out the Hyksos), and there is little evidence of occupation after that time. It may be that the Biblical writer in his description of Joshua's conquest unconsciously confused it with that of 1550. The recent excavations at Shechem and Hazor are equally unrewarding so far as an exact date for the Israelite conquest is concerned, but such evidence as there is again points to the end of the fourteenth century. I would accordingly lower my date for Joshua to *ca.* 1350 B.C. or slightly later, a hundred years or so before Moses. I still feel very strongly that Joshua must antedate Moses, because all the evidence for the date of Moses indicates, as definitely as circumstantial evidence can, that he lived *ca.* 1200 B.C. at the earliest (see pages 33 ff.; 43 f.); and Joshua was assuredly later than that. I also believe that the evidence indicates quite conclusively that Joshua was a tribal hero of Ephraim until he was magnified into the leader of all the Hebrews, both north and south; that is likewise the view of the two outstanding German historians, Albrecht Alt

and Martin Noth. I deal more fully with Joshua in my commentary on the Book of Joshua, to appear presently in the
annotated edition of *The Bible: An American Translation*.

We still have the Habiru-question with us, and two very
thorough treatments of the subject have appeared recently:
Moshe Greenberg, *The Hab/Piru* (1955), and Jean Bottéro,
*Le problème des Habiru à la 4ᵉ Rencontre Assyriologique
Internationale* (1954). Some additional occurrences of the
word are also to be found in Elena Cassin, "Nouveaux Documents sur les Habiru," *Journal Asiatique*, 1958, pp. 225-36.
These publications bring the references to the Habiru completely up to date, and there are scores of them. It is clear
from the records that the word *habiru*, or perhaps more
correctly *'apiru*, began as an appelative, but it is not so clear
what its meaning was, nor is it clear how the word eventually became a gentilic and came to be applied to the
people that we know as Hebrews. Despite the arguments of Greenberg to the contrary I still believe that
Joshua's followers and the Habiru had some vital connection with each other. It is a striking fact that amid all the
details in Josh. 1–12 about the conquest of the various regions of Canaan there is not a single word about the conquest
of the central highlands. And yet according to Josh. 10:7,
9, 15, 32; 19:1; 22:12; 24:1, the Hebrews kept passing at will
back and forth through the region, and this can only mean
that the people in possession of the highlands were friendly,
undoubtedly because they were of kindred stock, and
there is every reason to believe that they were the Habiru
people, who overran the region in the Tell el-Amarna period.
Hence it would not seem too bold to assert that the movement of the Hebrews under Joshua into the highlands of
Ephraim is to be connected with the Habiru movement into
the same region. The story as reflected in the Amarna letters

marks the beginning of the movement early in the fourteenth century, while the story in the Book of Joshua has to do largely with its final accomplishment toward the end of the century. This is also suggested by the fact that the recent excavations at Shechem show a surprising continuity into the period of the Hebrew occupation, with no evidence of violent destruction, as we have for the earlier period.

On page 52, I wrote in 1950 that the Eshnunna Code (now exhaustively treated by A. Goetze, *Annual of the American Schools of Oriental Research*, XXXI, 1956) was the oldest known to us at that time, but two years later a copy of a code promulgated by Ur-Nammu, the founder of the Third Dynasty of Ur (*ca.* 2070 B.C.), was discovered by Samuel N. Kramer and published by him in *Orientalia*, New Series, Vol. 23, pp. 40 ff.; see also his popular treatment in *From the Tablets of Sumer* (1956), pp. 47 ff. Unfortunately only a fragment of the code is preserved—a considerable part of the prologue, but only a few of the laws. A striking feature of the code is Ur-Nammu's concern for the poor, the father-less, and the widow, and the fact that the penalty for wrong-doing is a fine rather than physical retaliation. The code is written in Sumerian, the language of Ur at that time.

Some of my reviewers have contended that the Song to Deborah in Judg. 5 shows that Yahwism was the religion of the north from very early times, but does it? I think I have shown on page 144 that this is not the case at all. According to verses 4 and 5 Yahweh was not native to Israel but had to come on a long journey from his home in the south and on a special occasion to help his devotees in the north. This is made even more certain if we accept Albright's contention in *Bulletin of the American Schools of Oriental Research*, No. 62, p. 30, that the phrase "that is, Sinai" in verse 5 should be translated "the One of Sinai," meaning "the God of Sinai," and I locate Sinai on the western border of the land of Midian, just east of the Gulf of Aqabah (see pp. 36 f.). To be the god of a land the god had to reside in the land, and it is quite clear that Yahweh was not resident in the north in the time of Deborah. He was definitely a southern god, only just beginning to make his presence felt in the north, and the poem was written, among other things, to advance his cause in the north.

In the second edition of my book I was able to cite *Ancient Near Eastern Texts* (1950) for translations of ancient documents. This has now appeared in a second edition (1955), and more recently still in an abridged edition, *The Ancient Near East* (1958). Another work along the same line is *Documents from Old Testament Times* (1958), edited by D. Winton Thomas. It should also be noted that Jack Finegan, *Light from the Ancient Past*, has just been published in a second edition, and another recent book in the same field is G. Ernest Wright, *Biblical Archaeology* (1957). To note 71 on page 141 add now my commentary on the Song of Songs in *The Interpreter's Bible*, Vol. 5 (1956). For a striking parallel to the Song of Songs as I interpret it, see S. N. Kramer, *From the Tablets of Sumer* (1956), pp. 249 ff.

THEOPHILE J. MEEK

January 1, 1960

PREFACE TO THE SECOND EDITION

THE first edition of this book was exhausted some years ago and the continued demand has induced the publishers to issue a second edition. Since the original plates were melted down for bullets during the recent war, it was thought best to rewrite the whole volume, with the result that most of it is now entirely new, particularly Chapter I, where a more certain chronology of the ancient Near East has given us a more accurate perspective. The very recent discovery of new law codes has considerably altered Chapter II and new developments in other fields have necessitated many changes in the other chapters as well. Due attention has also been given to the many reviews of the first edition and the literature has been brought completely up to date. Hence the volume can no longer bear the subtitle, *The Haskell Lectures for 1933-34*, although it has grown out of those lectures.

In the Preface to the first edition I seemed to speak rather disparagingly of the documentary hypothesis of the Hexateuch, but I did not mean to repudiate the theory entirely. However, I have always felt that the hypothesis, as usually understood, is too artificial, and after an exhaustive study of all the ancient literatures of the world H. M. and N. K. Chadwick have come to the same conclusion in their extensive work, *The Growth of Literature* (2 vols., 1936). As I state several times in this edition, as likewise in the earlier one, I believe that there was a stock of southern traditions and a treatment of tradition from the southern point of view, and this cycle of traditions may well be called J, but I am not sure that it was ever a formally written document or anything more than a collection of traditions. Similarly, I believe that there was a specifically northern, or E, cycle of traditions, which is retained only in small part as it came eventually to be absorbed into J to make the document JE. So complete was this fusion that I have always regarded it as impossible, except in a few instances, to separate E from J, and I am not at all sympathetic with such analyses as that of the *Polychrome Bible* or the recent work of C. A. Simpson, *The Early Traditions of Israel* (1948). I feel that the Swedish school, despite their manifest extremes, have made some contributions to the solution of the problem, and my own theory I would label the stratum hypothesis, rather than the documentary. In short, it agrees almost exactly with that expressed by Aage Bentzen in his *Introduction to the Old Testament*, II (1949), 9-80.

I have discussed a number of the problems in the book with my colleagues, particularly Professor Ronald J. Williams, who also read the first draft of Chapter I. I am again indebted to my wife for assisting me in the preparation of the indexes and the correction of the proof, and likewise to Professor Williams.

THEOPHILE J. MEEK

University of Toronto
April 15, 1950

PREFACE TO THE FIRST EDITION

EVER since the publication of an article on the origin and history of the Hebrew Sabbath in the *Journal of Biblical Literature* some twenty-two years ago I have been intensely interested in Hebrew Origins, and when the invitation came to deliver the Haskell Lectures at Oberlin College for the year 1933-34, I welcomed it as an opportunity to gather together my ideas on the subject and present them to a critical public. The material, as conditioned by its presentation to a lay audience, is semipopular in character, but at the same time it is sufficiently technical and original, I trust, to interest the specialist as well. In Lectures I and III, I have changed my views slightly from their original form and somewhat expanded them, but the rest of the material remains much as it was delivered.

The book is fully documented with references, as I feel all books should be. The translations of ancient documents, which appear rather frequently in the text, are my own and in each case I have had particularly in mind the accurate reproduction of the original. The Old Testament quotations agree in the main with my translations in *The Bible: An American Translation* (revised edition of 1935), except that I have substituted "Yahweh" for the less correct but more popular "Lord." Every statement of importance is supported by documentary authority and to follow the argument of the book it is important that these be consulted. For the Old Testament citations the reader unacquainted with Hebrew is referred to the revised translation noted above because of its greater accuracy of text and translation. All the Old Testament references are given in accordance with the English numbering of chapters and verses rather than the Hebrew. In the transliteration of certain Hebrew letters I am not altogether consistent; for example, I transliterate *nephesh* on page 81, whereas on page 49 I give the root of *mishpāṭîm* as *shāpaṭ* rather than *shāphaṭ*, so that the lay reader may not query the additional *h*; and on page 7 I transliterate *ʿabir* rather than *ʿabbir* to indicate the philological identity with *ḫabiru*.

In these later days of Old Testament research the older documentary hypothesis is being seriously questioned. I occasionally use the documentary symbols, J, E, D, and P, but in no instance have I used an argument that is dependent upon the documentary hypothesis. I am not committed to any particular point of view, but in these Lectures I have attempted with completely open mind to ascertain the facts of Hebrew origins in so far as these may be revealed in the Hebrew documents themselves and in the excavations. Any light wherever found has been welcomed, and archaeology, the history of religions, the ancient records of the whole Near East, and many another field have been combed for what they might have to offer. Some readers may think that I have not been positive enough in my statements, but where the evidence is not conclusive, it is assuredly fairer to be candid. And after all, no amount of dogmatizing can make certainty out of what is merely possible, or at best only probable.

In this, as in all my publications, I am greatly indebted to my wife for reading both manuscript and proof, always a most tedious and thankless task. To the faculty of the Graduate School of Theology, Oberlin College, I am under special obligation for the honor that they did me and the delightful hospitality that they showed me on the occasion of my visit.

THEOPHILE J. MEEK

University of Toronto
February 1, 1936

CHAPTER ONE

The Origin of the Hebrew People

THE origin of the Hebrew people, as it came to be told traditionally, was a simple one. The first Hebrew was Abram (also called Abraham), who migrated from Ur of the Chaldees to Harran, and from there by command of God to the promised land of Canaan. After a brief sojourn in Egypt he and his family settled at Hebron in southern Canaan and lived there on friendly terms with the natives. There the family grew and prospered, remaining aloof from the resident population and marrying only among themselves or with their kinsmen in Harran. In the days of Jacob, however, there came a famine in the land, and learning of the high estate to which his son Joseph had risen in Egypt,[1] whither he had been sold by his jealous brothers and where now food was to be had, Jacob was moved to migrate thither with all his family. Here the newcomers were made so welcome and found conditions so propitious that they grew to be a considerable people. Presently, however, "a new king rose over Egypt who had no knowledge of Joseph" (Ex. 1:8), so that the Hebrews were compelled to do forced labor for the Egyptians and were reduced to virtual servitude, until a

---

[1] We have knowledge of three other Hebrews who rose to positions of great power in the ancient Near East; see J. Lewy, *Hebrew Union College Annual*, XIV (1939), 618 f., and notes 25 and 26 below.

deliverer arose in the person of Moses, who was commissioned
by God to lead his people back to the Promised Land. On
the way God gave the people through Moses at Sinai the
laws that were to guide them in their future state. Moses,
however, was not permitted to lead the people into Canaan
himself, but died in Moab, so that the actual conquest was
under the leadership of Joshua. That conquest was immediate
and complete. The Canaanites were exterminated and the
land was divided by lot among the several tribes. The people
now had a land of their own and in due time they demanded
and received a king in the person of Saul. Out of small
beginnings under the guidance of God a new nation was
born, a unique nation, the chosen of God to make him known
to the world.

But this account is true neither to the biblical records nor
the extra-biblical. It is fancy, not fact; it is a beautiful epic
that was told with enthralling interest, but it is not sober
history. In a sense, however, it is history, history idealized
and personified. It is tradition, but in tradition there is always
much of history. As T. Eric Peet has well said, "Tradition is
often incorrect in detail, its chronology is generally poor, it
telescopes and duplicates, and its geography is rarely consistent. But in most cases, in which archaeology has permitted
a test, the central facts of tradition are found to contain some
kernel of truth."[2] I would say "a considerable kernel of
truth." All of biblical tradition cannot be accepted as fact,
but facts do lie behind and within the biblical records, and
it is the task of the historian to discover these facts and give
them their true setting. And that is no easy task, and larger
knowledge does not always help that task, but complicates
it and makes it more difficult, because the more we know the
less we know we know; or, to put it in another way, the more
we know the more we know there is to know. And so it is

[2] *Egypt and the Old Testament* (1923), p. 64.

with Hebrew origins. The passing years have brought us larger knowledge, but as old problems were solved new problems were uncovered, so that even yet we cannot speak with certainty on the question. However, we do know more than we used to, and the picture, once faint, is rapidly becoming clearer and more distinct.

The period around 1750 B.C. was a most unsettled one in the Near East, with a multitude of little states in continual conflict with one another and frequently changing status. How unsettled it was is shown by the letters excavated at Mari, one of which, addressed to the king of Mari, reads as follows: "There is no king who is powerful on his own. Ten to fifteen kings follow Hammurabi, king of Babylon; a like number Rim-Sin, king of Larsa; a like number Ibal-pi-el, king of Eshnunna; a like number Amut-pi-el, king of Qatna, while twenty kings follow Yarim-Lim, king of Yamkhat."[3] The more important states of the time, as shown by the Mari letters, were Alalakh, Ugarit, Qatna, and Byblos in the west; Harran, Carchemish, and Aleppo in the north; Ashur on the upper Tigris; Mari on the middle Euphrates; Eshnunna and Babylon in central Babylonia; Isin and Larsa toward the south. Scattered among these rival states were the Hurrians. As early as 2200 B.C., in the Old Akkadian period, they had begun to push out of the Caucasian highlands into northern Mesopotamia and by 1800 B.C. they had infiltrated into southern Mesopotamia as well and were beginning their movement into the west. A more serious political menace was the invasion of the Gutians, who were able to hold sway over the country for more than a hundred years, *ca.* 2190-2065 B.C. The first of these alien invaders seem

[3] See G. Dossin, *Syria*, XIX (1938), 117 f. For the bibliography of the Mari letters see *Jaarbericht Ex Oriente Lux*, No. 10 (1946), p. 431. For the conflicts among the many states of the time see R. T. O'Callaghan, *Analecta Orientalia*, 26 (1948), pp. 23 ff. For the chronology of the ancient Near East see the tables in O'Callaghan, *op. cit.*, pp. 10, 81 and 98.

not to have established an empire, but they did spread rapidly
over the whole of the Near East, interspersed among other
ethnic groups or settled in colonies of their own. Mitanni in
northeastern Syria, when we know it (*ca.* 1500-1370 B.C.),
was a Hurrian state in population, but its rulers were Indo-
Aryans. Frequent references in the Boghaz-köi archives indicate that Hurrians flanked the Hittite Empire to the
southeast, and Hurrians in large numbers we know were
settled in northern Mesopotamia, particularly in Nuzi and
Arrapkha, owing their allegiance, at least in the fifteenth
century, to the king of Mitanni.[4] Hurrian texts of *ca.* 1800
B.C. have been found at Mari[5] and Hurrian names appear
even earlier throughout Mesopotamia to show the presence
of the people there from an early age. For their presence in
Syria we have not only the witness of Hurrian glosses and
personal names in the Tell el-Amarna letters, but actual
Hurrian texts, discovered at Ras Shamra.[6] In Palestine we
have the evidence of Hurrian names in the tablets excavated
at Taanach[7] and Hurrian names in the Old Testament,[8] along
with the actual mention of the people under the name *Hôrî*
(Horite), the exact Hebrew equivalent of the cuneiform
Hurru (Hurrian).[9] Indeed so largely were Hurrians settled

[4] See E. A. Speiser, *Journal of the American Oriental Society*, XLIX
(1929), 269-275; R. H. Pfeiffer, *Harvard Semitic Series*, IX (1932), No. 1.
For the date see I. J. Gelb, P. M. Purves, and A. A. MacRae, *Nuzi Personal
Names* (1943), p. 1.

[5] See F. Thureau-Dangin, *Revue d'Assyriologie*, XXXVI (1939), 1-28.

[6] E.g., C. H. Gordon, *Analecta Orientalia*, 25 (1947), Texts 4, 7, 31, 34,
45, 50, 61, and 106.

[7] See A. Gustavs, *Zeitschrift des Deutschen Palästina-Vereins*, L (1927),
7 ff.

[8] See W. Feiler, *Zeitschrift für Assyriologie*, XLV (1939), 216-229.

[9] E. A. Speiser, *Annual of the American Schools of Oriental Research*,
XIII (1933), 29 ff., has given good grounds for the belief that "Hivite"
in the Old Testament is sometimes a scribal error for "Horite," so that
references to the Horites are even more numerous than our present text
indicates. See also O'Callaghan, *op. cit.*, p. 54, n. 8.

in Palestine that the Egyptians, beginning with the Eighteenth Dynasty, regularly called it Huru.[10] In Egypt, too, there were Hurrian settlers, but not in any great number, as the paucity of Hurrian names suggests,[11] because the movement had pretty well spent itself by the time it reached Egypt.[12]

On the heels of the Hurrians there came *ca.* 1720 B.C. a great horde of peoples known as the Hyksos, a term that is not ethnic, as Hurrian is, but merely descriptive. Manetho, the Egyptian historian, interpreted the word as meaning "shepherd kings," which is not very wide of the actual meaning, "rulers of the foreign lands (the desert)." By the time of the Eighteenth Dynasty, however, the word had lost its original significance and had come to mean Asiatic foreigners in general. The Hyksos do not represent a single ethnic group, for their personal names indicate different national stocks. Most of them were Semites, but some were Hittites, and some were undoubtedly Hurrians.[13] The Jewish historian, Josephus, believed that they were Hebrews. They were manifestly a conglomerate mass of heterogeneous elements, who entered Egypt in successive waves at a time when she was weak from internal discord and internecine warfare. Manetho describes their invasion in these words: "There was

[10] See A. H. Gardiner, *Ancient Egyptian Onomastica*, I (1947), 180* ff. The word used to be vocalized as *Ḥaru*, but the correct vocalization would seem to be *Ḥuru* (despite Gardiner's preference for *Ḥor*), the exact equivalent of cuneiform *Ḥurru*.

[11] See O'Callaghan, *op. cit.*, p. 45, n. 2.

[12] The bibliography on the Hurrians is now very extensive; the more recent writings are W. F. Albright, *From the Pyramids to Paul*, ed. L. G. Leary (1935), pp. 9 ff.; A. Goetze, *Hethiter, Churriter und Assyrer* (1936); A. Ungnad, *Subartu* (1936); A. Alt, *Der Alte Orient*, XXXIV, 4 (1936), pp. 19 ff.; I. J. Gelb, *Hurrians and Subarians* (1944); E. A. Speiser, *Introduction to Hurrian* (1941); *Journal of the American Oriental Society*, LXVIII (1948), 1-13; O'Callaghan, *op. cit.*, pp. 37 ff.

[13] For recent discussions of the Hyksos see R. M. Engberg, *The Hyksos Reconsidered* (1939); H. Stock, *Ägyptologische Forschungen*, No. 12 (1942); O'Callaghan, *op. cit.*, pp. 45, 75 f.

a king of ours whose name was Timaios, in whose reign it came to pass, I know not why, that God was displeased with us, and there came unexpectedly from the east men of ignoble race who had the temerity to invade our country, which they easily subdued without a battle. When they got our rulers under their power, they savagely burned down our cities and demolished the temples of the gods and used all the inhabitants in a most barbarous manner; for they slew some and led the children and wives of others into slavery."[14] Under the alien rule of the Hyksos the Egyptians quickly dropped their differences, united under Amosis against the common foe, and drove them out of the country to the lands whence they had come, Palestine and Syria. Thither the Egyptians followed to complete their destruction, conquering as they went, until by the time of Tuthmosis III, *ca.* 1490-1436 B.C., they found themselves in possession of a great empire stretching all the way to the Euphrates, and thus including all of Palestine and Syria.

With the overthrow of the Third Dynasty of Ur in Mesopotamia, *ca.* 1960 B.C., by invading swarms of Elamites over the Zagros Mountains in the east, there came other, more vigorous swarms of Amorites from the west to contest the control of the land and some of these eventually established the First Babylonian Dynasty, *ca.* 1830 B.C., but this attained no great power until a century later. The effect of all these inroads into the lands of the Fertile Crescent by so many different peoples was to add still further to the complexity of the ethnic stocks that went into the making of the so-called Semitic peoples, and it was amid this welter of diverse nationalities rapidly commingling that the Hebrew people were born.

The first person to be called a Hebrew (*'ibrî*) in the Old

---

[14] Quoted by Josephus, *Contra Apionem*, i. 14.

Testament is Abram in Gen. 14:13, and the word is manifestly used here, not as an ethnic term, but as an appellative,
even as the Septuagint translates it, ὁ περάτης; and the meaning in both Greek and Hebrew is "one who crosses (from
place to place), a transient, a nomad." The root in Hebrew
is ʿābar, in its transitive sense, "to cross," in its intransitive
sense, "to be a crosser, a transient, a nomad." The word
ʿibrî is strictly a gentilic in Hebrew, but without the gentilic
ending it is found as the name of the eponymous ancestor of
the Hebrew nation, Eber (ʿēber, Gen. 10:21, 24 f.; 11:14
ff.; I Chron. 1:18 f.), which manifestly goes back to an
earlier form ʿabir(u), just as melek goes back to an earlier
form milk, and that to malik.[15] Now the exact equivalent
of ʿabir(u), and hence of ʿēber and ʿibrî, in cuneiform is
ḫabiru (nom. sing.), ḫabirū (nom. pl.), ḫabirī (gen.-acc.
pl.), and it so happens that this word appears in cuneiform
literature from one end of the Near East to the other, from
the twentieth century down to the eleventh. The word is
usually written phonetically ḫa-bi-ru, but interchanging
with this at times is SA.GAZ (variant, GAZ), which may be
the logographic writing of the same word, but this is not
absolutely certain.[16] The chief occurrences of ḫabiru and
SA.GAZ, where they appear to be the same, are as follows:

[15] Cf. F. M. T. Böhl, Kanaanäer und Hebräer (1911), pp. 85 f.; E. A.
Speiser, Annual of the American Schools of Oriental Research, XIII
(1933), 40; W. F. Albright, The Archaeology of Palestine and the Bible
(1932), pp. 206 f.

[16] Discussed, e.g., by E. Dhorme, Revue Biblique, XXXIII (1924), 12 ff.;
Böhl, op. cit., pp. 87 ff.; F. Schmidtke, Die Einwanderung Israels in Kanaan
(1933), pp. 46 ff. The equation is based on the apparent interchange of
SA.GAZ and Ḫabiru in the Boghaz-köi texts and the Tell el-Amarna letters;
e.g., the enemies of Abdi-Heba are called SA.GAZ in AO 7096, I, 21 (edited
by F. Thureau-Dangin, Revue d'Assyriologie, XIX [1922], 98 ff.), whereas
they are called Ḫabiru in Abdi-Heba's own letters (J. A. Knudtzon, Die
El-Amarna-Tafeln [1915], Nos. 285-290). Both terms have clearly very
much the same meaning and must refer to the same people.

(1) in texts of the Larsa dynasty at the end of the twentieth century, where both terms appear;[17] (2) in a letter of the nineteenth century excavated by the Oriental Institute of the University of Chicago at Alishar in Asia Minor, with *ḫabiru* alone;[18] (3) in a letter of Hammurabi toward the end of the eighteenth century, with SA.GAZ alone;[19] (4) in letters of the time of Hammurabi discovered at Mari, on the middle Euphrates, with *ḫabiru* alone;[20] (5) in the Akkadian texts of the fifteenth century excavated in the Hurrian city of Nuzi, with *ḫabiru* alone;[21] (6) in the Hittite texts

[17] V. Scheil, *Revue d'Assyriologie*, XII (1915), 114 f.; E. M. Grice, *Records from Ur and Larsa* (1919), Nos. 33, 46, 47, 50-53. A slightly earlier occurrence of SA.GAZ alone, in an uncertain context, is H. de Genouillac, *Textes cunéiformes*, V (1922), Pl. XLV, No. 6165, Obv. 3 and 9, dated in the eighth year of Amar-Sin, third king of Ur III, early in the twentieth century B.C.

[18] I. J. Gelb, *Inscriptions from Alishar and Vicinity* (1935), No. 5, Obv. 9. Discussed at length by J. Lewy, *Archives d'histoire du droit oriental*, II (1938), 128-131.

[19] L. W. King, *Letters and Inscriptions of Hammurabi* (1898), No. 35, line 8; translated by A. Ungnad, *Babylonische Briefe aus der Zeit der Hammurapi-Dynastie* (1914), p. 25.

[20] See E. Dhorme, *Revue de l'histoire des religions*, CXVII (1938), 174-176; C. F. Jean, *Revue des études sémitiques*, 1938, p. 132.

[21] Published by E. Chiera, *Publications of the Baghdad School: Texts*, V (1934), Nos. 447 f., 450, 452-456, 458-461, 463-465; E. R. Lacheman, *ibid.*, VI (1939), Nos. 610 f., 613; *Journal of the American Oriental Society*, LV (1935), Pls. I and II. Discussed at length by J. Lewy, *Hebrew Union College Annual*, XIV (1939), 587-623; XV (1940), 47-58. Lewy has well demonstrated that the Hebrews in Nuzi were not actual slaves, but I am not ready to follow him in his interpretation of the opening clause of the so-called Hebrew slave contracts, which regularly runs as follows: "In the matter of X, a Hebrew from the country of Y: his own self (*var.*, his mouth and his tongue) caused him to enter the house of Z for service." The personal name at the beginning is in the casus pendens, the following conjunction is explicative (hence the colon in our translation), and *ramānšuma* ("his own self") is the subject and not the object of the verb, as shown by the fact that the verb always remains singular even when two Hebrews are making the contract and the verbal suffix is singular when one person is making the contract and plural when there are more than one. In a language that has the niphal (reflexive) stem the verbal suffix could not possibly be reflexive. The phrase seems to mean that the

of the fourteenth and fifteenth centuries excavated at Boghaz-köi in Asia Minor, where both terms appear;[22] (7) in a Hittite translation of the romance of Naram-Sin, with SA.GAZ alone;[23] (8) in the Tell el-Amarna letters excavated in Egypt, where both terms appear, but ḫabiru alone in the letters from Jerusalem;[24] and finally (9) as a gentilic, ḫa-bir-a-a, in two texts of the time of Ninurta-tukul-Ashur, king of Assyria ca. 1132 B.C.,[25] and in a Babylonian text of the eleventh century.[26] In some of these documents SA.GAZ seems to interchange with ḫa-bi-ru, but it does not necessarily follow that SA.GAZ in every instance is to be interpreted as ḫabiru, because the only definitely attested equivalent of the logogram is ḫabbatu, "plunderer, brigand, nomad,"[27] but that after all seems to be the meaning of ḫabiru although

---

Hebrew himself is initiating the contract, being forced as a poor immigrant to sell his services wherever he can and make the best bargain that he can.

[22] *Keilschrifttexte aus Boghazköi*, I, No. 1, Rev. 50; No. 2, Rev. 27; No. 3, Rev. 5; No. 4, Col. iv, 29; III, No. 3, Col. i, 7; No. 46, Obv. 39; IV, No. 10, Rev. 3; V, No. 3, Col. i, 56; No. 9, Col. iv, 12; *Keilschrifturkunden aus Boghazköi*, III, No. 7, Rev. 4; VII, No. 42, Obv. 1; VIII, No. 83, 9; IX, No. 34, Col. iv, 14; *Hittite Texts in the British Museum*, No. 6, Obv. 18; No. 37, Obv. 4. To these references add those of A. Goetze, *Bulletin of the American Schools of Oriental Research*, No. 79 (1940), p. 34, n. 14.

[23] E. Forrer, *Die Boghazköi-Texte in Umschrift*, II (1926), No. 5, Rev. 10.

[24] The references to SA.GAZ known at the time are given in J. A. Knudtzon, *Die El-Amarna-Tafeln* (1915), pp. 1146 ff., and those to ḫabiru on pp. 1574 f.

[25] H. Rawlinson, *Cuneiform Inscriptions of Western Asia*, IV (2nd ed., 1875), Pl. 34, No. 2, l. 5, and T. G. Pinches, *Journal of the Royal Asiatic Society*, 1904, p. 415, line 11. Transliterated and translated by E. F. Weidner, *Archiv für Orientforschung*, X (1935), 2-6; cf. B. Landsberger, *ibid.*, pp. 140-144. .

[26] H. Hilprecht, *Old Babylonian Inscriptions chiefly from Nippur*, II, Part 2 (1896), No. 149, Col. i, 22. The text has been transliterated and translated by W. J. Hinke, *A New Boundary Stone of Nebuchadnezzar I* (1907), pp. 190 ff.

[27] See Rawlinson, *op. cit.*, II (1866), Pl. 26, 13 g-h; R. C. Thompson, *Reports of the Magicians and Astrologers* (1900), No. 103, Obv. 7.

this comes from inference only, because no certain root for
the word has as yet been found in Akkadian. Wherever used,
ḫabiru is a term of reproach, and just so is its equivalent
in Hebrew, *'ibrî*—"a degrading derogatory appellation, a
mark of inferiority denoting an alien, a barbarian, a Bedouin
. . . a mock-name that ridiculed its bearers," as Rabbi Parzen
has well demonstrated.[28] It was like the name "Christian"
given to the early followers of Jesus or the epithet "Cynic"
hurled in derision at Antisthenes and his followers. Wherever
we meet them the Habiru are aliens, men without a
country,[29] adventurers, soldiers of fortune, selling their services where best they can and thriving best in war. In Babylonia they were mercenaries, as they were among the Hittites and Hurrians in southern Asia Minor. Among the
more peaceful Hurrians at Nuzi and Arrapkha they had to
sell themselves into virtual slavery in order to get a living,
either to private individuals or to the state. Amid the tur-
moil in Syria and Palestine in the Tell el-Amarna age they
were particularly in their element and are found allied sometimes with the loyalists, but more frequently with those
revolting against Egyptian rule, or making raids on their

[28] *American Journal of Semitic Languages*, XLIX (1933), 258. B. Landsberger, *Kleinasiatische Forschungen*, I, 2 (1929), p. 322, has suggested that
SA.GAZ is a pseudo-logogram derived from Akkadian *šaggašu*, "slayer,
brigand," and this would seem to be confirmed by the spelling SAG.GAZ,
in a text from Ras Shamra noted by A. Goetze, *Bulletin of the American
Schools of Oriental Research*, No. 79 (1940), p. 32.

[29] This is shown, among other things, by the fact that when the word
ḫabiru came to be made into a gentilic (see notes 25 and 26 above) the
ending was added, not to a geographical name, as was usual, but to the
name of the people because the Habiru had no country, to the name of
which the gentilic ending could be added. Likewise, in the treatises cited
in notes 41 and 42 below all the gods, who are invoked to attest the
treaties, are connected with various states except "the gods of the Habiru,"
again because they had no country of their own. Suggestive, too, is the
fact that the Habiru are represented in the texts from Nuzi as coming
from various foreign countries, but never from one of their own.

own account. They entered the land as soldiers of fortune, making common cause with the rebels, and they ended by conquering some of the land for themselves (the region north of Jerusalem) and settling down in it.

But not only are the Habiru found in cuneiform literature, they appear in Egyptian as well, because scholars are now pretty well agreed that the Egyptian word *'apiru* is the exact equivalent of the cuneiform *ḫabiru* and the Hebrew *'ibrî*.[30] The only difficulty about the identification philologically is that *p* is not the regular representation of foreign *b* in Egyptian. However, the word *ḫabiru* was probably mediated to the Egyptians through the Hurrians, because the word appears in a bilingual text from Ras Shamra as *'prm* (plural of *'apiru*), the Ugaritic equivalent of [LÚ.MEŠ]SAG.GAZ,[31] and Ugaritic, we know, was much influenced by Hurrian, which did not distinguish between voiced and voiceless stops and hence was responsible for confusion in the rendering of *b* and *p*.[32] Even the Hurrian goddess, *Ḫebat*, appears in the alphabetic texts from Ugarit sometimes with *b* and sometimes with *p*, and in Egyptian she appears as *Ḫepa*, as evidenced by such personal names as *Putu-Ḫepa* and *Gilu-Ḫepa*. All of this shows that there is no occasion at all to take the Hebrew *'ibrî* and the cuneiform *ḫabiru* as secondary formations from an original *'iprî* and *ḫapiru* respectively,[33] and this is confirmed by the occurrence of the

[30] See J. A. Wilson, *American Journal of Semitic Languages*, XLIX (1933), 275 ff., and B. Gunn, *Annual of the American Schools of Oriental Research*, XIII (1933), 38, n. 93. These discussions were written quite independently of each other and yet they are identical in their conclusions, a striking evidence of their validity. See also A. H. Gardiner, *Ancient Egyptian Onomastica*, I (1947), 184*, n. 1.

[31] See, e.g., A. Goetze, *Bulletin of the American Schools of Oriental Research*, No. 79 (1940), pp. 32-34.

[32] See J. Lewy, *Hebrew Union College Annual*, XV (1940), 48, n. 7.

[33] So W. F. Albright, *Bulletin of the American Schools of Oriental Research*, No. 77 (1940), p. 33.

word in Assyrian as *ḫa-bi-ru*,[34] which cannot be read as *ḫa-pi-ru* because *bi* does not have the value *pi* in Assyrian.

The occurrences of the word *ʿapiru* in Egyptian are seven in number: (1) in the Memphis stela of Amenophis II (*ca.* 1436-1411 B.C.); (2) in the stela of Seti I (*ca.* 1303-1290 B.C.) excavated at Beisan in Palestine; (3) in Harris Papyrus 500, of the time of Seti I or slightly later; (4) in Leyden Papyrus I 348, of the time of Ramesses II (*ca.* 1290-1223 B.C.), the successor of Seti I; (5) in Leyden Papyrus I 349, of the time of Ramesses II; (6) in the Great Harris Papyrus, of the time of Ramesses III (*ca.* 1179-1147 B.C.); and (7) in the Wadi Hammamat Inscription, of the time of Ramesses IV, *ca.* 1145 B.C.[35] In all these occurrences the word is written in the "group writing," by which the Egyptians rendered foreign words and names. In the first inscription it has no determinative, but in the others it is determined with signs to indicate a foreign people; it is once determined with signs indicating men and women (Leyden I 349), but elsewhere with the sign for men alone. In the first inscription it is narrated that 3600 ʿApiru were made prisoners on the second campaign of Amenophis in Palestine and Syria, along with numbers of Retenu, Shosu, Hurrians, and Nugassians, and the word seems to have some ethnic force even though it has no determinative, but this inscription is sparing of determinatives. In four of the passages the ʿApiru are represented as doing heavy labor on public works, along with mercenaries and others; in Harris Papyrus 500 an ʿApiru is mentioned along with mercenaries,

---

[34] See O. Schroeder, *Keilschrifttexte aus Assur verschiedenen Inhalts* (1920), No. 42, Col. ii, 9.

[35] The references for Nos. 2-7 are given in the works cited in note 30 above. The text of the first inscription has been published by A. M. Badawi, *Annales du Service des Antiquités de l'Égypte*, XLII (1943), 1-23 and Pl. I; cf. Gardiner, *op. cit.*, p. 184*.

but the context is too broken to indicate his exact status, perhaps a stableman or groom. In the remaining passage, that of the Beisan stela, Seti I is apparently recording his conquest of the 'Apiru then molesting the district, as the Habiru did in the preceding century, the Tell el-Amarna period, but the context is too broken to make this a certainty.[36] The 'Apiru wherever found are clearly aliens, adventurers, wanderers, and the name is foreign and not Egyptian, identical in every respect with the Hebrew 'ibrî and the cuneiform ḫabiru.

That the word 'apiru, ḫabiru, was not an ethnic term originally, but an appellative, is confirmed by an examination of all the ḫabiru names that we have, which unfortunately are few in number. They represent different nationalities, non-Semitic as well as Semitic, with a tendency for the latter to predominate.[37] But though the term had no ethnic content originally, tendencies early developed in that direction, as was natural under the circumstances. We see that in the Amenophis inscription and in Babylonia the Habiru had officers of their own (UGULA^{LÚ}SA.GAZ^{pl}),[38] just as the Amorites had (UGULA MAR.TU).[39] In Nuzi and Arrapkha the word ḫabiru, in the forms Ḫa-bi-ra and Ḫa-bi-i-ra, became a personal name, found some twenty-five times.[40] In southern Asia Minor the Habiru had evidently

[36] The text is published and discussed by A. Rowe, *The Topography and History of Beth-shan* (1930), pp. 29 f., Pls. 42-44; cf. W. F. Albright, *From the Stone Age to Christianity* (1940), p. 330, n. 6.

[37] See E. Chiera, *American Journal of Semitic Languages*, XLIX (1933), 117; A. Saarisalo, *Studia Orientalia*, V, 3 (1934), pp. 84-86.

[38] A. Ungnad, *Babylonische Briefe aus der Zeit der Hammurapi-Dynastie* (1914), No. 26, l. 8.

[39] This expression is quite common in the Hammurabi period; see, e.g., Ungnad, *op. cit.*, p. 250 under *aklum*; E. Forrer, *Reallexikon der Assyriologie*, I (1932), 447.

[40] See I. J. Gelb, P. M. Purves, and A. A. MacRae, *Nuzi Personal Names* (1943), p. 55.

some kind of social and religious organization of their own,
as is evidenced by the fact that their gods, the *ilāni Ḫabiri*,[41]
were invoked along with the gods of the Hittites and Hurrians in attesting treaties.[42] In the three texts of the twelfth
and eleventh centuries the name appears definitely as a gentilic, *Ḫabirayu*, and thus it does eventually in the Old
Testament, *'Ibrî*. The name began as an appellative, with
no ethnic connotation whatever, but it ended as a gentilic,
and then specifically as the ethnic name of a group of people
whom we know as the Hebrews.

It has long been the custom to make Abraham, the first
person to be called a Hebrew in the Old Testament, a contemporary of Hammurabi, king of Babylon *ca.* 1728-1686
B.C.[43] The basis of this has been the identification of Amraphel in Gen. 14:1 with Hammurabi, and the other kings
mentioned in that chapter with contemporaries of his. Although these identifications are now known to be false, the
date for Abraham may still be close to that of Hammurabi,
ca. 1750 B.C. If the Benjaminites of the Mari letters are to
be identified with the Hebrew tribe of Benjamin,[44] this

[41] Also written in Hittite. For a tabular presentation of the occurrences
see A. Jirku, *Der Alte Orient*, XXIV, 2 (1925), p. 18. Cf. B. Landsberger,
Kleinasiatische Forschungen, I, 2 (1929), pp. 326 ff.; E. Dhorme, *Revue de
l'histoire des religions*, CXVIII (1938), 171 f. Note also the occurrence
of the god name *ḫa-bi-ru* in a list of gods and temples, O. Schroeder,
Keilschrifttexte aus Assur verschiedenen Inhalts (1920), No. 42, Col. ii, 9;
also the occurrence of *'prw* (*'apiru* ?) as an element in Canaanite names of
the Late Bronze Age; see W. F. Albright, *Bulletin of the American
Schools of Oriental Research*, No. 81 (1941), p. 20.

[42] For an English translation of these treaties see D. D. Luckenbill,
American Journal of Semitic Languages, XXXVII (1921), 161 ff.

[43] For this date see, e.g., W. F. Albright, *Bulletin of the American
Schools of Oriental Research*, No. 88 (1942), 28-33; F. Cornelius, *Klio*,
XXXV (1942), 1-16; B. L. van der Waerden, *Jaarbericht Ex Oriente Lux*,
No. 10 (1946), pp. 414-424.

[44] See G. Dossin, *Mélanges Syriens offerts à M. R. Dussaud*, II (1940),
981-996.

would make at least some of the Hebrews contemporary with Hammurabi, since the letters belong to his time. This is also the date indicated by the Old Testament itself—the three generations of Abraham, Isaac, and Jacob, plus 430 years, before the Exodus (Ex. 12:40; Gen. 15:13), which we date *ca.* 1200 B.C.;[45] and it has other considerations in its favor, like the evidence of ancient documents recounting movements of peoples from the east and north into Syria and Palestine at that time, and the evidence of excavations in Trans-Jordan and the Dead Sea area, which seem to set the nineteenth century as the upper limit for the age of Abraham.[46] This date of *ca.* 1750 B.C. for Abraham would make the first migration of the Hebrews into Palestine contemporaneous with and a part of the Hurrian migration to the west, and this would seem to accord with the facts as we know them.

It has long been noted by scholars that there are certain details in the stories of the early Hebrew patriarchs that do not fit into a purely Semitic background because we have no Semitic parallels, but with our enlarged knowledge of the Hurrians we now have exact Hurrian parallels. I note only three or four of these; others may be consulted in the writings of C. J. Gadd, S. Smith, E. A. Speiser, and C. H. Gordon.[47] From Hurrian parallels we get an entirely new

[45] See pp. 34 ff. below.
[46] See W. F. Albright, *The Archaeology of Palestine and the Bible* (3rd ed., 1935), pp. 133 ff., 208 ff., 239 ff.; *Annual of the American Schools of Oriental Research*, VI (1926), 13 ff.
[47] C. J. Gadd and S. Smith, *Revue d'Assyriologie*, XXIII (1926), 126 f.; S. Smith, *Journal of Theological Studies*, XXXIII (1932), 33 ff.; E. A. Speiser, *Annual of the American Schools of Oriental Research*, XIII (1933), 44; *Mesopotamian Origins* (1930), p. 162; *Journal of the American Oriental Society*, LII (1932), 365; C. H. Gordon, *Revue Biblique*, XLIV (1935), 34-41; *Bulletin of the American Schools of Oriental Research*, No. 66 (1937), pp. 25-27; *Biblical Archaeologist*, III (1940), 1-12. See also R. T. O'Callaghan, *Catholic Biblical Quarterly*, VI, 4 (1944), pp. 391-405.

translation for Gen. 31:14-16, according to which Rachel
and Leah addressed their husband Jacob as follows: "Have
we any longer share or heritage in our father's estate? Are
we not considered foreigners by him? For he sold us and
then completely used up the money for us as well. In fact, all
the property which God has taken away from our father
really belongs to us and our children; so now, do just what
God has told you to do."[48] Hebrew ideas of land tenure, recorded in Num. 36:9 and illustrated by the story of Naboth's
vineyard (I Kings 21), must have been an inheritance from
the Hurrians, among whom the principle of the inalienability
of real property was very strong. Rachel's theft of her
father's household goods, the teraphim (Gen. 31:19), had
long been a puzzle to scholars, but we know now that
according to Hurrian law this ensured title to her father's
property for her husband Jacob. Esau's renunciation of his
birthright for a consideration (Gen. 25:31-34) was likewise
unparalleled until we found the same thing occurring among
the Hurrians. These and similar analogues between the
early Hebrews and the Hurrians, along with the occurrence
of Hurrian names and references to the Hurrians in the Old
Testament, indicate quite clearly that the two migrations
went together. Hurrians and Habiru, or Hebrews, were
found together in Mesopotamia and it is likely that they
would be found together in the west, the Hebrews manifestly in a minor role as hangers-on and adventurers.

These first wanderers into Palestine were not conquerors,
but immigrants into a new land; *gêrîm* the Old Testament
calls them. They were not numerous enough or nationally
minded enough to hew out a home of their own as a nation,
but they lived and mingled on friendly terms with the

[48] Discussed at length by M. Burrows, *Journal of the American Oriental
Society*, LVII (1937), 259-276.

natives. Just so they are represented in the early patriarchal narratives. The importation of a wife from Harran for Isaac (Gen. 24) and Jacob's marriages there (Gen. 29) suggest, however, that connections were maintained with the original stock and that the earlier migration was supplemented by others in successive waves over a considerable period of time. Amid these migrations came the Hyksos avalanche from the north, carrying some of the Hebrews into Egypt. This again is reflected in the Old Testament in the story of Abraham's visit to Egypt (Gen. 12:10 ff.), duplicated by the account of Isaac's migration to Gerar (Gen. 26:1 ff.), along with the story of Joseph's sojourn in Egypt and the migration eventually of all his family thither to join him in his semiregal estate. Here we have a reflection of the successive waves by which the Hyksos entered Egypt, and it is not without significance that one of the Hyksos kings bore the name of Jacob-har, indicating that Jacob was a good Hyksos name and suggesting too that the Hebrews participated in the Hyksos regime in Egypt, as does the Joseph story in general. The Jewish historian, Josephus, definitely connects the Hebrews with the Hyksos invasion. Both the Hebrews and the Hyksos were predominantly Semitic and the age of the Patriarchs corresponds with that of the Hyksos. The references in the Old Testament story to horses and chariots indicate a period not earlier than the Hyksos when these were first introduced into Egypt, and the allotment of the land of Goshen to the Hebrews would seem to reflect the distribution of the land among the Hyksos conquerors. The Old Testament locates the land of Goshen (probably the Wadi Tumilat[49]) in close proximity to the Egyptian capital, and the Hyksos period, when Avaris was the capital, fulfills that condition as no other period

[49] See T. Eric Peet, *Egypt and the Old Testament* (1923), pp. 78-82.

does. Another indication of the connection of the Hebrews
with the Hyksos is the antiquarian gloss in Num. 13:22,
stating that Hebron was built seven years before Zoan in
Egypt (i.e., Tanis-Avaris), which can refer only to the
founding of the Hyksos capital there *ca.* 1720 B.C.[50]

Hence there is every reason to believe that Hebrews
constituted part of the conglomerate mass of Hyksos who
invaded Egypt, but to affirm with Josephus, as some scholars
do, that the Exodus is to be identified with the expulsion
of the Hyksos *ca.* 1560 B.C. does not follow at all. The
Hebrews who went with the Hyksos to Egypt must have
had an exodus, but it can scarcely have been the Exodus
recorded in the Bible. No people who had been in Egypt
as conquerors and masters would have represented their
sojourn there as servitude, as the Hebrews have throughout
all their literature. The milieu of the Exodus, as represented
in the Bible, and that of the expulsion of the Hyksos are so
completely different that the one cannot possibly be identified with the other. Furthermore, if we put the Exodus *ca.*
1560, it leaves the people wandering in the wilderness for
more than a century even if we put the conquest of Jericho
at its earliest possible, but most improbable date, 1450 B.C.
So the Hyksos came and they went, and with them went
those early Hebrews.

A little more than a hundred years after the expulsion
of the Hyksos from Egypt came a really serious incursion
of Hebrews, or Habiru, into Syria and Palestine, gaining
impetus as Egyptian prestige declined, as it did in the reign
of Amenophis III (*ca.* 1397-1360 B.C.), and more particularly in that of his son, Amenophis IV (Akhenaten), who

[50] See K. Sethe, *Zeitschrift für ägyptische Sprache*, LXV (1930), 85 ff.;
cf. E. Meyer, *Geschichte des Altertums*, I, 2 (2nd ed., 1909), § § 160, 305 f.,
308; W. F. Albright, *Journal of the Palestine Oriental Society*, I (1920),
64 f.

was more concerned with religious reform than with the maintenance of an empire. From the Tell el-Amarna letters and other sources we learn that Syria was seething with intrigue and revolt against Egyptian rule even earlier than the time of Amenophis III, and all this became more intense as time went on and Egypt failed to give the support to the loyalists that the occasion demanded. Under the circumstances it was only natural that the kingdoms of Hatti and Mitanni, bordering Syria in the north, should have taken a hand in the matter, professedly in the interests of their Egyptian ally, but as a matter of fact in their own interests. To add to the confusion of the situation and attracted by its opportunities, soldiers of fortune like the SA.GAZ (probably to be identified with the Habiru, as already noted) appeared on the scene, sometimes selling their services to a loyal governor like Biryawaza,[51] but more frequently to one who was secretly disloyal like Abdi-Ashirta,[52] or making raids and conquests on their own account.[53] Frequent are the appeals to Egypt for help, each governor accusing the other of disloyalty, and frequent are the warnings that the SA.GAZ are overrunning the whole land; but appeals and warnings alike fell on deaf ears, until in the reign of Amenophis IV Hatti stepped in and added most of Syria to her domain, so that the Habiru had to look elsewhere for a home.[54]

Under Amenophis III Palestine had remained fairly loyal

[51] See J. A. Knudtzon, *Die El-Amarna-Tafeln* (1915), No. 195. For the reading "Biryawaza" in place of the earlier reading "Namiawaza" see F. Thureau-Dangin, *Revue d'Assyriologie*, XXXVII (1940), 171; *Archiv für Orientforschung*, XIV (1942), 142.

[52] See Knudtzon, *op. cit.*, Nos. 71 and 82.

[53] See Knudtzon, *op. cit.*, Nos. 73, 74, and 77.

[54] For a running digest of the Tell el-Amarna letters see A. T. Olmstead, *History of Palestine and Syria* (1931), pp. 155 ff. For the most recent translation of selected letters see W. F. Albright, in *Ancient Near Eastern Texts*, ed. J. B. Pritchard (1950).

to Egypt, but as the north fell away, the native governors
in the south also began to dream of independence; intrigue
and dissension developed apace among them, and then open
revolt. It was these conspirators and rebels who helped to
bring the Habiru into the country to assist them in their
revolt, and in return for their services they gave them certain regions for their own, so Abdi-Heba, loyal governor
of Jerusalem, tells us in his several letters.[55] Over and over
again he warns Akhenaten that if help is not immediately
forthcoming the whole land will be lost to the Habiru, and
to emphasize the urgency of his appeal he frequently adds
a postscript addressed to the king's scribe.[56] "The Habiru
are devastating all the lands of the king," he writes to the
king on one occasion. "If troops are provided this year, the
land will remain the king's, my lord's; but if no troops are
provided, the lands of the king, my lord, will be lost."[57]
And again, "The land of the king is lost to the Habiru. And
now in fact a city of the territory of Jerusalem by the
name of Bêt-Ninurta, a city of the king, has been captured
from the people of Kilti. Let the king listen to Abdi-Heba,
your servant, and send troops that he may restore the king's
land to the king. But if no troops are provided, the land will
be lost to the Habiru."[58] And finally in desperation he writes,
"If no troops are provided this year, then let the king
send an officer to bring me with my brothers to himself, that
we may die with the king, our lord."[59] But the troops were

[55] Knudtzon, *op. cit.*, Nos. 285-290.
[56] One of these (Knudtzon, *op. cit.*, No. 286, ll. 61-64) reads as follows: "To the scribe of the king, my lord, thus (speaks) Abdi-Heba,
your servant: Bring the words clearly to the king, my lord: All the lands
of the king, my lord, are being lost."
[57] Knudtzon, *op. cit.*, No. 286, ll. 56-60.
[58] Knudtzon, *op. cit.*, No. 290, ll. 12-24.
[59] Knudtzon, *op. cit.*, No. 288, ll. 57-61. In place of "to himself" the text
has "to me," but this is clearly a scribal error.

not sent, and the Habiru got a permanent foothold in the land, a foothold that included presently cities like Jericho, Shechem, Gibeon, Mizpeh, and Shiloh. In the Tell el-Amarna archives we have not a single letter from any of these cities, as we do from surrounding cities like Megiddo, Akko, Gezer, Askelon, Lachish, and Jerusalem, presumably because they had already revolted or were being overrun by the invading Habiru by that time. Indeed Mut-Baal in one of his letters tells us explicitly that all the cities of the Ghôr (the Jordan valley and beyond, written ^{mât} ga-ri), Udumu, Aduri, Araru, Meshtu, Magdalim, Hinyanabi, and Zarki, were hostile, while Hawini and Yabishiba were conquered.[60] In another of the Amarna letters Abdi-Heba tells us even more explicitly that Shechem threw in its lot with the Habiru, giving them everything,[61] and he uses the word ḫabiru here with the determinative of country (ki) as well as people (amêlûti),[62] indicating that they now had a land of their own, and he warns the Egyptian king in his several letters that they are in danger of taking all the land.

This contemporaneous account of the settlement of the Habiru in Palestine so exactly parallels the Old Testament account of the Israelite conquest of Jericho and the invasion of the highlands of Ephraim under Joshua that the two manifestly must have reference to the same episode. The name of Joshua as a leader appears in both accounts, if we accept Yashuya as the cuneiform equivalent of Joshua (Yehoshuʿa),[63] but there is no ground for identifying the

[60] See Knudtzon, op. cit., No. 256, ll. 22-28. For the location of the cities see A. H. Godbey, New Light on the Old Testament (1934), p. 94. The earlier identification of ^{mât}ga-ri with the Negeb is clearly wrong.

[61] See Knudtzon, op. cit., No. 289, ll. 24 f.

[62] The logogram SA.GAZ is likewise used in two instances with both determinatives, Knudtzon, op. cit., No. 215, l. 15, and No. 298, l. 27.

[63] It is to be noted, however, that the cuneiform lacks the laryngal of the Hebrew.

two men, as A. T. Olmstead has ventured to do.[64] Both accounts reflect the same political situation in Palestine: petty kings intriguing, allying, and warring against one another. Both represent some of the native princes as making alliances with the invaders; for the actions of Labaya, Milkili, Tagi, and others, reported in the Tell el-Amarna letters as allying themselves with the Habiru, are quite like Gibeon's alliance with the Hebrews, as recorded in Josh. 9:3 ff. The Old Testament says explicitly that the Hebrews "did not conquer Bethshean and its dependencies, nor Taanach and its dependencies, nor the inhabitants of Dor and its dependencies, nor the inhabitants of Megiddo and its dependencies" (Judg. 1:27), nor did they "evict the Canaanites who lived in Gezer" (Judg. 1:29), nor did they "evict the inhabitants of Akko, nor the inhabitants of Sidon, nor those of Ahlab, nor those of Achzib, nor those of Aphik, nor those of Rehob" (Judg. 1:31), nor did they "evict the inhabitants of Beth-shemesh, nor the inhabitants of Beth-anath" (Judg. 1:33), nor did they conquer Harheres, Aijalon, and Shaalbim (Judg. 1:35);[65] and this is precisely the evidence of the Tell el-Amarna letters. The Hebrews at first were able to conquer only the Jordan valley and the eastern highlands of Ephraim,[66] and only gradually did they extend their occupation westward. The so-called "conquest" was neither complete nor immediate. The Old Testament picture here, as so frequently elsewhere, is very much foreshortened.[67] The

[64] *History of Palestine and Syria* (1931), p. 197.

[65] Cf. similar statements in Josh. 13:13; 15:63; 16:10; 17:11 f., 14 ff.; Judg. 1:21, 30; 3:1-6.

[66] The earliest Old Testament narratives have nothing to say about the conquest of the country to the south and west of Gibeon. Even after the defeat of the five kings the camp remained at Gilgal (Josh. 10:43), so that the expedition must have been little more than a raid; cf. W. O. E. Oesterley and T. H. Robinson, *An Introduction to the Books of the Old Testament* (1934), pp. 72 f.

[67] Cf. J. E. McFadyen, "Telescoped History," *Expository Times*, XXXVI (1925), 103 ff.

"conquest" was rather a gradual infiltration of the Hebrews into the country by small groups or clans,[68] and it must have continued over a century or more before they had made any considerable portion of the land their own.[69] The account in the Tell el-Amarna letters marks the beginning of the movement, while the Old Testament account has to do largely with its final accomplishment, the end product. That the two accounts are not contemporaneous is indicated by the fact that the Canaanite kings mentioned in the two bear altogether different names and so cannot be of the same time.[70]

Investigations in Trans-Jordan show that this region probably fell into the hands of the Hebrews before 1400 B.C., at the beginning of the Amarna period.[71] The date given for the fall of Jericho by its recent excavator, John Garstang, is 1407 B.C.,[72] and in this he has the support of the eminent British archaeologist, Alan Rowe,[73] and the two American archaeologists, G. E. Wright, and W. F. Albright, who have given the matter most attention and were long opposed to Garstang's date, have finally settled on a date just a little lower than his.[74] The stela of Seti I discovered at Beisan indi-

[68] I once had a student describe it in these words: "The Hebrews gained the ascension in the land of Palestine by a policy of gradual insinuation." Modern parallels drawn from the infiltration of Arabs from the desert and their gradual transition from nomadic to seminomadic, to agricultural life, are given by J. Garstang, *The Heritage of Solomon* (1934), pp. 42 ff.

[69] As a matter of fact the Hebrews did not gain complete ascendancy in Palestine until the time of David, *ca.* 960 B.C.

[70] See C. F. Burney, *Israel's Settlement in Canaan* (3rd ed., 1921), p. 92, for the names in detail.

[71] See A. Bergman, *Journal of the American Oriental Society*, LIV (1934), 169 ff.

[72] See his *Foundations of Bible History* (1931), pp. 61 f., 146 f.; *Quarterly Statement of the Palestine Exploration Fund*, 1935, pp. 61 ff.; *Annals of Archaeology and Anthropology*, XX (1933), 3 ff.; XXI (1934), 99 ff.; *American Journal of Semitic Languages*, LVIII (1941), 368 ff.

[73] *Quarterly Statement of the Palestine Exploration Fund*, 1936, p. 170.

[74] W. F. Albright, *Bulletin of the American Schools of Oriental Research*, No. 74 (1939), pp. 18 ff.; G. E. Wright, *ibid.*, No. 86 (1942), pp. 32 ff.

cates that the ʻApiru, or Hebrews, were certainly in the neighborhood at that time, *ca.* 1300 B.C., and they seem to have come from the East Jordan. This is not absolutely certain because the stela is badly preserved, but it would seem to be confirmed by the second stela of Seti I found at the same place, which distinctly refers to an invasion by tribes from the east side of the Jordan.[75] The excavations at Shechem seem to show a somewhat later date than 1400 B.C. for its occupation by the Hebrews,[76] and the excavations by W. F. Albright at Bethel indicate quite definitely a date in the thirteenth century for the conquest of that city.[77] The strength to which the Hebrews had grown by that time is shown by the evidences of the most terrific conflagration indicated by any excavation in the whole of Palestine.[78] In the Old Testament there is an elaborate account of the capture of Ai (Josh. 7:2-8:29) and only a brief reference to that of Bethel (Judg. 1:22-25), but the excavations at Ai show that the site was unoccupied from the Early Bronze Age to Early Iron I (i.e., from *ca.* 3000 to *ca.* 1200 B.C.).[79] Hence there was nothing at Ai to capture and destroy when the Hebrews came in, while Bethel was thoroughly burned and shortly afterwards rebuilt by the conquerors. The Old Testament has apparently confused Ai with Bethel, which is little more than a mile away. The excavations at Bethel show a

[75] See A. Rowe, *The Topography and History of Beth-shan* (1930), p. 29.

[76] The excavation of Shechem was not very well conducted and the results are disappointing. For a critical review see J. Hempel, *Zeitschrift für die alttestamentliche Wissenschaft,* LI (1933), 156-169. See also W. F. Albright, *Archaeology and the Religion of Israel* (1942), p. 188, n. 40.

[77] *Bulletin of the American Schools of Oriental Research,* No. 56 (1934), pp. 9 ff.; No. 58 (1935), pp. 10 ff.

[78] *Ibid.,* No. 56 (1934), p. 9.

[79] *Ibid.,* p. 11. Also reported to the writer by a private communication from Professor O. R. Sellers at the time of the excavation.

slight conflagration in the Late Bronze Age, which may possibly be the result of the occupation of the city recorded in
Judg. 1:22-25, while the later and much more severe conflagration in the thirteenth century may be that recorded in
Josh. 7:2-8:29, with Bethel to be substituted for Ai.[80] In any
case the evidences of the several excavations in Palestine go to
show that northern towns like Jericho, Hazor,[81] Shechem,
and Bethel were captured somewhat earlier than southern
towns like Beth-zur, Kirjath-sepher (probably Tell Beit Mirsim), and Lachish.[82] In fact everything goes to show that
the first conquests of the Hebrews were in the north and
they must have been there in considerable numbers even as
early as Amenophis II if his statement is correct that he captured 3,600 'Apiru on his second campaign. Unfortunately
he does not tell us exactly where he made the capture, but
it must have been on the northern fringes of Palestine or in
southern Syria because this seems to have been the northern
limit of his campaign.

These early invaders of Palestine were not an ethnic unit,
but a composite group, perhaps more Aramean than anything else, if we can trust the statement in Deut. 26:5, "A
nomad Aramean was my father."[83] The Old Testament represents them as invading the land loosely organized as allied
tribes. Their common cause against a common foe tended to
unite them more closely and in due course a confederacy or

[80] The tendency in recent years has been to interpret the story of Ai as
aetiological, with no basis in fact whatever, but the story would seem to
be too elaborate in its details to be purely aetiological, and it is more
likely that it was transferred from Bethel to Ai to explain the impressive
ruin at Ai, which means "Ruin." Cf. W. F. Albright, *Bulletin of the
American Schools of Oriental Research*, No. 74 (1939), pp. 14-17.

[81] John Garstang dates the conquest of Hazor *ca.* 1400 B.C., *The Foundations of Bible History* (1931), pp. 381-383.

[82] On these southern sites see pp. 39 f. below.

[83] See further pp. 185 ff. below.

amphictyony[84] of some of the tribes (probably only the Joseph tribes at first)[85] was organized by Joshua at Shechem near Mount Gerizim. Here a covenant was made, a simple code of laws promulgated, and a loosely organized state or amphictyony established, modeled in some respects after the pattern of the Canaanite state and incorporating some Canaanite civil and ritual law.[86] In this northern confederacy we have the beginning of what is later to be known as Israel. The early *gêrîm*, or immigrants, had now become a people; a rebirth had taken place; the name of Jacob was changed to Israel.

Numerous passages in the Old Testament show that Shechem was intimately associated with covenant-making and lawgiving and was once the political and religious center of the north, even as it is for the Samaritans down to the present day. Its patron god was Ba'al-berith, "Lord of the Covenant" (Judg. 8:33; 9:4), also called El-berith, "God of the Covenant" (Judg. 9:46). Here stood a sacred terebinth, variously called the "Terebinth of the Lawgiver" (Gen. 12:6; Deut. 11:30) and the "Terebinth of the Soothsayers" (Judg. 9:37), and its site today is called Balāṭa, "Terebinth," where the excavations by the Germans uncovered what may be the ancient shrine.[87] It was at Shechem that Jacob is recorded in

[84] For this type of organization with the early Hebrew tribes see especially M. Noth, *Das System der zwölf Stämme Israels* (1930), pp. 39-60; also the literature cited by J. Pedersen, *Israel: Its Life and Culture,* III-IV (1947), 677, n. 1 to p. 85.

[85] It was only gradually that the other tribes joined or were absorbed into the confederacy. In fact some of the Habiru or Hebrews never joined at all, as is clear from such passages as I Sam. 13:6 f.; 14:21, which distinguish between the Hebrews who became Israelites and those who remained Hebrews.

[86] See pp. 69 ff. below.

[87] The excavators differ among themselves as to whether a temple was excavated at Shechem; see W. F. Albright, *Archaeology and the Religion of Israel* (1942), p. 188, n. 40. That it was a temple would seem to be

Gen. 33:20 to have erected an altar which he called *El-elohe-Israel*, "El, the god of Israel"; and it was here, according to Gen. 34, that a covenant was concluded between the Shechemites and the Hebrews, involving alliance and intermarriage. It was here that the Israelites gathered to determine whether Rehoboam should be accepted as king (I Kings 12:1 ff.), and it is here that Joshua's covenant-making and lawgiving are staged in Josh. 24:1 ff.; 8:30 ff., and Deut. 27:1 ff. Hence it is not surprising to find scholars suggesting that Shechem was the original home of the Hebrew Torah as against Sinai-Horeb or Kadesh, in that the Shechem story is manifestly the earlier. Indeed a goodly number, e.g., Holzinger, Staerk, Steuernagel, Luckenbill, Waterman, and Pfeiffer, have argued very convincingly that the Book of the Covenant (Ex. 20:22-23:33), in whole or in part, originally stood in Josh. 24, constituting the "Book of the Law of God" mentioned in verse 26. The story of the double giving of the Torah, first by Moses at Sinai-Horeb (Ex. 19 ff.), and later by Joshua at Shechem or Gerizim (Josh. 8:30-35; 24:1 ff.; cf. Deut. 11:29 f.; 27:1 ff.), as indicated by the Old Testament narratives, would seem to be the result of a prejudiced Judean interpretation of the events, because it is of course natural that the Judeans would not take kindly to Israelite precedence in lawgiving and accordingly subordinated Joshua to Moses. We need to remember that our Old Testament records have come down to us through Judean and not Israelite hands, and in the very nature of the case they are decidedly Judean in their interpretation of history. In the present instance this is clearly shown by the Judean alteration of the text in three of the passages cited, Deut. 11:29 f.; 27:4, and

---

confirmed by the excavation of a temple at Megiddo, similar in plan; see G. E. Wright, *Journal of the American Oriental Society*, LXX (1950), 59.

Josh. 8:30. In the first passage that part of verse 30 which
would locate Gerizim somewhere near Jericho (in territory
not so definitely Israelite as Shechem) is clearly a Judean
gloss, and in the other two passages "Ebal" has very plainly
been substituted for "Gerizim," and the Samaritan Pentateuch has correctly "Gerizim."

Just what laws constituted this covenant code promulgated
by Joshua at Shechem in setting up the Israelite amphictyony, it is impossible to say with certainty. Some, like
Eduard Meyer, would identify them with the curses in
Deut. 27 because of their supposed primitive character;[88]
others, we have noted, would see in them some or all of the
laws in the Book of the Covenant. In any case there was a
covenant and a simple covenant code, and with that a new
people, the *běnê Yiśrā'ēl* or Israelites, came into being.

While this section of the Habiru migrants were taking
advantage of unsettled conditions in Palestine to carve out
for themselves a homeland, or the beginnings of one, in the
north, the mass of the migrating hordes had perforce to seek
home and pasturage elsewhere. The push was westward
and in that direction they continued, but southern Palestine
was an obstacle in their pathway because they could not
conquer it. They made an attempt, as described apparently
in Num. 14:39-45; Deut. 1:41-44,[89] but they were driven
back, and so had to make a circuit southward to mingle
with the tribes of Kenites, Calebites, Jerahmeelites, and
others in the grasslands of the Negeb. Some of the more
venturesome spirits pushed their way to the very borders of
Egypt and by a benevolent government they were allowed
entrance into the Wadi Tumilat, the land of Goshen of the
Old Testament. That this was not an unusual privilege ac-

---

[88] *Die Israeliten und ihre Nachbarstämme* (1906), pp. 542 ff.
[89] This narrative in its present context places the attempt after the
Exodus from Egypt, but it does not seem to have much point there and
could well have occurred earlier.

corded Bedouin tribes is clear from a number of Egyptian documents, e.g., a letter of an Egyptian frontier official of the Nineteenth Dynasty stationed at the eastern entrance to the Wadi Tumilat, in which he reports as follows: "We have finished passing the Bedouin tribes of Edom by the fortress of Merneptah, belonging to Tjeku [a district in the Wadi Tumilat], toward the pools of Pithom of Merneptah, belonging to Tjeku, in order to feed themselves and to feed their flocks."[90] It is a well-established fact that from 1500 to 1200 B.C. there was a considerable population of foreigners in Egypt of both high and low estate.[91] This was particularly true of the time of Amenophis III and IV, when this Hebrew migration seems to have occurred. In fact, one of the chief administrators of Amenophis IV, often mentioned in the Tell el-Amarna correspondence, was Yanhamu, a Semite. Hence we have plenty of parallels for the entrance of a foreign people like the Hebrews into Egypt and for the hospitality accorded them.

The contention that only a part of the Hebrews went to Egypt at this time, a part only of the southern group and not of the northern, seems best to accord with the known facts in the case. It is clear from Judg. 1 that the Hebrew tribes did not invade the country as a united whole, but individually and in groups, and a critical reading of the book of Joshua reveals the same situation.[92] Apart from the number in Ex. 12:37 ("about 600,000 men on foot besides the dependents"), based on the census in Num. 1-4 and 26, which unquestionably is late and may be the census taken by David (II Sam. 24), wrongly placed here,[93] all the records suggest

[90] Papyrus Anastasi, vi, 4, 14.

[91] See, e.g., J. H. Breasted, *History of Egypt* (2nd ed., 1949), pp. 446 ff.

[92] Cf. e.g., C. F. Burney, *Israel's Settlement in Canaan* (3rd ed., 1921), pp. 1-58; G. E. Wright, *Journal of Near Eastern Studies*, V (1946), 105-114.

[93] This suggestion was made by W. F. Albright, *Archaeology and the Bible* (1932), p. 158, but its validity is questioned by H. M. and N. K. Chadwick, *The Growth of Literature*, II (1936), 698, n. 2.

that the number in Egypt was comparatively small and hence not the whole nation. From Ex. 1:10 we infer that the Hebrews were a small community. According to Ex. 1:15 they were so few that two midwives were sufficient for their needs, and even P holds that only seventy went to Egypt (Gen. 46:27). The Wadi Tumilat even today with modern irrigation can support only a few thousand people, and the wanderings of the Hebrews through the wilderness would have been quite impossible for a large number; also, nomadic bands are never large. The genealogies in I Chron. 1-8 ignore the Exodus altogether and that would suggest that there was a continuous line of Hebrews in Palestine who never went to Egypt, and likewise does Gen. 38 with its story of Judah, at a very early period intermarrying and settling down with the Canaanites.[94] The pentateuchal narratives presuppose that Kadesh was already in Hebrew hands at the time of the Exodus, manifestly in the hands of those who did not go to Egypt. Judges 11:26 affirms that Hebrews had been living continuously in certain cities in Trans-Jordan for three hundred years before Jephthah, and that would carry us back to ca. 1400 B.C., some two hundred years before the Exodus. Zilpah and Bilhah, the mothers of four of the Hebrew tribes (Asher, Gad, Dan, and Naphtali), are said by the biblical writers to be concubines, which shows that these tribes were of alien origin, and this is most easily explained as the absorption of native Canaanite elements. Seti I (ca. 1303-1290 B.C.) and Ramesses II (ca. 1290-1223 B.C.) mention the tribe of 'Isr, identified by most scholars with Asher,[95] as settled in northern Palestine in their day. The tribe was adopted into

[94] Cf. Eduard Meyer, Die Israeliten und ihre Nachbarstämme (1906), pp. 104, 204 f., 433; O. Procksch, Die Genesis (1913), p. 205; J. Skinner, International Critical Commentary on Genesis (1910), pp. 449 f.
[95] See, e.g., A. H. Gardiner, Ancient Egyptian Onomastica, I (1947), 192.*

the Israelite confederacy founded by Joshua, but clearly belonged to the Canaanite stock. We have already noted that Seti I in one of his stelas found at Beisan records the presence of 'Apiru or Hebrews in the neighborhood of that city, and he antedates the Exodus by something like a century. Finally there is the clear statement of the Merneptah stela (*ca.* 1220 B.C.) that a people in Palestine by the name of Israel were raided by him,[96] proving beyond any possibility of doubt that there were Israelites there at that time and the Exodus had not as yet taken place. All the evidences, then, would seem to indicate quite definitely that there were Hebrews in Palestine, particularly in northern Palestine, all the time that there were Hebrews in Egypt and that only a comparatively small group ever went to Egypt.[97]

Exactly what Hebrews did go to Egypt is difficult to say, but the evidences point strongly to the tribe of Levi. Both Moses and Aaron were traditionally Levites and chief shamans of the Levites, and there is good ground for accepting that tradition.[98] If with Wilhelm Rudolph[99] we assign Ex. 2:1 ff. to J, our oldest source tells us that they were Levites. More explicit than this, the Chronicler says that Moses was the son of Amram, a Levite (I Chron. 6:3; 23:13), while P gives the names of both his parents, Amram and Jochebed, both of whom are said to be Levites (Ex. 6:20; Num. 26:59). Another evidence for the presence of Levites in Egypt is I Sam. 2:27 f., where Yahweh is represented as addressing Eli,

[96] For the latest English translation of this stela see J. A. Wilson, in *Ancient Near Eastern Texts*, ed. J. B. Pritchard (1950).

[97] This, too, is the opinion of practically all scholars today, but they differ as to whether it was a northern or a southern group that went to Egypt.

[98] See T. J. Meek, *American Journal of Semitic Languages*, LVI (1939), 113-117.

[99] *Beihefte zur Zeitschrift für die alttestamentliche Wissenschaft*, LXVIII (1938), 3 ff.

the priest at Shiloh, through a man of God in the following words: "I did indeed reveal myself[100] to the house of your father when they were in Egypt subject[101] to the house of Pharaoh; and I chose him out of all the tribes of Israel to be my priest, to go up to my altar, to burn incense, to wear the priestly apron [the ephod] before me; and I committed to the house of your father all the fire-offerings of the Israelites." The "house of your father" here can be none other than the house of Levi, as scholars have agreed,[102] and the fact that the passage is probably late does not invalidate the statement that Levi was once in Egypt. If it was a new tradition that the author was initiating here, he would have been more explicit in his reference and actually named Levi, but he is clearly giving expression to a generally accepted fact and so did not need to be too explicit. In further support of the sojourn of Levites in Egypt is the striking fact that many of them bear Egyptian names; e.g., Moses, Assir, Pashhur, Hophni, Phinehas, Merari, and Puti-el in its first element.[103] This would indicate that the Levites at least were once resident in Egypt, so long in fact that they came to give Egyptian names to their children,[104] with the result that these became traditional in their families. For example, Assir appears as the name of at least two Levites (Ex. 6:24 = I Chron. 6:22 and I

[100] So Greek; the Hebrew indicates that the clause is to be read as a question, but the two texts, as a matter of fact, carry the same meaning, since the Hebrew is a rhetorical question suggesting an affirmative answer and should be translated into English, "Did I not reveal myself?" See R. Gordis, *American Journal of Semitic Languages*, XLIX (1933), 212 ff.

[101] Omitted in the Hebrew text, but found in the Greek.

[102] See, e.g., E. Dhorme, *Les livres de Samuel* (1910), p. 39.

[103] See, e.g., M. Noth, *Die israelitischen Personennamen* (1928), p. 63; W. Spiegelberg, *Orientalistische Literaturzeitung*, IX (1906), 109; W. F. Albright, *Journal of the Palestine Oriental Society*, I (1920), 64, n. 2; A. H. Gardiner, *Journal of the American Oriental Society*, LVI (1936), 191-197.

[104] Similarly, the Hyksos adopted Egyptian names as a result of their sojourn in Egypt, several of them, for example, bearing the name Apophis.

Chron. 6:23, 37), the name Pashhur is borne by some four different Levites (see, e.g., Jer. 20:1; 21:1; 38:1; Ezra 2:38), and Phinehas was the name of three others (see, e.g., Judg. 20:28; I Sam. 1:3; Ezra 8:33).[105] That the Levites alone of the Hebrews were in Egypt is suggested, but of course not proved, by the further striking fact that they alone possess Egyptian names, not a single one being found in any of the other tribes. It is true that the account of the Exodus, as we have it now in our Bibles, seems to represent all the tribes as being in Egypt and all as a unit wandering through the wilderness, because this was the later interpretation. As the various tribes and groups of tribes became consolidated into a national unit, as they did by the time of David, the traditions of each became the common possession of the whole, and as the tribes and their traditions fused into one, the various episodes naturally became the experience of the nation as a whole; the experience of each became the experience of all.

Under a benevolent government the Hebrews that did go to Egypt grew and prospered, but with the overthrow of the Eighteenth Dynasty and the violent reaction against the policy of its later kings that developed with the establishment of the Nineteenth Dynasty, their happy lot was changed to one of oppression. This is the record of the Old Testament and the testimony also of the inscriptions of the Nineteenth Dynasty already noted.[106] From these we learn that Ramesses II, like his successors, Ramesses III and IV, used 'Apiru to perform heavy labor on public works along with mercenaries and others.[107] We know that the early years of Ramesses II were much devoted to building operations in the eastern

---

[105] See further on the Levites in Egypt T. J. Meek, *American Journal of Semitic Languages*, LVI (1939), 117-120.

[106] See p. 12 above.

[107] Similarly, according to Manetho, the Hebrews had to work in the quarries for the Egyptians; see Josephus, *Contra Apionem*, i. 26, 27.

Delta, in cities like Pi-tum and Pi-Ramesses (the Hebrew Pithom and Raamses), and these are the very cities which the Pharaoh of Ex. 1:11 forced the Hebrews to build for him. We know, too, that Pi-Ramesses as the name of a city appears first in the time of Ramesses II and was the name given by him to the ancient city of Avaris (later still called Tanis=Hebrew Zoan),[108] and it is not without significance that the city of Pi-Ramesses is mentioned in the Beisan stela of Ramesses II (line 10).[109] Hence there can be no question that the biblical writer of Ex. 1:11 identified the Pharaoh mentioned there with Ramesses II; he was "the new king who had no knowledge of Joseph" (Ex. 1:8) and proceeded to oppress the people. Ramesses II accordingly must have been the Pharaoh of the oppression, as tradition has long maintained, and the Exodus could not have occurred earlier than his reign, *ca.* 1290-1223 B.C. A date as late as this, however, conflicts seriously with that of the fall of Jericho, for we have already noted that Jericho must have fallen to the Hebrews close to 1400 B.C. Out of this dilemma there are only two avenues of escape, both of them quite drastic: either to deny the historicity of Ex. 1:11, as some scholars do,[110] or to assign the conquest of Jericho to an invasion that antedated the Exodus, as we have done, because the fall of Jericho cannot possibly be brought down to a date as late as Ramesses II and there is no good reason to doubt the historicity of Ex. 1:11. In that case Joshua has to be dissociated

[108] See A. H. Gardiner, *Ancient Egyptian Onomastica*, I (1947), 169*, 171* ff., 199* ff.; 278* f.

[109] Translated provisionally by A. Rowe, *The Topography and History of Beth-shan* (1930), pp. 35 f.; translated most recently by J. A. Wilson, in *Ancient Near Eastern Texts*, ed. J. B. Pritchard (1950).

[110] The different theories regarding the Exodus are well presented with full documentation by H. H. Rowley, *Bulletin of the John Rylands Library*, XXII, No. 1 (1938). See also the article on the Exodus by the present writer, to appear presently in the *Encyclopaedia Britannica*.

from Moses or from the capture of Jericho; he cannot possibly be both the successor of Moses and the conqueror of Jericho, if the Exodus occurred *ca.* 1200 B.C. and the fall of Jericho *ca.* 1400 B.C., as there is every reason to believe. He is so inextricably connected with Jericho that we have to dissociate him from Moses, and again we would account for the disorder in the Old Testament narratives by the fusion of the different sagas of the several groups that eventually coalesced to make the Hebrew people.

For the enslaved Hebrews in Egypt a deliverer arose in course of time in the person of Moses, who took advantage of the chaotic state of affairs that developed in Egypt after the death of Seti II (*ca.* 1194 B.C.)[111] to lead his people out, or such of them as could or would follow him. It is clear from the Old Testament account that not all were ready to do so, and an inscription of Ramesses IV, already noted,[112] records the presence of 'Apiru in Egypt as late as his reign (*ca.* 1145 B.C.), some time after the Exodus had taken place. Under the leadership of Moses and in the name of their god Yahweh the Hebrews that went with Moses saved themselves from further bondage by bounding back to the desert from which they had come and with whose spirit they were still more akin than with that of the more cultivated Egyptians. Retracing their earlier steps, they were led out of reach of the Egyptians "by the desert road to the Yam-Suph" (Ex. 13:18) rather than by the northern route directly to Palestine (Ex. 13:17), and the context shows that the Yam-Suph, or Sea of Reeds, intended here is the same as the one in Ex. 23:31, Num. 21:4, 1 Kings 9:26, and other passages; viz., the

[111] That this was a period of absolute anarchy, which lasted for a generation, is clearly stated in the Great Harris Papyrus; see J. H. Breasted, *Ancient Records of Egypt*, IV (1906), 198 f.

[112] See p. 12 above.

EDWARD MINER GALLAUDET MEMORIAL LIBRARY   108348
GALLAUDET COLLEGE
WASHINGTON, D. C.

eastern arm of the Red Sea known to us as the Gulf of Aqabah.[113] Here they mingled again with their kinsmen whom they had left behind in the Negeb when they originally went to Egypt.

The Negeb, never able to support a large population, was filled to overflowing with this sudden rush of newcomers, and a part of the enlarged population had of necessity to seek a homeland elsewhere. Sensing the opportunities of the occasion, Moses put himself at the head of this overflow as chief shaman, or *kāhin,* and organized his followers into a confederacy or amphictyony, even as Joshua had done, and many another in similar circumstances both before and after. He made the old tribal god Yahweh the god of the amphictyony, and in his name he made a covenant with the people and proceeded to collect the various laws, customs, and traditions of the uniting tribes into one confederate code. Tradition connects these events with Sinai-Horeb and Kadesh, but unfortunately it is impossible to determine exactly what occurred at each site[114] and it is equally impossible to determine their location. Phythian-Adams and Winnett[115] have given strong reasons to show that the name of the sacred mountain in the original tradition was Horeb and that it was situated on the western border of the land of Midian (so Ex. 3:1), just east of the Gulf of Aqabah. By the time of P it had come to be called Sinai and was identified with a

---

[113] The Yam-Suph of Ex. 14 and 15 was situated of course on the border of Egypt and is usually identified with the Red Sea and so translated, but this identification is by no means certain. For the name in Egyptian records see A. H. Gardiner, *Ancient Egyptian Onomastica,* II (1947), 201* f.

[114] Cf. R. H. Pfeiffer, *Introduction to the Old Testament* (1941), pp. 145 f., 170 f.

[115] W. J. Phythian-Adams, *The Call of Israel* (1934), pp. 131-133; *The Fulness of Israel* (1938), pp. 92-94; F. V. Winnett, *The Mosaic Tradition* (1949), pp. 72-76, 100-102, 117.

mountain in what is today known as the Sinaitic peninsula, and there it remains in tradition down to the present day. However, this is the last place in the world to which Moses would have led his people because it was a region held in force by the Egyptians from early dynastic times as its most important source of mineral wealth (copper and turquoise). Kadesh is even more difficult to locate than Sinai-Horeb, because of the conflict in tradition,[116] but whatever its location it was intimately connected with the formation of the southern confederacy. It was for a long time the site of the Hebrew encampment according to the Old Testament (Num. 20:1 ff.; Deut. 1:46), and here was situated the En-mishpat, the "Fountain of Judgment" (Gen. 14:7), where the people were wont to gather for *tôrôth* or oracular decisions. Here also was Meribah, the "Place of Litigation" (Num. 27:14; Deut. 32:51), another name suggestive of lawmaking and lawgiving.

Just what laws are to be attributed to Moses it is impossible to say.[117] They may have included a part of the Book of the Covenant, as many scholars believe; and the two decalogues of Ex. 20:2-17 and Ex. 34:17-26 are intimately associated with Moses. It is inconceivable, however, that either of the decalogues is now in its original form or wording,[118] and the reconstruction of the original is of necessity largely speculative. In Ex. 20:2-17=Deut. 5:6-21 many scholars would

[116] See Winnett, *op. cit.*, pp. 95 ff.; Phythian-Adams, *op. cit.*, pp. 69, 133, 195 ff., both of whom would identify Kadesh with Petra. Ever since H. C. Trumbull, *Kadesh Barnea* (1884), it has usually been identified with modern 'Ain Qadis or that general neighborhood.

[117] So also A. Bentzen, *Introduction to the Old Testament*, I (1948), p. 112: "That *Moses* has been a lawgiver should not be doubted, but it is impossible to trace one single element of the law *in its present form* back to him."

[118] Even the arrangement of the decalogue in Ex. 20 is different in different traditions; see A. Bentzen, *op. cit.*, p. 52.

delete verse 4, the prohibition of images, as late and read verses 2 and 3 as two laws: (1) "I am Yahweh your God who brought you out of the land of Egypt, out of a state of slavery." (2) "You must have no other gods beside me." But this is impossible; both grammar and syntax require the translation, "Since I, Yahweh, am your God, who brought you out of the land of Egypt, out of a state of slavery, you must have no other gods beside me," the first clause being clearly a circumstantial clause, with subject first as against the usual word order of predicate first.[119] As a matter of fact there is no assurance whatsoever that the early arrangement of the laws was in decads; it is found nowhere else and it is more likely to be late than early, a purely mechanical arrangement that smacks of artificiality.

But whatever the confederate code instituted by Moses consisted of, it had the effect of uniting kindred tribes into a more or less consolidated whole, and under the stimulus of that union the confederate tribes gradually pushed their way to the north, from Kadesh to Beersheba, to Hebron, until finally they controlled most of the land south of Jerusalem between the Dead Sea and Philistia, in which latter region certain "Peoples of the Sea" (known to us as the Philistines) had just recently established themselves.[120] That this invasion took place close to 1200 B.C. is evidenced by the archaeological explorations of Nelson Glueck in Edom and Moab, where the most thorough investigation showed no trace of

---

[119] See T. J. Meek, *Journal of the American Oriental Society*, LVIII (1938), 126 f.

[120] For these peoples see, e. g., *Cambridge Ancient History*, II (1931), 275-294; J. Garstang, *The Heritage of Solomon* (1934), pp. 230 ff.; A. H. Gardiner, *Ancient Egyptian Onomastica*, I (1947), 190*-205.* They invaded Egypt *ca.* 1175 B.C., but Ramasses III was able to drive them off. He was not able, however, to prevent some of them, the Pulestiu or Philistines, from carving out a homeland for themselves along the southwest coastland of Canaan.

a sedentary occupation from the nineteenth century until the thirteenth.[121] Hence, if there were settled peoples there at the time of the Hebrew invasion, as the Old Testament affirms, the invasion could not have occurred before the thirteenth century at the very earliest. This is strikingly confirmed by the excavations in southern Palestine, those of Albright in Tell Beit Mirsim (apparently ancient Debir, later called Kirjath-sepher),[122] and those of Sellers at Beth-zur,[123] which indicate that the Hebrew occupation of these cities occurred *ca.* 1200 B.C. The site that has given us archaeological data that we can date almost to the year is Tell ed-Duweir (ancient Lachish) and these place the capture of that city by the Hebrews at the very end of the thirteenth century. The exact date is almost certainly given by a hieratic inscription from the fourth year of some pharaoh whose name is unfortunately not preserved, but must be either Merneptah, Siptah, or Seti II.[124] This agrees too with the

[121] See *Bulletin of the American Schools of Oriental Research*, No. 55 (1934), pp. 3-21; *Annual of the American Schools of Oriental Research*, XIV (1934), 1 ff.; XVIII-XIX (1939), 268; *The Other Side of the Jordan* (1940), pp. 114-157. According to Glueck, there was a sedentary occupation in the region of the Negeb from the twenty-third to the nineteenth century B.C., followed by a complete break until the period from the thirteenth to the eighth century. The most intensive sedentary occupation was found in the twelfth century, when the copper mines of the region were extensively worked.

[122] See W. F. Albright, *The Archaeology of Palestine and the Bible* (1932), pp. 93, 100 ff.; *Annual of the American Schools of Oriental Research*, XII (1932), 52 ff.; XVII (1938), 76 ff.

[123] See O. R. Sellers, *The Citadel of Beth-zur* (1931), p. 9.

[124] See W. F. Albright, *Bulletin of the American Schools of Oriental Research*, No. 74 (1939), pp. 20-22, with the literature there cited. The excavations at Lachish show that the city enjoyed unbroken security under Egyptian suzerainty down to the end of the Nineteenth Dynasty and there are indications that this extended into the Twentieth Dynasty as late as Ramesses III, *ca.* 1160 B.C. We know definitely that Lachish was still in the hands of the Egyptians in the Tell el-Amarna period, although Abdi-Heba of Jerusalem accuses the city, along with Gezer and Askelon, of being friendly with the Habiru, supplying them with food, oil, and

biblical setting of the invasion in the Iron Age (cf. Josh. 6:24; 17:16, 18), which began close to 1200 B.C.[125] Likewise, the references to the Philistines (Ex. 13:17; 23:31), who we know entered Palestine *ca.* 1190 B.C., suggest the same period. That the Hebrews did not extend their conquests to the sea must be due to the fact that the Philistines got there first; otherwise there would have been nothing to stop them. Except for a brief revival of power in Palestine in the early years of Merneptah, Egypt lost all control of the country, and this was the one occasion when it could fall an easy prey to invaders like the Philistines and Hebrews. Furthermore, the fact that the Old Testament retains no remembrance of Egyptian rule in Palestine must indicate that the Hebrews had no experience of it and they must have invaded the country when Egyptian control had declined to the vanishing point, viz., in the Tell el-Amarna period in the north and in the period after Ramesses II in the south.

The preparations for the southern invasion are recounted in Num. 13, while the invasion itself is briefly recounted in Num. 21:1-3; Josh. 15:14-19; Judg. 1:1-21,[126] from which narratives it is clear that the invasion was from the south northward.[127] These southerners were the people known

---

other necessities; see J. A. Knudtzon, *Die El-Amarna-Tafeln* (1915), No. 287, ll. 14-16. The excavations at Tell el-Hesi, now identified with Eglon rather than Lachish, as used to be the case, were conducted too early to be altogether scientific and the publication of the results was too inadequate to determine with any certainty the date of its conquest by the Hebrews.

[125] See, e.g., G. E. Wright, *American Journal of Archaeology*, XLIII (1939), 458-463.

[126] In Judg. 1:1-21 v. 8 is to be deleted as contrary to fact and contradicted by v. 21, and in the latter verse "Benjamin" is to be changed to "Judah," to accord with its doublet, Josh. 15:63.

[127] It is true that according to Judg. 1:16 the starting point was the "City of Palms," by which term Jericho may have been intended, but it could equally well or better apply to Beersheba or some other southern

later as Judah, after the name of the strongest tribe, because
it is clear from the narratives that it was with this tribe that
the Levites, Simeonites, Kenites, Calebites, and others amalgamated to make the southern confederacy.[128] In the genealogies Reuben appears regularly as the first-born (see, e.g.,
Gen. 35:23), suggesting that as a tribe Reuben was the oldest
and strongest of all, but its arrogance brought about its
downfall (Gen. 49:3 f.; cf. 35:22). It never rose beyond
the seminomadic stage; it appears as one of the weakest of
the tribes when reliable history begins, and it disappeared
entirely by the middle of the ninth century. On the other
hand, Judah is represented as an aggressive, growing tribe
from the very beginning, "a lion's whelp who has grown up
on prey," before whom all the others bow in submission
(Gen. 49:8-12); and its primacy among the tribes is indicated by the further fact that traditionally it was selected
by Yahweh as the one to be the first to invade the land (Judg.
1:1 f.; cf. also 20:18). There may also be a suggestion here
of the great antiquity of Judah, certain elements of which
were native to the land. Indeed Gen. 38 says distinctly that
Judah early separated from his brother Hebrews, intermar-
ried with the natives, and settled down with them, thus making his settlement in Palestine date from patriarchal times.
In that case Judah was actually the first of all the tribes to
occupy the land.

According to the Old Testament, Reuben settled north-

---

city, where palms are more numerous. Garstang's contention, *Foundations
of Bible History* (1931), p. 215, that the movement was *upwards* and so
must have been from Jericho and not from the south is by no means so
cogent as he maintains, because identically the same verb, "to go up," is
used for the movement from the south, e.g., in Num. 13:17, 21 f.; 14:40 ff.
Jericho would be a most unlikely, if not impossible, starting point for an
invasion of the Negeb round about Arad, some seventeen miles south of
Hebron.

[128] See also pp. 114 f., 125 ff. below.

east of the Dead Sea (Num. 32:37 f.; Josh. 13:15-23), but
in ancestry it is joined with Simeon, Levi, and Judah as a
Leah tribe (Gen. 29:32; 35:23). The earliest traditions
emphasize its arrogance (Gen. 49:3 f.; 35:22). It was un-
co-operative (Judg. 5:15 f.) and in Num. 16 there is the
record of a dissension within the tribes, fomented by the
Reubenites, Dathan and Abiram. In this we have doubtless a
reminiscence of the separation of Reuben from the southern
group, apparently in the form of an expulsion. Thus ex-
pelled, the Reubenites migrated northward around Edom
and through Moab, eventually landing northeast of the Dead
Sea. The record of that migration is then to be found in
Num. 21-25 (cf. Deut. 2-3). In these narratives, as in most
of the others, it is professedly the whole Hebrew people
that are concerned, but it is clearly only a part of them,
and the group that best fits the situation is the tribe of
Reuben. They alone migrated from the south to settle in the
north and so weak were they that they could not plow
their way ruthlessly through a land strongly held, but had
to make a circuit to reach their homeland. Even there they
were not able to maintain themselves for long and by the
middle of the ninth century, as already noted, they had
completely disappeared.

Thus the facts of history and archaeology, as well as the
Old Testament sagas and narratives, would force us to find
the origin of the Hebrew people in several distinct groups.
(1) One was the far north: Asher, Dan, Naphtali, Issachar,
and Zebulun,[129] all of whom were more native than Hebrew

[129] According to the Old Testament, Dan first attempted to settle in
the Shephelah, but was ousted from there and had to seek a homeland in
the north (Judg. 1:34; 18:1-31). This, too, may have been the experience
of Naphtali (cf. Deut. 33:23), traditionally connected with Dan as the
second son of Rachel's handmaid, Bilhah (Gen. 30:7 f.; 35:25). Cf. also
C. Steuernagel, *Die Einwanderung der israelitischen Stämme in Kanaan*,
(1901), pp. 28 f.; C. F. Burney, *Israel's Settlement in Canaan* (3rd ed.,
1921), pp. 23 ff., 50 ff.

and became Hebrew only as they were drawn into the
Hebrew confederacy by a common peril, beginning about
the time of Deborah with the menace from Sisera. The Old
Testament accordingly represents the first three as the sons
of concubines and the last two as belated sons of Leah,
and all of them are represented as living as best they could
among the Canaanites, with the chief cities unconquered
(Judg. 1:30-36). (2) Another group was located in east
central Palestine: Machir, Gilead, and Gad (joined later by
Reuben) in the East Jordan, and Ephraim, Manasseh, and
Benjamin in the highlands of the West Jordan. Here they
were hemmed in by a belt of Canaanite cities stretching
across the plain of Esdraelon and southward through the
Shephelah—cities like Bethshean, Ibleam, Taanach, Megiddo,
Dor, Bethhoron, Bethshemesh, and Gezer. (3) In the south
was still another group: Judah, Simeon, and Levi, with related tribes like the Kenites, Calebites, Kenizzites, and Jerahmeelites. These made their way by gradual conquest through
the Negeb into the southern hill country, but they were
unable to occupy the Maritime Plain or the belt of Canaanite
territory which ran through Jerusalem and thus separated
them from the northerners.

The settlement of the northern, or Israelite, group, as it
became, occurred during the century or two beginning
about 1400 B.C., while the southern, or Judean, group came
in about 1200 B.C. This has the support of history and
archaeology and apparently that of biblical chronology as
well. It is true that too much reliance cannot be placed on
chronological data in the Old Testament and at best they
are only approximate; but it is not a little startling to discover that we have evidences for both dates, 1400 and
1200 B.C. According to I Kings 6:1, the Exodus from Egypt
occurred 480 years before the building of Solomon's temple,
which was begun *ca.* 960 B.C., thereby putting the settle-

ment in Canaan *ca.* 1400 B.C. Similarly, according to Judg. 11:26 there were three hundred years between Jephthah, *ca.* 1100 B.C., and Israel's occupation of the East Jordan, giving us again the date 1400 B.C. On the other hand, Gen. 36:31-39 names eight Edomite kings as having ruled between the conquest and the accession of Saul, *ca.* 1020 B.C. If we allow an average reign of twenty or twenty-five years for each of the eight kings, we would get *ca.* 1200 B.C. as the date of the conquest. Furthermore, according to the Greek and Samaritan versions of Ex. 12:40 and one statement in Josephus (*Antiquities*, II, xv, 2) the total length of the Hebrew sojourn in Egypt was 215 years.[130] If we take this as calculated from the time of Amenophis III and IV, when according to our thesis the Hebrews of the Exodus entered Egypt, this would again give us a date of *ca.* 1200 B.C. for the Exodus. The 430 years of the Hebrew text and the four hundred years of Gen. 15:13 and two passages in Josephus (*Wars*, V, ix, 4, and *Antiquities*, II, ix, 1) may be explained perhaps as reckoned from some time in the Hyksos period when the first Hebrews went to Egypt. The Bible has unquestionably telescoped the earlier and the later sojourns into one and foreshortened history, as ancient records so frequently do.

The more the records are studied, the clearer it is that there are two cycles of traditions concerning the Hebrew entry into Palestine. According to one, the entry was from the east across the Jordan, and in this Joshua is the leading figure; the tribes are Israelites; and the conquests are in the north. According to the other, the entry was from the south and it is associated with Judah, Simeon, Caleb, Othniel, and other related tribes, with Moses as the leading figure. The first invasion was manifestly Israelite, and the second Judean.

[130] See, e.g., S. R. Driver, *The Book of Exodus* (1911), pp. 101 f.

The Old Testament narrative, as we have it now in its later nationalized form, has dovetailed the two conquests into each other as the work of a single people,[131] resulting naturally in a good deal of confusion and inconsistency. For example, according to Josh. 15:15-19 and Judg. 1:11-15 Kirjath-sepher or Debir was captured by Othniel, whereas according to Josh. 10:38 f. it was captured by Joshua. Judges 1 distinguishes definitely between the conquest of the south by Judah and its confederates (vv. 1-21) and the conquest of the north by the Israelite tribes under the leadership of Joshua (vv. 22-36); but the later, more elaborate, idealized, and nationalized account in the Book of Joshua tends to combine the two conquests into one and ascribe most of the glory to the Israelite hero Joshua.[132] It is to be noted, however, that his glory is only a reflected one from the southern hero, Moses, and he acts, not on his own initiative, but on directions handed down from Moses; and this is what we would expect, because the narrative in its present traditional form has come down to us through Judean hands. The north receives its mead of credit, but the greater glory

[131] This was a natural process as north and south united to form a single people. The early literature of the Old Testament is full of indications that the traditions of the two peoples were fused together to make a common history, in part consciously as nationalistic propaganda to unite the two peoples and in part unconsciously as a result of that union. If the two peoples were to become one, they must be made one in the past as well as in the present.

[132] Hence Caleb's conquest of Hebron (Josh. 15:13 f.) and Othniel's conquest of Debir (Josh. 15:15-19; Judg. 1:11-15) are credited to Joshua in Josh. 10:36-39. Even Deborah's victory over the Canaanites at a much later date is attributed to Joshua, for Jabin, king of Hazor, mentioned in Josh. 11:1, can be none other than the king of the same name, place, and nationality mentioned in Judg. 4:2. For an analysis and appraisal of the narratives in Joshua and Judges see, e.g., C. F. Burney, *Israel's Settlement in Canaan* (3rd ed., 1921), pp. 1-58. For an attempt to compose the differences between Josh. 10 and Judg. 1 see G. E. Wright, *Journal of Near Eastern Studies*, V (1946), 105-114.

after all goes to the south. That the northern hero, Joshua, should have become the national hero of the conquest and "Israel"[133] the national name of the people as a whole may be surprising, but it was doubtless due to the fact that the first union of north and south occurred under Saul, a northerner, and the further fact that Israel throughout the union was the greater in territory, numbers, wealth, culture, and hence in prestige. It was not until the time of David that Judah forged to the front and then for a short period only.

To put the settlement of Israel in the north some two hundred years before that of Judah in the south seems best to account for the cultural superiority of the north over the south. Two hundred years' earlier settlement in agricultural life and closer contact with the more cultured Canaanites would give the northerners no little advantage over their kinsmen to the south. It would also seem to be the only way to account for the differences in the Hebrew language as used in north and south; for the dialectal differences we know now were considerable.[134] It was likewise because north and south were two separate groups that we have the division into Rachel and Leah tribes in the genealo-

[133] It is to be noted that "Israel" in the Old Testament, and likewise in modern writings, is sometimes used for the north alone and sometimes for the nation as a whole, whereas "Judah" is never used otherwise than in its local sense. It is also to be noted that the modern name of the Jewish state is "Israel." For a study of all the occurrences of the name Israel in the Old Testament see G. A. Danell, *Studies in the Name Israel in the Old Testament* (1946).

[134] These are apparent, for example, from a comparison of the Hebrew of the Israelites as revealed in the Samaritan version of the Pentateuch and on the ostraca excavated in the north with that of the Old Testament, which is almost wholly Judean. Cf. also Judg. 18:3, where it is recorded that the Danites recognized the Levite from Judah by his accent: "As they came near the house of Micah, they recognized the accent of the young Levite." Another reference to dialectal difference, this time between the Gileadites and Ephraimites, is Judg. 12:6.

gies,[135] and for the same reason there was no appeal by Deborah to the southern tribes, Judah, Simeon, and Levi, when the northern tribes were menaced by the Canaanites under Sisera (Judg. 5). They belonged to the south and at that time had no concern in the affairs of the north. The settlement of the two groups at different periods and under different leaders, and with different cultural and religious attainments, would also account best for the continued friction between them when they did come together,[136] and it is the only way to account for the fact that Rehoboam had to go to Shechem to receive, if he could, the kingship of Israel (I Kings 12:1). Only for a brief period were they ever united and then not very closely, when they were engaged in a common cause against a common foe, the Philistines. As soon as this pressure was removed in the time of David, their differences quickly reappeared.[137] Internal dissension developed and grew in intensity until the two peoples on the death of Solomon split definitely into the two kingdoms of Israel and Judah and went their separate ways. Not even the long reigns of David and Solomon or the reorganization of the state by Solomon could weld the two peoples into a homogeneous kingdom or make Israel feel that it was one with Judah. As two peoples they began; as two peoples they insisted on living, even to the bitter end. Instead of healing their differences, time only seemed to intensify them, so that in the days of Jesus a Jew, if he could

[135] There is ground for the belief that the earliest traditions represented Israel and Judah as brothers, which would make still clearer the distinction between the two groups that bore their names. Cf. Eduard Meyer, *Die Israeliten und ihre Nachbarstämme* (1906), p. 425.

[136] For this in the early period see I Chron. 5:1 f.; II Sam. 19:41-43.

[137] Cf. also W. O. E. Oesterley and T. H. Robinson, *A History of Israel*, I (1932), 135 f.; J. N. Schofield, *The Historical Background of the Bible* (1938), pp. 142 f.

prevent it, would have no dealings whatsoever with a Samaritan.[138]

[138] The outline of this interpretation of early Hebrew history was presented by the writer as long ago as 1920 in an article entitled "A Proposed Reconstruction of Early Hebrew History," *American Journal of Theology*, XXIV (1920), 209-216. It is an interpretation that has become increasingly popular as best fitting all the evidences in the case. The chapter should be read in conjunction with the article on the Exodus prepared by the present writer for Encyclopaedia Britannica, Inc. It might also be compared with two articles by H. H. Rowley, "Israel's Sojourn in Egypt," *Bulletin of the John Rylands Library*, XXII (1938), No. 1, and "Recent Discovery and the Patriarchal Age," *ibid.*, XXXII (1949), No. 1. A feature of these articles is their complete documentation, but the interpretation of the data is very different from that presented here. The same author's Schweich Lectures, *From Joseph to Joshua* (1950), appeared too late to be utilized in the writing of this chapter. Most of the archaeological material used in this book is well presented by Millar Burrows, *What Mean These Stones?* (1941); C. C. McCown, *The Ladder of Progress in Palestine* (1943); Jack Finegan, *Light from the Ancient Past* (1946).

CHAPTER TWO

The Origin of Hebrew Law

UNTIL comparatively recent years the Hebrew Torah was the only Oriental code of laws that we possessed, and we could say little about its origin because we had no other with which to compare it. Thanks, however, to the spades of the excavators we now have several other Oriental codes.

The work of the excavator has much of drudgery in it, but this is more than compensated for by the thrills of new discoveries. In the most unexpected places and at most unexpected times finds of tremendous importance are continually being made. So it was with the discovery of the famous Code of Hammurabi, king of Babylonia, *ca.* 1728-1686 B.C.[1] This was found, not in Babylonia, but in the old Elamite capital, Susa (the Shushan of Esther and Daniel), whither it had been carried from Babylonia by some Elamite conqueror (apparently Shutruk-Nahhunte, *ca.* 1207-1171 B.C.) as a trophy of war, in turn to be carried off by French archaeologists and deposited in the Louvre in Paris as a trophy of archaeology. Its discovery occurred in the winter of 1901-2 and quite took the world by storm, so important

---

[1] The best edition is that by A. Deimel, *Codex Hammurabi* (1930). The most recent translation is that by T. J. Meek, in *Ancient Near Eastern Texts,* ed. J. B. Pritchard (1950).

was it and so enlightening for the understanding of Hebrew law. Originally it contained about three hundred laws and it has a prologue and an epilogue.

The discovery of Hammurabi's lawbook only whetted the appetite of scholars for other Semitic codes, but none was forthcoming for many years. Partial copies of the Hammurabi Code were found to fill part of the gap in the original stela;[2] groups of laws in both Babylonian and Sumerian were discovered; and there appeared clear indications from various sources that the Assyrians must have had a law code of their own, but this was not found until the German excavators at Ashur unearthed it just before World War I. This was another tremendously important discovery, but because the nations at the time were more concerned in destroying one another than in learning from one another or the past, the contents of the code were not made public until 1920.[3] The laws are preserved to us, not on a stela as in the case of Hammurabi's laws, but on clay tablets, many of which are unfortunately badly broken, and the lacunae have not as yet been completely filled. Hence we do not have the code in its entirety, but only in a more or less fragmentary state. The original code may go back to the fifteenth century B.C., but our copies date from the time of Tiglath-pileser I, *ca.* 1112-1074 B.C.

Besides this Middle Assyrian Code we have three very fragmentary tablets containing Old Assyrian laws of ap-

[2] The last seven columns of the obverse, from the end of § 65 to the beginning of § 100, were chiseled off by the Elamite plunderer to make room for an inscription of his own, but this was never inserted.

[3] O. Schroeder, *Keilschrifttexte aus Assur verschiedenen Inhalts* (1920), Nos. 1-6, 143, 144, 193. Additional texts have since been published by E. F. Weidner, *Archiv für Orientforschung*, XII (1937), 50-54 and 4 plates. The most recent translation is that by T. J. Meek, *op. cit.*, pp. 180-188. For an earlier translation of the Schroeder texts and an exhaustive commentary see G. R. Driver and J. C. Miles, *The Assyrian Laws* (1935).

proximately the twentieth century B.C.[4] Their provenance is uncertain because they were dug up by natives, but both script and language indicate that they belong to the same time and place as the Old Assyrian tablets found in Asia Minor. Hence they are not the law of Assyria proper, but of an Assyrian trading colony in Asia Minor. They are too fragmentary to enter into our discussion here.

A fourth collection of laws known to us, the Hittite Code, was found by Professor Hugo Winckler of Berlin in his excavations at Boghaz-köi in Asia Minor, the site of the capital of the ancient Hittite Empire, in 1906-7, together with many other documents of that great empire. This code, like the Assyrian, is written on clay tablets (partly broken) in the cuneiform script, but in a language unknown at the time of discovery and only deciphered in 1915 by Professor F. Hrozný of Prague. As discoverer, Professor Winckler had first claim on the publication of the tablets, but sickness prevented him from accomplishing this, and the law code was accordingly not published until after his death, a part of it in 1921,[5] and the rest in subsequent years.[6] It was first translated by Professor Hrozný in 1922,[7] and has most recently been translated into English by Albrecht Goetze.[8] The Hittite Code in its present form comes from some time between 1400 and 1200 B.C.

Scholars presently came to suspect that there were codes

[4] Two of the tablets were published by G. Contenau, *Tablettes cappadociennes publiées avec inventaire et tables* (1920), Nos. 112 and 123. The other tablet was published by F. J. Stephens, *Journal of the Society of Oriental Research*, XI (1927), 122, No. 19. The tablets have most recently been translated by Driver and Miles, *op. cit.*, pp. 276-279.

[5] *Keilschrifttexte aus Boghazköi*, VI (1921), Nos. 2-26.

[6] *Keilschrifturkunden aus Boghazköi*, XIII (1925), Nos. 11-16; XXVI (1933), No. 56; XXIX (1936), Nos. 13-38.

[7] *Code hittite provenant de l'Asie mineure* (1922).

[8] In *Ancient Near Eastern Texts*, ed. J. B. Pritchard (1950).

earlier than any of these when fragments of laws were identified as connected with Lipit-Ishtar, fifth king of the dynasty of Isin, *ca.* 1868-1857 B.C.,[9] more than a hundred years before the time of Hammurabi. Then in 1947 Francis R. Steele and Samuel N. Kramer discovered four fragments of a Sumerian code among the tablets in the University Museum of Philadelphia,[10] which had been excavated by the University of Pennsylvania Expedition to Nippur some fifty years earlier. Upon further examination these turned out to be fragments of the code of Lipit-Ishtar, and this in turn led to the identification of a number of previously published tablets as belonging to the same code and eventually a partial restoration of the text was achieved,[11] with a sum total of about 400 lines, containing 38 laws, out of an estimated original of 1,200 lines or a little more than 100 laws. Like Hammurabi's lawbook, the Lipit-Ishtar Code has a prologue and an epilogue, similar in content to those of Hammurabi. It may have been published on a stela originally, but all that we have now are copies on clay tablets, rather badly preserved.

Scholars had scarcely recovered from the excitement of this vastly important discovery, when another was announced in 1948 of even greater significance. Two tablets were unearthed by an Iraqi expedition at Tell Abu Harmal on the southern outskirts of Baghdad, which turned out to be two recensions apparently of the Code of Bilalama, king of Eshnunna *ca.* 1930 B.C., shortly after the fall of the Third Dynasty of Ur.[12] This makes it the oldest code known to

[9] See A. Boissier, *Babyloniaca*, IX (1926), 19-22.

[10] See F. R. Steele, *American Journal of Archaeology*, LI (1947), 158-164.

[11] See F. R. Steele, *ibid.*, LII (1948), 425-450 and Pls. XXXIX-XLV. A more recent translation is that by S. N. Kramer, in *Ancient Near Eastern Texts*, ed. J. B. Pritchard (1950).

[12] Published by A. Goetze, *Sumer*, IV (1948), 63-102 and Pls. I-IV. A later translation appears in *Ancient Near Eastern Texts*, ed. J. B. Pritchard (1950).

date, nearly a hundred years older than that of Lipit-Ishtar. Like the Hammurabi Code, it is written in Old Babylonian, but there is every indication that it is based on Sumerian prototypes, which go back to the Third Dynasty of Ur or perhaps to Urukagina, the reforming king of Lagash, ca. 2370 B.C. Unfortunately only a part of the original code is preserved, some 60 laws in all. The prologue is quite short and is preserved only in part; if there was an epilogue, it has been lost.

Finally there is a small collection of Neo-Babylonian laws, which were published as long ago as 1889,[13] but have only recently been translated into English.[14] Only 9 laws out of a total of approximately 16 have been preserved. Since the collection is later than the Hebrew Code and hence could not have affected the latter, it is not pertinent to our purpose here.

No Egyptian lawbook has as yet been discovered, with the exception of a very fragmentary civil code of the Ptolemaic period,[15] which is too late for our purpose. Numerous contracts, court decisions, and the like are of course known to us from the early period and these naturally give us considerable information about the laws of Egypt,[16] but we have no code to compare with the Hebrew Code. Hence the only Oriental codes known to us to date are the city code of Eshnunna, the city code of Lipit-Ishtar, the imperial code of Hammurabi, the Middle Assyrian Code, the Hittite Code, and the Hebrew Code, together with a few

[13] Published by F. E. Peiser, *Sitzungsberichte der Preussischen Akademie der Wissenschaften*, 1889, pp. 823-828 and Tafel VII.

[14] T. J. Meek, in *Ancient Near Eastern Texts*, ed. J. B. Pritchard (1950).

[15] W. Spiegelberg, *Aus einer ägyptischen Zivilprozessordnung der Ptolemäerzeit* (1929).

[16] See, e.g., A. Scharff und E. Seidl, *Ägyptologische Forschungen*, No. 10 (1939); E. Seidl, in *The Legacy of Egypt*, ed. S. R. K. Glanville (1942), pp. 198-217.

Old Assyrian laws and the small Neo-Babylonian collection. Since the Hebrew Code is later than the first five, our task is to compare it with these to see if it was in any way derived from them, but before doing that we need to make some remarks about all six codes in general. In the first place, they are strictly not codes at all, although for the sake of convenience we shall continue to call them codes. The first code in the strict sense of the word was not prepared until many centuries later, not until the time of the Twelve Tables of Rome in the fifth century B.C. The Oriental codes are merely collections of precedents (i.e., case law), and "precedents" is one of the terms used in the Hebrew law to describe its ordinances, *mishpāṭîm*, "judgments, decisions, precedents" (see, e.g., Ex. 21:1), from the root *shāpat*, "to judge, decide." Various precedents are set forth as illustrations of the administration of justice, but these precedents are not at all exhaustive of the various kinds of cases that might arise. It is true that none of the codes has come down to us in its entirety and some omissions are doubtless due to this, but they were manifestly not intended to be exhaustive, but merely illustrative of the general procedure to be followed. For example, in the Hammurabi Code we have no specific laws regarding willful murder, buying on credit, loans, and many another matter, but we know from the contract tablets of the time that all these things were provided for by law. Similarly, in the Hebrew Code we have no laws whatsoever defining marriage rites and terms, and yet the Hebrews married and gave in marriage, all in accord with established law, as we know from references like Ex. 22:17; Gen. 34:12; I Sam. 18:25, where the marriage price is referred to (mistranslated "dowry" in the Authorized Version); Ex. 22:16; Deut. 20:7; 22:23 ff.;

Lev. 19:20, where a betrothal is presupposed; and Gen. 24:22, 53; 34:12, where the giving of presents is mentioned.[17]

Another thing that we need to note about these Oriental lawbooks is that they consist of old and new material, as all lawbooks do; i.e., they were not created in a day out of nothing, but were the accumulation of centuries of legal procedure, slowly but continually modified and changed as new situations arose. This is very manifest in the Hittite Code, in which some laws contain the statement that formerly the penalty was, for example, 30 oxen (§ 57), but now the penalty is 15 oxen (the later penalty being always more lenient). Furthermore, we have different redactions of the code preserved to us, representing different periods in its development, and likewise in the case of the Middle Assyrian Code. In the case of the Hammurabi Code we know now that it was not the original creation of Hammurabi and his lawmakers, because a number of the laws are little more than translations from the Lipit-Ishtar Code or earlier Sumerian laws, or adaptations from the Eshnunna Code.[18] Indeed this was doubtless in Hammurabi's own mind when he said in the prologue to his code, "When Marduk commissioned me to guide the people aright, to direct the land I established law and justice in the language of the land [*ina pî mâtim*],

[17] For an exhaustive, fully documented discussion of the Hebrew marriage rites and customs, deduced largely from the Old Testament narratives, see E. Neufeld, *Ancient Hebrew Marriage Laws* (1944).

[18] For a comparison of the Hammurabi Code with that of Eshnunna see F. R. Steele, *American Journal of Archaeology*, LII (1948), 446-450. For previous comparisons see W. Eilers, *Der Alte Orient*, XXXI, Heft 3/4 (1932), pp. 6 ff., who cited all the relevant literature known at the time, together with detailed references in his translation of the laws in question. For a comparison of the Hammurabi Code with that of Bilalama see J. Miles and O. R. Gurney, *Archiv Orientální*, XVII (1949), 178 ff., who find a very close resemblance between the two codes, both in subject matter and in style.

thereby promoting the welfare of the people." What Hammurabi did was to bring together the various laws of his empire representing various cultures, reduce them to a common language, and make them a more or less consistent whole, but not wholly consistent, because the Oriental mind is not quite so logical as the Occidental, and inconsistencies appear in Hammurabi's laws as they do in most. For example, the penalty for theft in § 7 is death (so also in § 6 for stealing something and selling it), but in § 8 it is merely severalfold restitution, and death only if the thief has nothing wherewith to make restitution. This and other inconsistencies in the code, Paul Koschaker would explain as due to interpolations,[19] but however they got into the text they represent different periods of legislation. Likewise the Hebrew Torah is not one consistent whole, the creation of a single legislator, Moses, or anyone else. Law does not originate in that way. It comes into existence slowly to meet the ever-changing needs of the time, and this is more evident in the Hebrew Torah than in any of the other codes, because we have here not one book but several, separated by many centuries of time. These, as generally recognized, are the Book of the Covenant (Ex. 20:22-23:33), now incorporated in the fusion of a northern, or E, collection of laws with a southern, or J collection; the Deuteronomic Code of the seventh century B.C.; the Holiness Code of the sixth century (Lev. 17-26); and the Priestly Code of the fifth century (parts of Ex., Lev., Num.). Nor can we say that these several codes are each the product of a single pen in a single age, because several different styles of drafting the laws occur in each. New and old material is found in all of

---

[19] *Rechtsvergleichende Studien zur Gesetzgebung Hammurapis* (1917), *passim.*

them, even the latest,[20] so that the Torah, as we have it, is the accumulation of centuries, a legislative snowball that has rolled down the avenues of time, gathering more and more material from various sources the further it rolled and taking on new forms with every change in the course. Through centuries of time the various codes, each in turn a growth over a period of time, have fused together and have been fused together to make our present composite and very complicated Torah.[21] Hence our task to discover its origin is no easy one.

Still another thing we have to note regarding all six Oriental codes: none of them is arranged in completely logical order. The Oriental mind is no more systematic and orderly than it is consistent. In the earliest Hebrew laws, however, we can discern an arrangement in decalogues. Indeed the laws of Ex. 20:2-17 = Deut. 5:6-21 are called a decalogue in Deut. 4:13 and 10:4; the laws of Ex. 34:17-26 are likewise ten in number; and on the basis of these two decalogues some scholars (e.g., L. B. Paton, C. A. Briggs, C. F. Kent, and Leroy Waterman)[22] would arrange all the

[20] So J. Wellhausen himself recognized, *Prolegomena zur Geschichte Israels* (6th ed., 1905), pp. 346, 364, cf. 421, but critics of Wellhausen regularly ignore this or are ignorant of it. On the textual analysis of ancient codes see D. Daube, *Studies in Biblical Law* (1947), pp. 74-101.

[21] Many parallels to this in ancient literature could be cited, of which it is sufficient to note the identical history of the Vedas in the Rig-Veda, the Yajur-Veda, the Sama-Veda, and the Atharva-Veda. They originated approximately in this order, but new and old material is found mixed in all of them, the latest as well as the earliest. For an attempt to determine the special origin and place in life of the laws of the Hebrews see Martin Noth, *Die Gesetze im Pentateuch: Ihre Voraussetzungen und ihr Sinn* (1940). See also A. Bentzen, *Introduction to the Old Testament*, I (1948), 213-232, and Gunnar Hylmö, *Gamla testamentets litteraturhistorica* (1938), frequently cited by Bentzen.

[22] Of these Waterman's study is the most recent, "Pre-Israelite Laws in the Book of the Covenant," *American Journal of Semitic Languages*, XXXVIII (1921), 36-54.

laws of the Book of the Covenant into decads, each falling
into two pentads; but this can only be done by such
arbitrary methods and such rearrangement of the text as to
be highly speculative. There was unquestionably some
arrangement at some time in decads, but whether this was
early and whether the decads in turn were divided systemati-
cally into pentads is more than questionable.[23] The early
Hebrews were no more systematic than their neighbors.

Furthermore, it is presuming a great deal to believe that
we have many of the laws in their original form. Laws are
tenacious and change slowly, but they do change, and as
they become utterly outworn, they give way to new laws.
Hence there is probably comparatively little in the Book
of the Covenant, as we have it now, in its original form.
Much of the material has been modified, old matter has
been lost, and new matter has been added, and the history
of the Covenant Code is a long and complicated one, as
Morgenstern, Pfeiffer, and others[24] have conclusively
demonstrated, so complicated in fact that no two scholars
are agreed on it and the recovery of the original is really
impossible.

With these general observations out of the way we are
now in a position to compare the Hebrew Code with the
others to see what relationship there may be between it and
them. In the first place, it is to be noted that there is some
agreement in terminology, in the technical terms used, particularly between the Hebrew Code and the Hammurabi

---

[23] See also p. 38 above, and A. Bentzen, *op. cit.*, pp. 221 ff.

[24] J. Morgenstern, "The Book of the Covenant," *Hebrew Union College
Annual*, V (1928), 1-151; VII (1930), 19-258; VIII-IX (1931-32), 1-150;
R. H. Pfeiffer, "The Transmission of the Book of the Covenant," *Harvard
Theological Review*, XXIV (1931), 99-109; *Introduction to the Old Testa-
ment* (1941), pp. 211-226; H. Cazelles, *Études sur le Code de l'Alliance*
(1946); F. V. Winnett, *The Mosaic Tradition* (1949), pp. 30-56.

Code, but this is not nearly so extensive as some scholars have maintained. The most striking of these is the use of *awêlum*, "man," in the Hammurabi Code in the technical sense of "free man, seignior, man of the highest class," and the identical use of *'îsh*, "man," in the Hebrew Code, e.g., in Ex. 21:7, 14, 16, 18, 20, 22, 26, 33, 35, appearing there as regularly as it does in the Hammurabi Code.[25] Indeed, so definitely technical is the latter term that it is used sometimes without the article when it strictly should have it, e.g., in Ex. 21:28, where we have the expression *'eth-'îsh*, which is an anomaly in Hebrew, since *'êth*, as the sign of the definite accusative, strictly requires that *'îsh* should be written with the article, *hā'îsh*. Furthermore, in this same chapter, verse 31, appears another technical expression that has its exact parallel in the Hammurabi Code, viz., *bēn*, "son," and *bath*, "daughter," which are ellipses for "the son of a man" and "the daughter of a man," and mean simply "free man" and "free woman" respectively,[26] exactly as the parallel expressions *mâr awêlim* and *mârat awêlim* do in the Hammurabi Code; cf., e.g., § § 203, 207, 209, and 251. This is a striking similarity

[25] The word *awêlum* is literally "man," but in the Babylonian and Assyrian codes it seems to be used in at least three senses: (1) sometimes to indicate a man of the higher class, a noble; (2) sometimes a free man of any class, high or low; and (3) occasionally a man of any class, from king to slave. For the last I use the inclusive word "man," but for the first two, since it is seldom clear which of the two is intended in a given context, I follow the ambiguity of the original and use the rather general term "seignior," which I employ as the word is employed in Italian and Spanish, to indicate any free man of standing, and not in the strict feudal sense, although ancient Babylonia and Assyria did have something approximating the feudal system, and that is another reason for using "seignior." In the Hebrew Code the word *'îsh*, corresponding to *awêlum*, I translate "man" rather than "seignior," because it accords better with the simpler social structure of the Hebrews.

[26] A. B. Ehrlich noted this many years ago in his *Randglossen zur hebräischen Bibel*, I (1908), 351. "Son" and "daughter" are here used in the common Semitic idiom, meaning "one belonging to, a member of" some particular class, in this instance the class "man."

that suggests some connection between the codes, but it is not safe to stress the point too much, because a common terminology is not necessarily a mark of dependence, as is well illustrated by the fact that the expression *pāleš pûlšāthâ*, "who makes a breach in a wall," in § 80 of the *Leges Constantini Theodosii Leonis*[27] is philologically identical with *pilšam palāšum*, "to make a breach in a wall," in CH 21,[28] but no one would venture to say that the Syriac writer was dependent for his language upon a code that had long since been lost. Some of the likenesses between the Hebrew Code and the Babylonian, as likewise the Syriac, are to be accounted for by the fact that all three are written in Semitic languages, and under such circumstances likenesses in terminology are bound to occur. The likenesses between the Hebrew and Babylonian codes in this respect are not frequent enough to suggest much in the way of dependence. A technical term like *dîn napištim* (CH 3), "a case involving life, capital suit," for example, is not found in the Old Testament at all, but rather strangely it is found in Mishnaic Hebrew as the name of one of the divisions of later Hebrew law, *dînê nĕpāšôth*, indicating Babylonian influence in that late period. The contact that the early Hebrews had with Babylonian culture was not direct as in the later period, but through the medium of the Canaanites, so that not too much influence is to be expected, and the differences are as apparent as the likenesses.

For example, a striking difference is the fact that in the Hebrew laws the hypothesis is set out as still in the future by the use of the imperfect tense, whereas in the Hammurabi

[27] See E. Sachau, *Syrische Rechtsbücher*, I (1907), 166.
[28] CH=Code of Hammurabi, while the following number is the paragraph number. Similarly, MAC=Middle Assyrian Code, and the following number is the paragraph number of Tablet A.

Code it is regularly stated as a fact in the past and the pre-
terite tense is used,[29] with only the occasional use of the
permansive (e.g., CH 126) and the present (e.g., CH
172).[30] An example is Ex. 22:1: "If a man steals an ox or a
sheep, and kills it or sells it, he must pay an indemnity of
five oxen for the ox, and four sheep for the sheep." With this
compare CH 8: "If a seignior stole either an ox or a sheep
or an ass or a pig or a boat, if it belonged to the church
(or) if it belonged to the state, he shall make thirty-fold
restitution; if it belonged to a private citizen, he shall make
good ten-fold." The only instances in the Hammurabi Code
where the present tense (corresponding to the Hebrew
imperfect) is used in the protasis is to indicate repeated or
continuous action, e.g., § 172, "If her children keep plaguing
her"; or to express a wish or desire, e.g., § 138, "If a man
wishes to divorce his wife." This difference in the formula-
tion of the laws of the codes would indicate that there is
no great dependence of the one upon the other, and this is
borne out by a detailed investigation of the several laws.

It is not our purpose to compare all six codes in great
detail because that would take too long and be too weari-
some. We shall content ourselves with a few examples from
the Hammurabi, Hittite, Middle Assyrian, and Hebrew
codes, since the others are too fragmentary for our purpose
and consist largely of material not in the Hebrew Code.
In the case of the Hittite Code we need not expect much
contact with the Hebrew Torah, even though there was
probably some Hittite blood in the Hebrew people. The
code reflects a degree of culture for the Hittites in which

---

[29] The same in general is true of the other Akkadian codes.
[30] The complete references are given by T. J. Meek, *Journal of Near
Eastern Studies*, V (1946), 65, notes 9 and 10 for the present tense and
n. 11 for the permansive. In note 10, however, "*i-ḫi-a-at* in § 186" should
be substituted for "*im-ta-gar* in § 149."

the agricultural, industrial, and commercial life of the people
was far beyond any that the Hebrews ever attained in Old
Testament times. The laws are accordingly more advanced
than the Hebrew laws, and the penalties are fines rather
than penalties based on the *lex talionis*. There is no law
strictly parallel to a Hebrew law and none that is particularly close. The nearest is § 197, "If a man seizes a woman
in the mountains, since it is the man's wrong, he shall
be put to death. But if he seizes her in the house, since it
is the woman's fault, the woman shall be put to death. If the
husband finds them and then kills them, he is not to be
punished." With this we may compare Deut. 22:23-27, "If
there should be a girl who is a virgin, betrothed to a husband, and a man chances upon her in the city and lies with
her, you must take them both out to the gate of that city
and stone them to death; the girl, because she did not call for
help although in the city, and the man, because he seduced
another's (prospective) wife. Thus shall you eradicate the
wicked person from your midst. If, however, it is in the
open country that the man chances upon the betrothed girl,
and the man seizes her and lies with her, then simply the
man who lay with her shall be put to death; you must do
nothing to the girl, since no sin deserving of death attaches
to the girl; for this case is like that of a man attacking another and murdering him, because it was in the open country
that he chanced upon her; the betrothed girl may have
called for help, but there was no one to save her." Both
laws give the woman the benefit of the doubt when the
crime is committed in the open country, but this slight
resemblance and others of a like nature throughout the
codes[31] are not strong enough to suggest any real dependence

---

[31] E.g., § 10 cf. Ex. 21:18 f.; §§ 105 f. cf. Ex. 22:5 f.; §§ 17 f. cf. Ex.
21:22-25; § 75 cf. Ex. 22:10-15; § 70 cf. Ex. 22:1-3; § 187 cf. Deut. 27:21;
Lev. 18:23; 20:15.

or close relationship. Hence the origin of Hebrew law is not to be found in the Hittite Code.

The resemblances between the Middle Assyrian Code and the Hebrew are not much greater. Again it is to be noted that the Assyrian code is legislating for a more advanced social order than are the early Hebrew laws, and the legislation is accordingly much more elaborate and detailed. There is one law, however, that the Assyrian and Hebrew codes have in common that is not found in any other, viz., that requiring the Levirate marriage.[32] This institution was a survival from primitive times[33] and it continued longer with the Assyrians and Hebrews than with any other people of the Near East. It was a custom of early Hebrew society, as we infer from Gen. 38:8, and it is found as a legal prescription for brothers "living together" (apparently on a joint estate) in Deut. 25:5-10, according to which a man is required to marry the wife of his deceased brother if the latter has been left without a son. A similar law obtained with the Assyrians (MAC 30), which reads as follows: "If a father has conveyed (or) brought the betrothal gift to the house of his son's (prospective) father-in-law, with the

[32] § 193 in the Hittite Code has been cited by some (e.g., by G. A. Barton, *Semitic and Hamitic Origins* [1934], p. 368) as evidence that the Levirate was required by the Hittites, but this is not so and is based on a wrong translation. The law reads as follows: "If a man has married [*lit.,* taken] a woman, then the man dies and his brother marries his wife, then his father marries her; then again, if his father also dies and one of his brother's sons marries the woman whom he had married, (there is) no punishment." It is clear from this that the Levirate with the Hittites had become quite obsolete; so obsolete and out of favor that a law had to be formulated to make it legal if someone did follow it.

[33] Scholars differ in their opinions regarding the origin of the Levirate, but all of course are agreed that it was a survival from primitive times. For my own part I feel that it was a survival from early ancestor worship, when it was thought necessary for a man to have a son to perform the worship due him after his death. For a recent discussion see E. Neufeld, *Ancient Hebrew Marriage Laws* (1944), pp. 23-55, together with the literature there cited.

woman not yet married to his son, and another son of his, whose wife is living in her father's house, died, he shall give his dead son's wife in marriage to his other son, to the house of whose (prospective) father-in-law he brought (the gift)"; i.e., the Levirate was to be enforced even though other marriage plans had been made for the deceased man's brother. The law goes on to say that these arrangements may be annulled if the parties to the contract so desire, showing that the institution was becoming obsolete. Similarly, in the Hebrew law provision was made whereby one could be released from the obligation of the Levirate, but not without considerable odium to himself (Deut. 25:7-10; cf. Ruth 4:4-10, where the obligation is transferred to another).[34] Another Assyrian law (MAC 33), whose interpretation is not absolutely certain because it is broken in part, requires that if there should be no brother-in-law to marry the widow, or he in turn has died, she is to be given in marriage to her father-in-law, providing he is alive. In the light of this law we can see the justification for Tamar's trickery whereby she was enabled to marry her father-in-law Judah, when he procrastinated about letting her have another of his sons after the death of the first two (Gen. 38).[35]

Another ancient institution that the Hebrews and Assyrians preserved in common, as against the Babylonians and Hittites,[36] was the type of marriage in which the woman continued to live in her father's house after her marriage

[34] It was not until the time of Lev. 18:16 and 20:21 apparently that the Levirate was completely outgrown by the Hebrews, because that law, as ordinarily interpreted, forbids a man to marry his brother's widow, but it is not certain that this is the correct interpretation. The reference may be to having intercourse with the wife of a brother still living.

[35] Cf. also the Hittite law quoted in note 32 above.

[36] The last sentence in § 27 of the Hittite Code may possibly reflect the errēbu type of marriage, but this is questionable.

and, closely related to that, the *errēbu* type, in which a father who had no son, but only a daughter or daughters, selected a husband for his daughter with the arrangement that the son-in-law should join his household and perpetuate his family like a true son.[37] There are a number of laws in the Middle Assyrian Code (§ § 25, 26, 30, 32, 33, 36, 38) in which the wife is represented as living in her father's house and these must reflect the *errēbu* type of marriage.[38] MAC 27, on the other hand, reflects the first type because the husband is represented as visiting his wife from time to time. Since only the merest fragments of the marriage laws of the Hebrews have been preserved to us, it is from the narratives that we learn that they, too, had both types of marriage. The first is found in Samson's marriage to the Philistine woman (Judg. 15:1) and the second is defined in Gen. 2:24: "That is why a man leaves his father and mother and clings to his wife, so that they form one flesh," and two very clear examples are the marriage of Moses with Zipporah (Ex. 2:16-22) and that of Jacob with Rachel and Leah (Gen. 29:16-30), where both fathers-in-law have daughters only and no son to perpetuate the family. The latter example also shows some parallels with the adoptive marriage of the Nuzians,[39] who were considerably influenced by the Assyrians. It was also the *errēbu* type of marriage that Abraham's slave must have had in mind when he asked

[37] See, e.g., Neufeld, *op. cit.*, pp. 56-67, together with the literature there cited, particularly Millar Burrows, *Journal of the American Oriental Society*, LVIII (1937), 259-276; *The Basis of Israelite Marriage* (1938). As Neufeld has noted, *op. cit.*, pp. 63 f., the *beena* type of marriage is not to be confused with the *errēbu* type. The former seems not to have been found with the Hebrews, as used to be thought.

[38] See Neufeld, *op. cit.*, pp. 65-67, who notes, however, that the Assyrians were outgrowing this form of marriage and this would explain the lack of detailed legislation on the subject.

[39] See C. H. Gordon, *Bulletin of the American Schools of Oriental Research*, No. 66 (1937), 25-27.

in Gen. 24:5, "Suppose the woman is unwilling to follow me to this land, am I then to take your son back to the land that you left?"

The preservation of these old institutions, however, by Assyrians and Hebrews alike does not indicate dependence of the one upon the other, but the conservatism of both peoples. There is kindred legislation in the codes of the two peoples, but there is nothing to suggest that there was direct borrowing on the part of the Hebrew lawmakers from the Middle Assyrian Code. The two have slight points of contact, with a few general parallels,[40] but on the whole they are very different.

It is not until we come to compare the Hebrew Code with the Babylonian that we discover marked likenesses. Indeed, C. H. W. Johns has gone so far as to say in his Schweich Lectures, *The Relations between the Laws of Babylonia and the Laws of the Hebrew Peoples* (2nd ed., 1917), page 49, "It has been calculated that out of 45, or possibly 55, judgments preserved in this old Hebrew Law [i.e., the Book of the Covenant] 35 have points of contact with the Hammurabi Code and quite half are parallel." However, when one examines these parallels in detail the likenesses are not so close after all. Take, for example, the laws on theft (Ex. 22:1 ff.; cf. CH 6-13, 259, 260, 265). In some of the laws in the Hammurabi Code the penalty is severalfold restitution (§ 8) or a fine (§§ 259, 260, 265); but alongside these is preserved the older type of law which imposed the death penalty (§§ 7, 9, 10). Similarly, there are indications that in early times the Hebrews punished stealing by death, particularly the steal-

[40] § 8 cf. Deut. 25:11 f.; §§ 21, 50-52 cf. Ex. 21:22-25; § 20 cf. Lev. 18:22 and 20:13; § 47 cf. Ex. 22:18 and Lev. 20:27; §§ 12-17, 55 f. cf. Deut. 22:23-29; §§ 22-24 cf. Lev. 20:10-21; §§ 30 f., 33 cf. Deut. 25:5-10.

ing of sacred objects (cf. Gen. 31:32, re Laban's loss of his household gods; Gen. 44:9, re Joseph's stolen divination cup; Josh. 7:1 ff., re Achan's theft of the loot of Jericho that had been put under the ban). The development of the law was manifestly the same with the Hebrews and Babylonians: (1) theft was regularly punished by death; (2) the death penalty was confined to the theft of sacred or royal possessions (cf. CH 6, "If a seignior stole the property of church or state, that seignior shall be put to death; also the one who received the stolen goods from his hand shall be put to death"); (3) severalfold restitution or a fine came to be substituted for the death penalty. But that is the sort of development we would expect in a growing state and need not indicate imitation of one by the other. In the Hebrew legislation a distinction is drawn between the thief who keeps the stolen goods for himself and one who sells them to another. There is no indication of this in the Hammurabi Code and the penalties there are different from those prescribed in the Hebrew Code, and they vary with the social status of the offender,[41] as they do not in the Hebrew Code. The Hebrew legislation confines the punishment to the thief, although any suspected person must clear himself (Ex. 22:8), whereas the Hammurabi Code extends it to the purchaser of the stolen goods (the accessory after the fact) and to the person who pretends falsely to be the actual owner (§ § 9-13), and in certain instances (the stealing of a plow or a harrow, §§ 259, 260) the penalty is neither death nor restitution,

---

[41] The Hammurabi Code is frankly class legislation, but at the same time there is this to be said in its favor: it is fair. The penalties are lighter for crimes committed by one against another of lower class, and greater in the opposite case, but a man of lower class pays less for his offense when committed against one of his own rank, and fees for services are graded according to class; the lower the class the lower the fee.

but a money fine. This comparison of the Hebrew and Babylonian laws on theft is typical of all the others. Fundamentally the laws are the same, but in the details of their application they differ. The Babylonian legislation is more detailed and explicit than the Hebrew and reflects a much more advanced social order.

There is no doubt but that there is great similarity between the Hebrew and Babylonian codes. Both are the concrete expression of the same general principles of morality and justice, and a spirit of humaneness pervades both codes, even the Hammurabi Code. There is similarity in content and sometimes in terminology and arrangement. Certain laws follow one another in the same order in both. The principles of retaliation (*lex talionis*) and restitution underlie both codes (cf., e.g., CH 196, 197, 200, and Ex. 21:24 f.: "You must give life for life, eye for eye, tooth for tooth, hand for hand, foot for foot, burn for burn, wound for wound, lash for lash"). The institution of appearing before God for the oath of purgation (CH 20, 23, 103, 106, 107, 120, 126, 131, 206, 227, 240, 249, 266, 281; cf. Ex. 21:6; 22:8, 9, 11) is found in both, but more frequently in the Hammurabi Code. A goodly number of crimes are punished in the same or nearly the same way in both (e.g. unchastity, kidnaping, personal injuries, and goring by an ox). According to both a debtor unable to meet his debts could be sold into slavery, but must be released after a certain time (three years according to CH 117, six years according to Ex. 21:2). In both codes the penalty for sorcery and magic is death (CH 2; cf. Ex. 22:18; Lev. 20:27), as likewise in the Middle Assyrian Code (MAC 47); and both provide that it is not until the fifth year that the fruit of an orchard is to be used (CH 60; cf. Lev. 19:23-

25). All these similarities and others like them[42] can scarcely be regarded as wholly accidental. There must be some connection between the two codes, but the connection is not such as to indicate direct borrowing. No one today argues that. Whatever borrowing there was came indirectly, either through common inheritance or through Canaanite influence, or much more likely through both ways.

In emphasizing the latter of these ways Leroy Waterman[43] and A. T. Olmstead[44] have gone so far as to interpret the Book of the Covenant as nothing but a Canaanite code taken over bodily by the Hebrews with scarcely any vital change. Now, there is no question but that the Hebrews as a seminomadic, semicivilized people upon their entry into Palestine were tremendously influenced by the more civilized Canaanites and Amorites, deeply steeped in the culture of Babylonia. Hammurabi's dynasty in Babylonia was an Amoritic dynasty; intermittently from at least as early as Lugal-zaggisi, *ca.* 2370 B.C., down to the time of Hammurabi and later both Palestine and Syria were Babylonian spheres of influence, and even when the Hebrews arrived in the country the language of diplomacy still remained the Babylonian, as we know from the Tell el-Amarna letters, even though the country was under Egyptian sway. Hence much of Babylonian culture, including Babylonian law, must have been mediated to the Hebrews through the Canaanites, and the Canaanites also made some contributions of their own, as is attested among other things by the Hebrew adoption of the word ḥpṯ = Akkadian ḫupšu,

[42] The laws in the Hammurabi Code, which are in any way parallel to laws in the Hebrew Code, are indicated in the footnotes to the translation of the Hammurabi Code by the present writer in *Ancient Near Eastern Texts*, ed. J. B. Pritchard (1950).

[43] *American Journal of Semitic Languages*, XXXVIII (1921), 36 ff.

[44] *History of Palestine and Syria* (1931), pp. 103 ff.

meaning in Canaanite "peasant" or a semifree individual, which appears in Hebrew (Ex. 21:2, 5, 26 f.; Lev. 19:20; Deut. 15:12 f., 18) as ḥopšî, with the gentilic ending designating class and usually translated "free (from slavery)."[45] The laws that the Hebrews took over from the Canaanites were naturally those which they themselves had had no occasion to develop in their nomadic wanderings, viz., the laws of a settled community: laws concerning agriculture, damages, lawsuits, court cases, the giving of evidence, deposit, the goring ox, and the like. For comparison we may select from these the one concerning the goring ox. The Hammurabi Code (§ § 250-252) reads: "If an ox, when it was walking along the street, gored a seignior to death, that case is not subject to claim. If a seignior's ox was a gorer and his city-council [lit., gate] made it known to him that it was a gorer, but he did not pad its horns (or) tie up his ox, and that ox gored a member of the aristocracy to death, he shall pay one-half mina of silver. If it was a seignior's slave, he shall pay one-third mina of silver."[46] In closely parallel language the Hebrew law (Ex. 21:28-32) reads: "If an ox gores a man or a woman to death, the ox shall be stoned to death, but its flesh is not to be eaten; the owner of the ox is blameless. If, however, the ox has been a gorer for some time and its owner was warned, but still did not keep it in, and it kills a man or a woman, the ox shall be stoned and its owner shall also be put to death. If only a fine is imposed on him, he shall pay in redemption of his

---

[45] See I. Mendelsohn, *Bulletin of the American Schools of Oriental Research*, No. 83 (1941), pp. 36-39; E. R. Lacheman, *ibid.*, No. 86 (1942), pp. 36 f.

[46] Cf. § § 53-55 of the Eshnunna Code: "If an ox gored a(nother) ox to death, both ox owners shall divide the price of the live ox and the value of the dead ox. If an ox was a gorer and the city-council made it known to its owner, but he did not keep (the head of) his ox down and it gored a seignior to death, the owner of the ox shall pay two-thirds of a mina of silver. If it gored a slave to death, he shall pay fifteen shekels of silver."

life whatever amount is imposed on him. Whether it is a
free man or a free woman that it gores, he is to be dealt
with in accordance with this same precedent (*mishpāṭ*).
If the ox gores a male or a female slave, he shall pay their
master thirty shekels of silver and the ox shall be stoned."
Here we see the ancient Hebrew law actually in process
of change as it came into contact with the Babylonian
through the Canaanites. In accordance with the old desert
principle of *lex talionis* both the ox and its owner were to
be put to death, but under Canaanite influence the latter
penalty was commuted to a fine. The two laws are too
closely in accord to have arisen quite independently of each
other, and this is further indicated by the technical use of
'îsh ("man") and of *bēn* ("son") in the Exodus passage,
a phenomenon that we have already noted.[47]

Another law where we can see the adjustment of the
Hebrews to a new environment is Deut. 19:16-19: "If a
plaintiff with a grudge appears against a man to accuse
him falsely, the two parties to the dispute must appear before Yahweh, before the priests and the judges that are in
office at that time; and the judges shall make a thorough
investigation, and if it turns out that the plaintiff is false,
having falsely accused his fellow, you must do to him as he
meant to do to his fellow." Here the old order of procedure,
the oath of purgation before God, is replaced by the more
advanced method of trial before judges, exactly as in the
Babylonian law, CH 3 f.: "If a seignior came forward with
false testimony in a case and has not proved the word which
he spoke, if that case was a case involving life, that seignior
shall be put to death. If he came forward with (false)
testimony concerning grain or money, he shall himself bear
the penalty of that case." In all such laws, where the Hebrews had previously no occasion for legislative experience,

[47] See p. 59 above.

they were clearly influenced by contact with the Canaanites.

Albrecht Alt has gone so far as to maintain that we can determine quite exactly what laws were of Canaanite origin and what were native to the Hebrews.[48] He notes that there are two main types of pentateuchal legislation: (1) the casuistic, introduced by a conditional clause and found frequently in the Book of the Covenant, and (2) the apodictic type, which is a definite command or prohibition (e.g., Ex. 20:2-17; Lev. 18:6-23; Deut. 27:15-26). Since the former is general in the other Oriental codes and is based on a Sumerian prototype, it is likely to be of foreign origin with the Hebrews or influenced by foreign law, whereas the latter type is regarded as of native origin because it is more or less peculiar to the Hebrews, but Albright is definitely wrong in saying that it is unique and original with the Hebrews,[49] because the same type is found mixed with the casuistic, exactly as in the Hebrew Code, in the Eshnunna Code (§ § 1-4, 7 f., 10-13, 15 f., 19, 51 f.), in the Hammurabi Code (§ § 36, 38-40), in the Old Assyrian laws, in the Middle Assyrian Code (Tablet A, § § 40, 57-59; Tablet B, § 6), and in the Neo-Babylonian laws. It is true, however, that the apodictic type is found more frequently in the Hebrew Code than in the others and it is to be noted that all the parallels with other codes that we have cited so far are of the casuistic type, but in the next paragraph we cite one (Ex. 23:14-17) of the apodictic type. Hence the two types are no certain criterion as to what is native and what is not,[50] but they do sug-

[48] *Die Ursprünge des israelitischen Rechts* (1934).
[49] *From the Stone Age to Christianity* (1940), pp. 204 f.
[50] Note, too, the criticisms of I. Rapaport, *Palestine Exploration Quarterly*, 1941, pp. 158-167; M. David, *Tijdschrift voor Rechtsgeschiedenis*, XIV (1939), 20, n. 3; B. Landsberger, *Symbolae Koschaker* (1939), p. 223, n. 19.

gest that the apodictic is the more primitive and the more likely to be native. It is noteworthy, too, that most of the Hebrew civil law is of the casuistic type, while the ritual law is largely apodictic.

Some scholars like René Dussaud,[51] and to a lesser degree A. Lods,[52] maintain that the early Hebrew ritual law, like the civil, was taken over from the Canaanites, and this to some extent is undoubtedly true. There can be no question but that the Hebrews absorbed much of the Canaanite religion,[53] of which sufficient evidence can be found in the denunciations of the prophets; and with the Canaanite religion naturally went much of its practice and ritual,[54] such a law, for example, as Ex. 23:14-17: "Three times a year you are to hold a festival for me. You must keep the festival of unleavened cakes, eating unleavened cakes for seven days, as I commanded you, at the appointed time, the new moon of Abib (for it was then that you came out of Egypt); none may visit me empty-handed. There is also the harvest festival, that of the first-fruits of your labor, of what you sowed in the field; and the festival of ingathering at the inception of the year, when you gather in the fruit of your labor from the field. Three times a year all your males must visit the Lord Yahweh." Here, however, there

[51] *Les origines cananéennes du sacrifice israélite* (1921).

[52] "Éléments anciens et éléments modernes dans le rituel du sacrifice israélite," *Revue d'histoire et de philosophie religieuses*, VIII (1928), 399 ff.

[53] See, e.g., E. A. Leslie, *Old Testament Religion in the Light of its Canaanite Background* (1936); W. C. Graham and H. G. May, *Culture and Conscience* (1936).

[54] Note the parallels between Hebrew and Ugaritic cultic practices and terminology as pointed out, for example, by W. F. Albright, *Archaeology and the Religion of Israel* (1942), pp. 61, 92-94, 106, 127 f., 159. Cf. also T. H. Gaster, "The Religion of the Canaanites," *Forgotten Religions*, ed. V. Ferm (1950); J. H. Patton, *Canaanite Parallels in the Book of Psalms* (1944); A. Bentzen, *Introduction to the Old Testament*, I (1948), 216 ff., and the literature cited there.

is no bodily taking over of Canaanite law, but the adaptation of what was manifestly a Canaanite ordinance to the Hebrew background and the Hebrew god. Hebrew law did not become Canaanite overnight (fusions between peoples do not take place in that fashion), but Canaanite influence came gradually with give-and-take on both sides, and that in turn modified by influences from other sources, as the excavations in Palestine well demonstrate. These show a definite break between Canaanite (Late Bronze) and Hebrew (Early Iron) cultures with a number of differences between them, and they show in the period of fusion influences as well from Philistia, Phoenicia, and elsewhere.[55]

But not all the likenesses between Hebrew and Babylonian law are due to Canaanite influence on the Hebrews. Much is due to the fact that the Hebrews, Babylonians, and Canaanites, as Semitic peoples, alike were heirs of a common heritage of primitive Bedouin law,[56] and when one compares the laws that most closely agree, one will discover at once that in many instances they have to do with matters that are universally legislated for by primitive peoples; matters like murder, kidnaping, theft, incest, adultery, filial impiety, assault and battery; and most of the penalties attached to these in both the Hebrew and Babylonian codes still retain much of their primitive severity, with the *lex talionis* and blood revenge prominent in both. But with the likenesses there are differences, due to several reasons.

For one thing, the Babylonians and Hebrews settled in different parts of the world and came under vastly differ-

---

[55] See, e.g., W. F. Albright, *The Archaeology of Palestine and the Bible* (1932), pp. 101 ff., 154; *Annual of the American Schools of Oriental Research*, XII (1932), 53 ff.; O. R. Sellers, *The Citadel of Beth-zur* (1933), p. 9 *et passim*.

[56] On this point see, e.g., J. Garstang, *The Heritage of Solomon* (1934), pp. 199 ff.

ent influences. The Semites who moved into Babylonia as a conquering minority found a people much more highly cultured than did the Hebrews in Palestine, with commerce and agriculture developed to an almost unbelievable degree for that early age. It was in the interests of all that commerce and agriculture should be maintained and the rights of property holders protected. Hence the existing Sumerian law was very largely adopted. But it was also in the interests of the conquerors that the balance of power should be in the hands of the conquering *awêlum* class as against the *muškēnum*; hence the class legislation in the Hammurabi Code. The Hebrews, on the other hand, entered Palestine much more gradually and rather slowly adopted the settled life of the agriculturist. The transition in their case was accordingly more gradual and they clung more tenaciously to old nomadic laws and institutions. Hence a number of laws are to be found in the Hebrew Code (e.g., laws regarding food taboos, leavened bread, the first-born, first-fruits, the Levirate, etc.) that do not appear in the Babylonian Code, because they were outgrown; and many laws appear in the Babylonian Code (e.g., laws regarding wages, fees, hire, rent, land tenure, irrigation, navigation, adoption, and various trades and professions like those of the physician, veterinary, barber, merchant, broker, artisan, housebuilder, and shipbuilder) that do not appear in the Hebrew Code, because Hebrew life was not sufficiently advanced to demand them.

Furthermore, the lawmakers were different in the two codes and were actuated by different motives in large part. In Babylonia the lawmakers were the political rulers. With the Hebrews they were largely priests and prophets, the religious and moral leaders of the people.[57] Hence the one

[57] Cf. A. Bentzen, *Introduction to the Old Testament*, I (1948), 215 f.

code is largely economic and political, and the other moral and religious, with its place in life almost wholly cultic-theological.[58] The Babylonian motive was to maintain the economic prosperity of the country; the Hebrew motive was to better the social and religious life of the people. Accordingly, there are religious and moral laws in the Hebrew Code that are conspicuous by their absence in the Babylonian, and a spirit of kindness and humanity that is not nearly so prominent in the other, and much of the law is hortatory with no penalties attached. Where the Babylonian law definitely legislated for interest (CH 49-52, 88-102), the Hebrew Code even more definitely prohibited it (Ex. 22:25; Deut. 23:19; Lev. 25:35-38); where the Babylonian compelled the return of an escaped slave (CH 15-20), the Hebrew Code legislated exactly the opposite (Deut. 23:15 f.). Even when a law was taken over from the Babylonian, it came to be given a religious interpretation, as is well illustrated by a comparison of CH 60 with Lev. 19:23-25. CH 60 reads: "If, when a seignior gave a field to a gardener to set out an orchard, the gardener set out the orchard, he shall develop the orchard for four years; in the fifth year the owner of the orchard and the gardener shall divide equally, with the owner of the orchard receiving his preferential share." With this compare Lev. 19:23-25: "When you enter the land, and plant all kinds of trees for food, you must treat their fruit as uncircumcised, for three years to be held by you as uncircumcised and not to be eaten, and in the fourth year all their fruit is to be sacred, a praise-offering to Yahweh; it is only in the fifth year that you may eat their fruit, that their produce may enrich you, since I, Yahweh, am your God." Here the re-

---

[58] Discussed in great detail by Martin Noth, *Die Gesetze im Pentateuch: Ihre Voraussetzungen und ihr Sinn* (1940).

ligious interpretation given to the old Babylonian law by the Hebrew legislator is clearly manifest; and due apparently to this same religious influence we have a point in Hebrew law that stands in striking contrast with all the other codes, Babylonian, Hittite, and Assyrian alike. These all make elaborate provision for the widow, but the Hebrew Code makes no provision whatsoever, except in the case of the Levirate, and that was not to provide for the widow but to rear offspring for the deceased childless husband. In every code except the Hebrew the widow has rights of inheritance, but in the Hebrew legislation she is passed over completely;[59] and the widow did not even have the usufruct of her husband's property. Just why she was passed over so completely is not easy to explain, but must have been due to some religious motive. In common with the other Semitic peoples, the Hebrews regarded long life as a blessing and death before old age as a calamity, a retribution of God for sin; but the Hebrews alone extended that retribution apparently to include the wife, and to be left a widow was regarded as a disgrace (see, e.g., Ruth 1:20 f.; Is. 54:4), as it is to the present day in India. However, the widow was not absolutely prohibited from remarrying, as used to be the case in India, but the possibility of remarriage is mentioned rarely, only four times in the whole of the Old Testament (Lev. 21:14; Ruth 1:9, 13; Ez. 44:22), and in the whole of the Old Testament there are only two recorded instances of the actual remarriage of a widow not in the Levirate category, viz., the marriage of Abigail to David

[59] See, e.g., Num. 27:8-11: "If a man dies, leaving no son, you must transfer his heritage to his daughter. If he has no daughter, you must give his heritage to his brothers. If he has no brothers, you must give his heritage to his father's brothers. If his father has no brothers, you must give his heritage to the nearest relative in his family, and he shall take it over."

(I Sam. 25) and that of Bathsheba to David (II Sam. 11), and in each case David fell in love with the woman before her husband's death and it was only David's voluptuousness that brought about the marriage. The lot of the Hebrew widow was accordingly a most unhappy one, and so piteous did it become that undue severity and injustice against her were prohibited (Ex. 22:22; Deut. 27:19), and eventually under prophetic influence she was commended to the charity of the people (Deut. 10:18; 16:11, 14; 24:17, 19 ff.), along with the orphan, the resident alien (the gêr), and the Levite, and the religious tithes of every third year came to be assigned to these dependents (Deut. 14:28 f.; 26:12 f.). The orphan, with whom the widow is classed in this legislation, was manifestly not the orphaned son, because he was provided for by his father's estate (Deut. 21:15-17), but the orphaned daughter, who inherited only on the failure of sons (Num. 27:7-11). Some of the orphans may have been sons of penniless fathers, but most of them were doubtless orphaned daughters, or the children of sacred prostitutes, and hence called "fatherless" (yāthôm).

It was this same prophetic humanitarian influence at work that ameliorated the law in other ways. It came to the rescue of the resident alien, protected him in his rights, commended him to the charity of the people, and eventually gave him in the Priestly Code the status of a proselyte on an absolute equality with the native-born Hebrew (Ex. 12:49; Lev. 24:22; Num. 9:14; etc.),[60] but the tôshābh, "serf," corresponding closely to the muškēnum of the Hammurabi Code, was never raised to that level, even in the latest legislation (cf. Ex. 12:45; Lev. 22:10). Even the slaves had greater recognition, because they were regarded as members of their

[60] For this change in the status of the gêr see the present writer, Journal of Biblical Literature, XLIX (1930), 172-180.

master's households and were admitted to most of the privileges of the family, being admitted, for example, to the Passover (Ex. 12:44), as serfs and hired laborers were not, and being permitted, when the slave of a priest, to eat sacred food (Lev. 22:11), a privilege that was denied even to the free layman. The slave had rights in the Hebrew Code that he did not have in any of the others, and it was through prophetic influence that the Deuteronomic Code legislated that a slave upon his release was to be sent away with a bountiful supply of provisions (Deut. 15:13 f.) and that a fugitive slave was not to be returned to his master (Deut. 23:15), in direct antithesis to the regulations of all the other codes; and before long it was legislated that no Hebrew under any circumstances could be enslaved, but foreigners only (Lev. 25:39-46). It was this same influence, too, that brought about the prohibition of the sacred prostitutes (Deut. 23:17 f.), definitely recognized and provided for in the Hammurabi Code, and the prohibition of many another institution borrowed from the Canaanites, the use of the sacred pillar (*maṣṣēbāh*), the sacred pole ('*ăshērāh*),[61] and images, worship at the high places, human sacrifice, pagan mourning rites, and the like. Eventually this spirit reached such noble utterance as Ex. 23:4 f., "If you chance upon your enemy's ox or ass going astray, you must be sure to take it home to him. If you see the ass of one who hates you lying prostrate under its load, you must refrain from deserting him; you must be sure to help him get it up"; or Deut. 15:7-10: "If there is a needy person among you, any of your fellow-countrymen in any of the communities in the land which Yahweh your God is about to give you, you must not steel your heart nor shut your hand

[61] W. L. Reed, *The Asherah in the Old Testament*, (1949), would be more explicit and translate "Asherah-image" rather than "sacred pole."

against your needy countryman; but you must open wide your hand to him and freely lend him sufficient for the needs that he has. . . . You must give to him freely; and you are not to begrudge it when you give him something, because Yahweh your God for this very thing will bless you in all your work and all your undertakings"; or Lev. 19:34: "You must treat the proselyte who resides with you like the native born among you, and love him as one of your own."[62] Neither the Sumerians nor the Babylonians nor the Assyrians nor the Hittites in their codes ever reached to heights like that.

No Hurrian law code has as yet been discovered, but we have hundreds of legal texts from the Hurrians at Nuzi and in these we note a number of institutions that the Hebrews had in common with them. Since the Hebrews were in part of Hurrian extraction and were much influenced by them, as we have already noted,[63] there must have been Hurrian elements in their law as well. This is best illustrated by the laws in Ex. 21:2-11, Lev. 25:39 ff., and Deut. 15:12-18, for the elucidation of which we have to go to Hurrian legal practice, as Isaac Mendelsohn and Julius Lewy have clearly demonstrated.[64] The laws have to do

[62] Lev. 19:18 has usually been cited as superior to the above, "the noblest single expression of philanthropy to be found in Hebrew law, or anywhere else in the Old Testament," according to J. M. P. Smith, *The Origin and History of Hebrew Law* (1931), p. 78, but this estimate is based on a mistranslation, as A. B. Ehrlich has well shown, *Randglossen zur hebräischen Bibel*, II (1909), 65. The passage should be translated somewhat as follows: "You must not avenge yourself or bear a grudge against the members of your own nation, but you must love your fellow as one of your own," or more literally in the words of Ehrlich, "wie deinesgleichen." All that is expressed in this verse is national brotherhood, not international.

[63] See pp. 3 f., 15 f. above.

[64] Isaac Mendelsohn, *Journal of the American Oriental Society*, LV (1935), 190-195; *Slavery in the Ancient Near East* (1949), pp. 10-19; Julius Lewy, *Hebrew Union College Annual*, XIV (1939), 587-623; XV (1940), 47-58. For other points of contact between Hebrew and Hurrian

with the sale of Hebrews into conditional slavery, with self-sale, and voluntary slavery, which practices were not found in Babylonia or Assyria, but only with the Hebrews and Hurrians.

Our conclusions, then, after this rather extended comparison of the various codes and laws, are that the Hebrews were dependent for their legislation only to a very slight degree, if at all, upon the Hittite and Assyrian codes, but that they did draw to some extent from Hurrian and Canaanite law and indirectly from Babylonian.[65] Most of their law, however, was their own, the product of their own experiences in their nomadic wanderings and in Palestine, and what they did borrow they made their own. It was no slavish imitation of an uncreative people, but an imitation that improved what it took, and in the end what it did take became definitely Hebrew and did not remain Babylonian or Hurrian or Canaanite. It was Hebrew legislation suited to Hebrew needs, and under the influence of the prophets that legislation was sublimated and ethicized. Herein, as so often, the pupil surpassed the teacher.

---

legal practice see, e.g., C. H. Gordon, *Journal of the Palestine Oriental Society*, XV (1935), 29 ff.; *Journal of Biblical Literature*, LIV (1935), 139 ff.; *Revue Biblique*, XLIV (1935), 34-41; *Biblical Archaeologist*, III, 1 (1940); E. Neufeld, *Ancient Hebrew Marriage Laws* (1944), *passim*.

[65] Much more negative are the conclusions of the noted legal specialist, M. David, "The Codex Hammurabi and its Relation to the Provisions of Law in Exodus," *Oudtestamentische Studiën*, VII (1950), 149-178. On the other hand, A. van Selms, *Journal of Near Eastern Studies*, IX (1950), 65-75, traces a marriage law from the Lipit-Ishtar Code (§ 29) through the Hammurabi Code (§ 161) to Hebrew practice in the marriage of Samson to a Philistine woman (Judg. 14:1-15:8).

CHAPTER THREE

The Origin of the Hebrew God

A S WE tried to show in Chapter I, Israel and Judah were in their origin two separate and distinct peoples, as separate and distinct as the Babylonians and Assyrians, the Serbs and Bulgars, the Lowland Scotch and English, or any other two peoples of kindred ancestry similarly situated. Each developed more or less independently of the other, Israel in the north and Judah in the south; and only gradually did circumstances bring them together, and then came the inevitable clash of interests, religious as well as political. This is well illustrated by the literatures of the two peoples. There was a stock of southern traditions and a treatment of traditions from the southern point of view, and there was likewise a specifically northern cycle of traditions. These two streams are very manifest in all the Old Testament books from Genesis to Samuel, as has long been recognized by biblical scholars, but in the light of our present knowledge the fact takes on new significance. When Israel became extinct as an independent nation in 721 B.C. and the two peoples were drawn together, their traditions tended to unite and were eventually combined to make our present narratives, with the resultant confusion of the terms "Israel" and "Judah" and the obscuring in many places of things not in accord with the later Judean point of view. Hence there were racial and political jealousies, as well as religious, that have tremendously affected our Old Testament narratives.[1] Ancient writings were always written from a motive (racial, political, religious, or what not), but that motive in the very nature of the case was never the presentation of a coldly scientific and accurate narration of events. Our sources have come down to us through many different hands and each has invariably left its impress upon them. Stories were not fabricated out of whole cloth, but they were manipulated. They were retold, readapted, sometimes relocalized, and mingled with others until it is well-nigh impossible to recover the historical facts lying behind them. This is particularly true of our Old Testament narratives, as Stanley A. Cook has so well shown,[2] and constitutes the great obstacle in the way of discovering the origin of the Hebrew God.

Many definitions of religion have been offered by different scholars,[3] and I venture to add still another. Religion may be defined as man's belief that there is that in his environment which is greater than himself, and upon which he feels to some degree dependent, and with which he accordingly attempts to establish a relationship of mutual interest and goodwill. Just as soon as man developed to the point of reflective thought, just as soon as he became aware of his environment and his dependence upon it, he became religious. He sought a way of coming to terms with his environment in order to

[1] So also my colleague, F. V. Winnett, *The Mosaic Tradition* (1949), but to my mind he overstates the case, and he is more explicit as to where, how, and when the changes were made than I would ever venture to be.

[2] *Critical Notes on Old Testament History* (1907); cf. also his *Religion of Ancient Palestine in the Light of Archaeology* (1930), p. 8, and his article, "Simeon and Levi," *American Journal of Theology*, XIII (1933), 370 ff.

[3] For some of these see J. H. Leuba, *A Psychological Study of Religion* (1912), pp. 339 ff.

live, and later, as he developed beyond the point of satisfaction in mere physical life alone, in order to live more abundantly. Religion is, accordingly, the product of experience, a way of life which comes to be expressed in the many institutions that we call religious.

Man was religious long before he invented the art of writing, and so it is only in archaeological remains and in later survivals and reminiscences that he has left a record of his early religion. Of these two sources the latter is probably the more important, for in no realm of life is man so conservative as he is in religion. Religious institutions die hard; indeed, they rarely die at all, but are rather reinterpreted to suit new ideas and new situations. Probably no literature in the world is so full of these survivals and reminiscences as the Old Testament, and it is in these that we must find the origin of the Hebrew God.

To begin with, the Old Testament shows us quite clearly what the early Hebrew conception of deity was. The various words that are used for "god" by their root meanings all suggest that the earliest idea connected with deity was strength. The usual word, 'ēl, has "strong one" as its original meaning, and this still persists in a number of passages (e.g., Gen. 31:29; Deut. 28:32; Mic. 2:1; Prov. 3:27; Neh. 5:5; Ez. 31:11; 32:21; Job 41:25; Ps. 36:6). Another word, 'ĕlôhîm, is a plural form and besides meaning "gods," or as an intensive plural "god," it has the force of "strong, mighty"; e.g., in Gen. 23:6, where the Hittites at Hebron call Abraham "a prince of god," meaning "a mighty prince." 'Elyôn, a frequent appellation of deity, means "exalted one," and shaddai, another appellative, is the Babylonian šaddā'ū, the gentilic of šadū, šaddū,[4] the regular word for "mountain"

---

[4] See W. F. Albright, *Journal of Biblical Literature*, LIV (1935), 180 ff.; *From the Stone Age to Christianity* (1940), p. 326, n. 63.

and an appellative of deity suggesting strength, its root meaning being "great one, mighty one." Two other appellatives,
'ādôn and 'ădônāi, have as their meaning "master, lord." All
these terms for "god" in Hebrew confirm our suggestion that
the early motive of religion with the Hebrews, as with others,
was a sense of dependence upon that in the environment
which was strong and was superior to the ordinary powers
of man; and that is indicated too by the way in which
Hebrew expresses the idea of worship, viz., by such verbs as
"to fear," "to bow down to," and "to serve."

According to Gen. 33:20, when Jacob settled at Shechem,
he erected a maṣṣēbāh,[5] or sacred stone pillar there, and
called it El-elohe-Israel, i.e., "El, the god of Israel." According to Gen. 35:7, the sanctuary at Bethel was called El-
Bethel, i.e., "the god of Bethel," or "the god Bethel" (cf.
Gen. 31:13).[6] These and other references (e.g., Gen. 28:18;
Ex. 17:15; Judg. 6:24), suggest that an exceedingly early
form of the Hebrew religion was what we might call naturism or animatism; i.e., the belief that the phenomena of nature, both inanimate and animate, are possessed of magic
power which may influence the life of man and which in
turn may be influenced by human activity in various rites.
What primitive man was first conscious of was not the universe as a whole, but his immediate environment, the things
at hand among which he lived and moved and had his being.
He could not possibly know or think of the universe as a
whole, and he assuredly had no occasion and no urge to
think back of that universe to the First Cause and Creator
of all. Primitive man was practical, not speculative, and the
category of cause and effect simply did not exist in his psy-

[5] Reading this in place of mizbēah, "altar"; so all scholars since J. Wellhausen, Composition des Hexateuchs (1889), p. 50.

[6] For the god Bethel see J. P. Hyatt, Journal of the American Oriental
Society, LIX (1939), 81-98.

chology, as anthropologists have long since recognized. What he had to do was to live, and to live he had to come to terms with his environment, and in doing this he became religious. Primitive man had no conception of the regularity of nature (he had not lived long enough); he had no conception of forces and laws; the only activities of nature that he knew were those mysterious phenomena round about him which did things to him, and it was with these that he felt the necessity of establishing friendly relations. The very phenomena of nature were deity to him—the actual mountains, stones, springs, trees, animals, storms, and what not. They were greater than he; they controlled his destiny; upon them he was dependent; and their good-will was necessary to his well-being. He accordingly attempted to control them to his own advantage, and so gradually devised a system of control through the use of various rites and institutions. Thus is to be explained the origin of the rites that the Old Testament so frequently connects with sacred mountains, springs, trees, stones, and the like.[7]

Another form of early religion was ancestor worship, and of its origin and development there are clear indications in the Old Testament. Manifestly it began with the tendance of the dead. Primitive man did not know what death was, but whatever it was, it did not mean for him the cessation of life. He knew simply that his friend who had hunted with him yesterday was today still and cold. Something mysterious had taken place, but he thought of his friend still in terms of his old living self, because life was all that he knew, not death. His friend could no longer care for himself, that was

[7] For these see, e.g., L. B. Paton, *Annual of the American Schools of Oriental Research*, I (1920), 51 ff.; E. Dhorme, *L'évolution religieuse d'Israël* (1937), pp. 149 ff.; J. Pedersen, *Israel: Its Life and Culture*, III-IV (1947), 214 ff.; W. O. E. Oesterley and T. H. Robinson, *Hebrew Religion* (2nd ed., 1937), pp. 23-49.

clear; so his living relatives must provide for him the necessities of life, and thus arose the rite of offerings to the dead. The dead still lived on in another life, and in that other life they needed all that they had needed in this life, food and drink and raiment (cf. Deut. 26:14; Hos. 9:4; Jer. 16:7; Ez. 24:17; Tob. 4:17; Sir. 7:33). The belief in the reality of the other life arose not only from the impossibility of realizing the fact of death, but also from the experience of dreams. The dead appeared in dreams, and seemed just as real and alive as ever they had been. With this experience apparently came to man his first idea of spirit, which presently he applied to the phenomena about him; so naturism developed into animism or polydaemonism.

It was not the phenomena themselves now that were deity, but the spirits inherent in the phenomena; i.e., the mysterious forces of nature were personified. One proof of this is the fact that even modern man reacts in exactly the same way when he finds himself jostled about at the mercy of forces that he cannot control. The Gremlins of the airmen in the recent war were nothing other than personifications of the various forces that pestered the airman in his flying, and they were just as real to him as the gods and spirits were to his ancient forebears. In fact, a full-fledged cult of the Gremlins soon developed in the Air Force and even spread to the other services, for behind it all was a human need which the cult helped to meet—the need to mitigate a fear or to explain an otherwise unexplainable phenomenon. So it was with the ancient Hebrews. Everywhere in the environment were spirits or daemons or numina, benevolent or malevolent as suited their mood or character; and these in turn could be influenced by human rites and practices. Hence, instead of the phenomenon itself being worshiped, it was the spirit in the phenomenon, the phenomenon personified.[8] But spirit here is not to be understood as very different from matter. It is simply matter in a less compact form, rarefied and aeriform. The Hebrew words *nephesh* and *rûaḥ* well express the idea. They are both applied to man as well as to deity, and there is no clear distinction between them.[9] In a number of passages (e.g., Is. 26:9) they are synonymous; the root meaning of both is "breath" or "wind," and both are material.

It is the spirit part of man that slips out of the body part of him at death (cf., e.g., Gen. 35:18; I Kings 17:21; Eccl. 3:21; 12:7), and that lives on in the next life and appears in dreams, man's double, as it were, something like the Egyptian *ka*.[10] The dead, though inactive in the flesh, are more mysteriously active in the spirit, and presently partake of the character of deity, so that they are in turn influenced by that which they themselves influence. There was something strangely mysterious about death itself and about the individual after death, and mystery always breeds awe, reverence, and fear, which were the primary motives of early worship, as the Old Testament makes very clear. The transition to worship was an early and inevitable one. Upon the dead the living were to some degree dependent; so the experience of dreams of the dead seemed to indicate. The dead thus became controlling factors of life and must in turn be

---

[8] See, e.g., Gen. 28:22, where Jacob is represented as giving to the sacred pillar that he erected the name of Bethel, i.e., "the house of God," and contrast v. 18, where the earlier idea survives that the pillar itself is deity. Also note Gen. 28:19 in contrast with Gen. 35:7.

[9] See W. E. Staples, *American Journal of Semitic Languages*, XLIV (1928), 145 ff. Cf. also A. R. Johnson, *The Vitality of the Individual in the Thought of Ancient Israel* (1949), pp. 9-39, together with the authorities there cited, some of whom argue that "throat" or "neck" is the original meaning of *nephesh*.

[10] On this see H. Frankfort, *Kingship and the Gods* (1948), pp. 61 ff.

controlled. Hence the offerings of food, drink, and raiment
became something more than supplies for the sustenance of
the dead. They were offered in order to secure the interest
of the dead and their good-will, or in order to placate them
if for any reason they were evilly disposed. The dead were
thought of as semidivine beings, and before long they became full-fledged deities, and were worshiped as such.

With the Hebrews a highly elaborate cult of the dead
rather early developed, and its rites and institutions continued in vogue long after their original significance had
been forgotten, despite the efforts of some to get rid of
them. The Old Testament is full of references to the cult,
and the prophets were vigorous in their denunciation of it.
In I Sam. 28:13 the shade of Samuel is explicitly called
'ĕlôhîm, i.e., "god" (cf. also Is. 8:19). The 'ĕlôhîm of Ex.
21:2-6 (wrongly translated "judges" in some versions) were
probably the ancestral spirits of the house, although they
may have been the spirits of the threshold. The corpse was
unclean and hence taboo (Num. 19:14-16), as deity always
was. The graves of the patriarchs and others were sacred
shrines,[11] like the welis of modern Muslims; and the regular
equipment of a grave was the maṣṣēbāh, or sacred pillar, the
dwelling place of deity. In Amos 6:10 (translating, not "he
that burneth him," since cremation was abhorrent to the Hebrews and was inflicted only upon the worst criminals,[12]
but "he that maketh a burning [i.e., a sacrifice] to him");
in Jer. 34:5; 16:4 ff.; II Chron. 16:14; 21:19; Ez. 43:7 ff.;
Ps. 106:28, we have references to rites of worship to the
dead, and these continued even as late as the time of Is. 65:4.

[11] See, e.g., W. O. E. Oesterley, *Immortality and the Unseen World*
(1921), pp. 101 ff.; J. Pedersen, *Israel: Its Life and Culture*, III-IV (1947),
480 f. For the cult of the dead see also W. C. Graham and H. G. May,
Culture and Conscience (1936), pp. 24 ff. *et passim.*
[12] Cf. Lev. 20:14; 21:9; Josh. 7:25.

Scholars are pretty well agreed today that the teraphim (cf.
Gen. 31:30 ff.; II Kings 23:24; Ez. 21:21) were images of
the ancestors, and in Gen. 31:30 ff. they are explicitly called
"gods" (*'ĕlôhîm*). Necromancy in all its forms is clear evidence of belief in the divinity of the dead, and its practice,
we know, was prevalent with the Hebrews, even after it
came to be condemned by the more enlightened. The various
mourning rites, like kissing the corpse (cf. Gen. 50:1), wearing sackcloth (Gen. 37:34; II Sam. 3:31), veiling the head
(II Sam. 15:30; Jer. 14:3), cutting the flesh (Jer. 16:5 ff.;
41:5), cutting the hair (Amos 8:10; Is. 22:12), wailing
(Gen. 37:34; II Sam. 3:31 ff.), and fasting (I Sam. 31:13; II
Sam. 1:12), all had their beginnings in ancestor worship, as
scholars have long since noted,[13] and for this very reason
most of the rites came later into disrepute, were condemned
by the prophets, and prohibited by the later lawbooks (cf.
Deut. 14:1 f.; Lev. 21:5; 19:27 f.).

The next step in the early evolution of the Hebrew religion seems to have come with the development of the clan.
As the family revered its ancestors, so the clan came to revere
its ancestral heroes. These were first exalted and then deified
as the tutelary gods of the clan. Abraham, Isaac, and Jacob
became eponymous heroes to the Hebrews. Their graves
were shrines where there were rites of worship.[14] As Albrecht Alt has noted in the case of the ancient Nabateans
and Palmyrenians, and so also in the case of the Hebrews,[15]

[13] See, e.g., Oesterley, *op. cit.*, pp. 101 ff., 141 ff.; Pedersen, *op. cit.*, pp.
483 ff.; A. Lods, *Israel* (Eng. trans., 1932), pp. 218 ff. For archaeological
evidences of the cult of the dead with the Hebrews see E. L. Sukenik,
Memorial Lagrange, ed. L.-H. Vincent (1940), pp. 59-65.

[14] See, e.g., Oesterley, *op. cit.*, pp. 101 ff.; Pedersen, *op cit.*, pp. 206 ff.,
213, 480 f., 665 f.

[15] *Der Gott der Väter* (1929); cf. E. A. Leslie, *Old Testament Religion
in the Light of Its Canaanite Background* (1936), pp. 54 ff.; J. Lewy,
Revue de l'histoire des religions, CX (1934), 50 ff.; W. F. Albright, *Jour-*

the particular deity of a group was designated by the name
of the founder of the cult and his worship was participated
in by the clan whose members were supposedly connected
with the founder through blood relationship. Hence we have
frequent references in the early Old Testament to "the God
of Abraham," "the God of Isaac," and "the God of Jacob,"
indicating that these were originally three different gods,
each the eponymous god of his group. In Is. 63:16 the deifica-
tion of Abraham (cf. Luke 16:22 f.) and that of Jacob (Israel) seems to be implied. Other heroes like Enoch (Gen.
5:24) and Elijah (II Kings 2:11), paralleling the Babylonian
hero Ut-napishtim, did not die, but were transported to
heaven to live with God and apparently to *be* god or something approaching god. The same, too, seems to have been
the experience of Moses (Deut. 34:6). According to Rab-
binic tradition, his soul was separated from the body, not
by death but by the kiss of God, and went to live with the
angelic host in heaven.

It is clear from the Old Testament, then, that the early
Hebrew religion was a very primitive one and many of its
elements remained long in the popular religion despite the
efforts of priests and prophets to eradicate them. The religion was polydaemonistic and polytheistic, so the Old Testament itself explicitly affirms (Josh. 24:2; Gen. 35:2). The
world was full of spirits controlling and directing human
affairs. Some were inherent in natural phenomena; others
were the spirits of the departed. Some of the outstanding of
both classes rose eventually to the rank of gods, and were
given personal names; and as tribes developed, each tribe,
through accident or design, hit upon some one deity to be

nal of Biblical Literature, LIV (1935), 188 ff.; *From the Stone Age to
Christianity* (1940), pp. 187 ff.; H. G. May, *Journal of Biblical Literature*,
LX (1941), 123 ff.

its particular tribal god. It was as such apparently that the god Yahweh first appears on the pages of the Old Testament.

On the question of the origin of Yahweh opinion is much divided. Indeed, the Old Testament itself is not in complete accord in its own views. One document, the late Priestly, maintains that it was to Moses that God first made himself known as Yahweh, being previously known only as El Shaddai; see, e.g., Ex. 6:3, where Yahweh says to Moses, "I am Yahweh; I appeared to Abraham, Isaac, and Jacob as El Shaddai, but I did not make myself known to them by my name Yahweh." P, accordingly, does not use the name "Yahweh" in his narrative until he comes to this revelation to Moses. On the other hand, the J document asserts that Yahweh was not a new god at all, but a god long known to the Hebrew people, having his origin, not in the time of Moses, but in the dim distant past, in the time of Enosh; cf. Gen. 4:26: "Seth in turn had a son born to him whom he named Enosh. It was then that men began to call upon the name of Yahweh"; and Ex. 3:15,[16] where Yahweh says to Moses: "Thus shall you say to the Israelites: 'Yahweh, the God of your fathers, the God of Abraham, Isaac, and Jacob, has sent me to you.' This shall always be my name and this my designation throughout the ages."[17] In the E document there seems to be a confusion of these two opposing views. In its narrative up to the time of Moses it has a decided preference for the general term *'ĕlôhîm* to indicate "God" as against the specific name Yahweh, but after the time of Moses that preference to a large degree disappears. This suggests that E's idea was that God first revealed himself to Moses under the new name Yahweh, but at the same time he

[16] This verse is ordinarily ascribed to E, but its point of view is surely that of J.
[17] Cf. also Gen. 12:8; 13:4; 21:33; 26:25.

affirms that the god who appeared under this name to Moses was the same god whom his fathers, Abraham, Isaac, and Jacob, had worshiped (Ex. 3:6), and this after all is not greatly different from P's point of view, and neither view is altogether inconsistent with J. E and P interpret God as revealing himself first to Moses under the name Yahweh, but it is the same god as of old, only under a new name. J's contention is that he is not only the same god, but the same god under the same name, Yahweh, the name that he bore from the beginning, because Enosh originally must have signified the first man.

Where the Old Testament itself is divided in its views, it is of course inevitable that scholars will not agree. The theory that still prevails, but perhaps not with the vogue that it once had, is the Kenite hypothesis, first suggested in 1862 by R. Ghillany, writing under the pseudonym of R. von der Alm.[18] According to this theory, Yahweh was originally the tribal god of the Kenites, and was entirely unknown to the Hebrews until he was introduced to them by Moses, who first learned of him through his father-in-law Jethro, a Kenite. This has some support in the views of E and P, both of whom, as already noted, believed that God revealed himself under a new name to Moses, and the adherents of the Kenite hypothesis aver that a new name here means a new god. This can well be so, but it does not necessarily follow, nor was it the view of E and P, as is plain from their records. With the Semites a name was a description, a definition; it was also something without which a thing was nonexistent.[19] A new name for God might indicate the introduction of a

[18] *Theologische Briefe an den Gebilden der deutschen Nation*, I (1862), 216, 480.
[19] Cf. Babylonian Creation Story, I, 1 f.:
   When above the heavens had not been named;
   Below, the earth had not been called a name.

new god to fuse with and take the place of the old god, but it could just as well imply a new definition, a new significance, a new understanding of his being and power;[20] and in any case there is no absolute evidence that Yahweh was a new name to the Hebrews, first revealed to Moses. This is the view of E and P, but it is contradicted by J, who is our earliest and probably most reliable witness.

In Ex. 18:12 (E) there is an account of a sacrificial meal arranged by Jethro: "So Jethro, the father-in-law of Moses, procured a burnt-offering and sacrifices for God, whereupon Aaron came with all the elders of Israel to participate with the father-in-law of Moses in the meal before God." This is interpreted by the exponents of the Kenite hypothesis as the rite whereby the Hebrews were initiated into the new Yahweh cult by the Kenite priest, Jethro. But this is not so certain.[21] It is true that Jethro is called the priest of Midian (Ex. 18:1; cf. also 2:16; 3:1), but he is nowhere called the priest of Yahweh, and in Ex. 18 he is not explicitly represented as performing priestly functions, because verse 12 says simply that "he procured (*wayyiqqaḥ*)[22] a burnt-offering and sacrifices for God," and the word for "God" is here the general term *'ĕlôhîm* and not the specific name Yahweh. The verse does indicate, however, that Jethro arranged a sacrifice for Yahweh, in which "Aaron and all the elders of Israel" participated, and that would suggest that Jethro

[20] Note how the name of Abram was changed to Abraham, Sarai to Sarah, Jacob to Israel, and Saul to Paul. Cf. also the different names by which the Egyptian god Rē was known: Rē, Khepre, Harakhte, Atum, and Horus; see A. Erman, *A Handbook of Egyptian Religion* (Eng. trans., 1907), pp. 9 f.

[21] It is opposed, e.g., by A. R. Gordon, *The Early Traditions of Genesis* (1907), pp. 108 f.; W. J. Phythian-Adams, *The Call of Israel* (1934), p. 73; F. V. Winnett, *The Mosaic Tradition* (1949), p. 69.

[22] The Syriac and Targums, it is true, read *wayyaqrēb*, "he offered," but there is nothing to indicate that this was the original reading.

was joining the Hebrews in recognizing the might of Yahweh. Whether Reuel (Ex. 2:18; Num. 10:29) be regarded as a variant or a clan name of Jethro or as the name of his father,[23] it would indicate that Jethro was originally a worshiper of the god El, and in Ex. 18 he recognizes for the first time the god Yahweh; cf. vv. 3-11, where Jethro upon being told by Moses what Yahweh had done for his people exclaims, "Blessed be Yahweh, who delivered you from the power of the Egyptians and the power of Pharaoh, who delivered the people from under the power of the Egyptians! Now I know that Yahweh is greater than all other gods, in that his power has prevailed over them."[24] If Jethro had been a priest of Yahweh and the one who initiated the Hebrews into his cult, it would surely have been on that ground that Moses would have invited him to join them on their journey. On the contrary, he invited him solely on the ground that he knew the desert and its camping places, and so would prove an efficient guide (Num. 10:29-32).

The whole narrative in Ex. 18 is much better interpreted at its face value, as a record of the occasion when Moses was reunited with his family and father-in-law, on which occasion there was naturally great rejoicing, mutual recognition of the might of Yahweh, and kindly advice from the more experienced Jethro to his young son-in-law. The Old Testament, it is true, represents some of Jethro's tribesmen, the Rechabites,[25] as strong supporters of the Yahweh cult (II Kings 10:15-28; Jer. 35:6 ff.), but there is nothing to indicate anywhere that the cult originated with them.

The Kenite hypothesis owes much of its popularity to its supposed solution of the problem of the ethical superiority

[23] Discussed most recently by Winnett, *op. cit.*, pp. 62 ff.
[24] Reading ידו for זדו with A. B. Ehrlich, *Randglossen zur hebräischen Bibel*, I (1908), 331.
[25] So I Chron. 2:55.

of the Yahweh religion. It is said that the Hebrews' adoption of Yahweh, as likewise his adoption of them, was an act of choice, as if this were "a new thing in the history of religion," as claimed,[26] and the reason for the high ethical character of the Hebrew religion. However, the most casual study of the history of religions shows that peoples since the beginning of time have been borrowing their neighbors' gods, but these acts of choice have not been fraught with any "far-reaching consequences," such as are claimed for the Hebrews.[27]

It is difficult to understand how Moses could have induced his people to leave Egypt under the guidance of a god of whom they knew absolutely nothing and of whom they had had no previous experience, and yet that was not impossible, particularly if we understand that the Hebrews had been grievously oppressed in Egypt. They must, in consequence, have lost faith in their own tribal god and in the power of that god to protect and deliver them. Therefore, when Moses came to them with the word that there was a god in the desert interested in them, who would deliver them, and with whom they might enter into a covenant, it is possible that they would have listened to him. The story of the tribe of Dan in Judg. 17 f. furnishes a close parallel. There the tribe of Dan, reduced, probably through unsuccessful war

[26] Reiterated, e.g., by such writers as W. O. E. Oesterley and T. H. Robinson, *A History of Israel*, I (1932), 74; *Hebrew Religion* (2nd ed., 1937), pp. 147-150; G. A. Barton, *Semitic and Hamitic Origins* (1934), p. 343; E. A. Leslie, *Old Testament Religion in the Light of Its Canaanite Background* (1936), pp. 80, 83; and H. H. Rowley, *The Re-Discovery of the Old Testament* (1946), pp. 118 f.; but on their own pages these same writers give plenty of examples of the phenomenon with peoples other than the Hebrews. Barton, for example, maintains that Marduk, the national god of Babylon, was a god borrowed from Central Asia and not at all a native Babylonian god, not even a Semitic god (p. 272).

[27] Cf. also A. C. Knudson, *The Religious Teaching of the Old Testament* (1918), pp. 158 f.; J. M. P. Smith, *The Moral Life of the Hebrews* (1925), p. 65.

with the Philistines, to a mere fraction of its former self, is compelled to seek a new abode, away from the Philistine menace and far to the north. It has lost faith in its own god and migrates without the protection of a tribal deity. At the first opportunity, accordingly, it steals another god, that of Micah, and raises him to the status of its tribal god. Here we have a tribe adopting a deity hitherto unknown to it, adopting him in sheer desperation for want of any other god, and trusting that he will prove sufficiently powerful to protect the tribe and further its interests.

It is not altogether certain, however, that the Hebrews with Moses in Egypt, i.e., the Levites,[28] had absolutely no previous knowledge of Yahweh. The name of Moses' mother, Jochebed (יוכבד), is unquestionably a Yahweh name,[29] and this would imply that the family of Moses at least were worshipers of Yahweh. It is true of course that Jochebed appears as the name of Moses' mother only in P (Ex. 6:20; Num. 26:59), but it was clearly not coined by him, because P would not consciously have given a Yahweh name to anyone earlier than Moses and in common with his generation he was averse to the use of Yahweh as an element in personal names.[30] Hence there is good ground for the belief that Yahweh was early known to the Hebrews, at least in some circles close to Moses, but assuredly not very widely outside those circles. It is a striking fact that not a single personal name with Yahweh as an element appears with the Hebrews until Jochebed and very few thereafter until the time of David.[1]

[28] So we were led to conclude on pp. 31 ff. above.
[29] Some deny this, e.g., M. Noth, *Die israelitischen Personennamen* (1928), p. 111, but without good reason, for we have an exact parallel to the name in the Assyrian personal name, *Adad-kabit*, as H. Bauer has noted, *Zeitschrift für die alttestamentliche Wissenschaft*, LI (1933), 92 f.
[30] See G. B. Gray, *Studies in Hebrew Proper Names* (1896), pp. 181 ff., 190 ff., 257.
[31] See pp. 113 f. below.

Not too much should be made of the argument *e silentio*,
but at the same time personal names with ancient peoples
invariably reflect their religious beliefs, and the complete
absence of Yahweh names with the early Hebrews would
indicate quite clearly that there was no general worship of
Yahweh among them, although there may have been some
knowledge of him. What Moses did, as our earliest source J
definitely states and the others imply, was to build on whatever knowledge of Yahweh the people already had and per-
suade them to put such trust in him that they would hazard
everything in his name, even the venture into the unknown
wastes of the desert. And having done that with eminently
successful results, they were ready to accept Yahweh as God
and enter into covenant relations with him, join the other
worshipers of Yahweh in a great southern amphictyony, and
in fact become ardent champions of the Yahweh cult (Ex.
32:25-29).[32]

But irrespective of the part that Moses may have had in
the introduction or expansion of the Yahweh religion, we
are still faced with the problem of the origin of the god
Yahweh, and that problem the Kenite hypothesis has not
solved. At best it has simply carried Yahweh back to the
Kenites as their tribal god,[33] a thesis that could perhaps be
accepted, particularly if we make Cain the eponym of the
Kenites, as is usually done. According to Gen. 4:15, Yahweh
set his mark on Cain and this may indicate that Cain was an
early worshiper of him. But that does not give us the origin
of Yahweh. We must go back to a time before he became

[32] See pp. 125 ff. below.
[33] Cf. A. Guillaume, *Prophecy and Divination among the Hebrews and
other Semites* (1938), pp. 341 f.: "The Kenite hypothesis, it is true, pushes
its [Yahwism's] hypothetical beginning a stage further back; but only
into the darkness of the unknown."

the tribal god of any tribe. As we have already noted,[34] the earliest form of the religion of the Hebrews was probably naturism, which in course of time passed over into animism. Yahweh, like most gods, undoubtedly had his origin in nature, and if we were to derive his name from *hwy*, "to blow," = Arabic *hwy*, as many scholars do, this would indicate that he was originally a storm-god.[35] The derivation, however, is not certain, but apart from that numerous references in the Old Testament indicate that he was a storm-god to begin with, sometimes connected with earthquakes and volcanic eruptions,[36] and that his early habitat was in the southern desert, the Negeb.[37] This is precisely the representation of Yahweh that we have in the Song to Deborah,[38] which is generally regarded as the oldest writing in the Old Testament, Judg. 5:4 f.:

> O Yahweh, when thou camest forth from Seir,
> When thou marchedst from the steppes of Edom,
> The earth quaked, the heavens also shook,[39]
> The clouds too dripped water,

[34] See pp. 85 ff. above.

[35] W. F. Albright, *From the Stone Age to Christianity* (1940), p. 200, denies that Yahweh was a storm-god, but on p. 218 he says that he was. The many references from the Old Testament given below would seem to establish his stormlike character without any possibility of doubt.

[36] See W. J Phythian-Adams, *Journal of the Palestine Oriental Society*, XII (1932), 86-90. However, the volcanic features may be later accretions drawn from the imagery of the Day of Yahweh; see N. Glueck, *Journal of the American Oriental Society*, LVI (1936), 469 f. Cf. also J. Morgenstern, *Zeitschrift für Assyriologie*, XXV (1910), 139 ff.; XXVIII (1913), 15 ff.; Albright, *op. cit.*, p. 200.

[37] I use "Negeb" here in its broadest sense, to include Midian.

[38] This song is better called "the Song to Deborah" rather than "the Song of Deborah" because it is addressed to Deborah and is not by her. For its date see R. M. Engberg and W. F. Albright, *Bulletin of the American Schools of Oriental Research*, No. 78 (1940), pp. 4-9.

[39] So the Versions read in place of the Masoretic text, "the heavens also dripped."

some particular tribe as its tribal god; so he became a personal god, and was thought of in human terms, with form,
voice, thoughts, emotions, and everything else quite after the
order of man. Since those who adopted him were nomads or
seminomads, he, too, became nomadic and moved about with
his tribe in their nomadic wanderings. Because he was conceived of in human terms,[49] a tent was provided for him as
his habitation and he was transported from place to place in
a sacred box, or ark.[50] The very existence of tent and ark of
necessity preclude the possibility of his being anything other
than the tutelary god of one particular group of people,
whom he accompanied and guarded in their desert wanderings (Num. 10:35 f.). But even nomadic tribes have some
focal point. That focal point for the followers of Yahweh
doubtless varied from time to time, Sinai-Horeb or some
other holy place, but presently it came to be Kadesh, and
here for a time Yahweh was localized before his entry with
his people into the land of Palestine (Num. 20:1; Deut. 1:46).

But whence came Yahweh before settling at Kadesh, and
was he widely known before the time of Moses? Friedrich
Delitzsch, the noted Assyriologist, answered these questions
in his famous Babel-Bibel lecture before the German Kaiser

[49] To date, however, no certain pictorial representation of Yahweh has
been discovered despite the opinion of A. Lods, *Israel* (Eng. trans., 1932),
p. 459, that his figure appears on the seal of Elishama. The famous silver
coin in the British Museum, illustrated, for example, by S. A. Cook, *The
Religion of Ancient Palestine in the Light of Archaeology* (1930), Pl.
XXXII, used to be thought to picture Yahweh, because the inscription
above the figure supposedly read *Yahu* (*yhw*); but E. L. Sukenik has
conclusively shown that the three-letter stamp here and elsewhere is not
to be read *yhw*, but *yhd*, i.e., *Yĕhûd*, Aramaic for "Judah"; see *Journal of
the Palestine Oriental Society*, XIV (1934), 178 ff.; XV (1935), 341 ff.

[50] Cf. the migration of the Ruwala Arabs with their ark, or *markab*, at
their head so vividly described by C. R. Raswan, *The Black Tents of
Arabia* (1935), pp. 64 ff. Cf. also J. Morgenstern, *The Ark, the Ephod, and
the "Tent of Meeting"* (1945).

in 1902[51] by announcing that he had discovered the god Yahweh in cuneiform literature long antedating the time of Moses, antedating in fact the time of Abraham. The announcement made a tremendous stir throughout the world, but with our larger knowledge we know now that the personal name *Yawi-ilum*, which Delitzsch interpreted as "Yahweh is God," is a verbal form plus a divine name, a variant writing of *Yaḫwi-ilum*,[52] of which *Yawium* is a hypocoristicon and is not to be interpreted with Delitzsch as meaning "belonging to Yahweh." Another personal name that Delitzsch and others thought contained the god name Yahweh is *Yaum-ilum*, interpreted as "Yau (=Yahweh) is god," but we know now that the meaning is "God is mine," since *yaum* is the first person singular possessive pronoun, as Arno Poebel was the first to show.[53] Still another name in cuneiform that scholars have regarded as containing Yahweh as an element is *Aḫu-yami*, which occurs on a tablet found at Taanach, dated about 1400 B.C., but *Yami* appears nowhere else as the cuneiform equivalent of Yahu or Yahweh and it is only in late Babylonian that *m* was used to transcribe Canaanite *w*.[54] *Yaḫwi* and *yawi* could be the cuneiform equivalent of Hebrew *Yahweh* so far as spelling is concerned,

[51] Published under the title of *Babel und Bibel* (1902); translated into English by C. H. W. Johns, *Babel and Bible* (1903).

[52] Cf. Theo Bauer, *Die Ostkanaanäer* (1926), pp. 61, 74; W. F. Albright, *Journal of Biblical Literature*, LXVII (1948), 380.

[53] *University of Pennsylvania: The University Museum: Publications of the Babylonian Section*, VI, 1 (1914), p. 66, col. iii, l. 22; and for the corresponding *kūm*, "thine," see his *Grundzüge der sumerischen Grammatik* (1923), § 181 end. For the identification of this possessive pronoun B. Landsberger has usually been given the credit (so W. von Soden, *Zeitschrift für Assyriologie*, XL [1931], 193, n. 3), but the Landsberger identification did not come until 1924, *Zeitschrift für Assyriologie*, XXXV (1924), 24, n. 2.

[54] See W. F. Albright, *Archaeology and the Religion of Israel* (1942), p. 64; *Journal of Biblical Literature*, LXVII (1948), 380; G. R. Driver, *Zeitschrift für die alttestamentliche Wissenschaft*, XLVI (1928), 7, n. 1.

but they are verbal forms, as is shown conclusively by the personal name *Yawi-Dagan*.[55] Hence they cannot be divine names.

Another interpretation of Yahweh that used to be popular with Assyriologists is his identification with the Akkadian god Ea, who may possibly have been of West Semitic origin, as R. P. Dougherty suggests.[56] This theory gained some support from the Old Assyrian texts of Cappadocia and certain texts from Nuzi, where *Ya* seemed to appear occasionally as a variant writing of *Ea*,[57] and this of course is strikingly close to *Yah*, a variant writing of *Yahweh* in the Old Testament. The evidence is stronger for the Cappadocian texts than the Nuzi texts and can almost certainly be ruled out in the case of the latter. In any case, the two gods, Ea and Yahweh, are so absolutely different in their functions, as Dougherty himself has pointed out,[58] that they can scarcely be identified, and any similarity in name must simply be a coincidence.

As yet there is no absolute evidence for the occurrence of the name Yahweh in cuneiform literature earlier than the eighth century B.C.,[59] and no clear evidence for the occur-

---

[55] See Theo Bauer, *Die Ostkanaanäer* (1926), pp. 31, 74.

[56] *The Sealand of Arabia* (1932), pp. 189 f.

[57] The evidence from the Old Assyrian texts is rather slight, simply the occasional variant of *Ya* for *Ea* in personal names; see F. J. Stephens, *Personal Names from Cappadocia* (1928), pp. 74, 98; J. Lewy, *Mitteilungen der vorderasiatisch-aegyptischen Gesellschaft*, XXXIII (1930), 25 f.; P. van der Meer, *Une correspondance commerciale assyrienne de Cappadoce* (1931), pp. 123 f. In Hurrian names *ya* as a variant of *ea* always appears at the end and is manifestly the familiar hypocoristic ending, with *y* sometimes written as *e* (a common phenomenon in the Nuzi texts); see I. J. Gelb, P. M. Purves, and A. A. MacRae, *Nuzi Personal Names* (1943), p. 294.

[58] *Op. cit.*, pp. 184 ff.

[59] See D. D. Luckenbill, *American Journal of Theology*, XXII (1918), 24 ff.; S. Daiches, *Zeitschrift für Assyriologie*, XXII (1909), 125 ff.; G. R. Driver, *Zeitschrift für die alttestamentliche Wissenschaft*, XLVI (1928), 7 ff.

rence of the name outside the Old Testament earlier than
the ninth century (viz., on the Moabite Stone), with the
possible exception of the Ras Shamra texts, where some
scholars find the god *Yw*, whom they would identify with
Yahweh.[60] Nevertheless, we can doubtless assert with complete confidence that Yahweh was known by name at least
to most, if not all, the Hebrew tribes as the tribal god of one
of their number. In fact, he may have been known and revered as the great High God of all the tribes, and as a storm-
god he was doubtless worshiped by some and known by
many, even outside the Hebrew fold.

In the Old Testament the name "Yahweh" is written in
two different ways when standing by itself, יה and יהוה,
and in three different ways when used as an element in personal names, יה, יו and יהו, but never as יהוה. Outside the
Old Testament it is found in only two places as יהוה, on
the Moabite Stone and the ostraca from Lachish;[61] elsewhere
it always appears as יה and יהו, except that it appears once
in an Aramaic papyrus from Elephantine of 447 B.C. as

[60] See, e.g., C. H. Gordon, *Analecta Orientalia*, 25 (1947), p. 234, No.
858. On the other hand, W. F. Albright, *From the Stone Age to Christianity* (1940), pp. 197, 328, n. 83, would read *yr* in place of *yw* and deny
any connection with Yahweh. However, a careful study of the text does
not confirm this. The sign in question has clearly four wedges as against
five required for *r*, and a comparison between the writing of *w* and *r*
elsewhere in the tablet shows *w* to be the more natural reading; but even
so the context is too obscure to be made the basis for any conclusions
regarding a knowledge of the god Yahweh. So also R. de Langhe, *Un
dieu Yahweh à Ras Shamra?* (1942).

[61] Edited by H. Torczyner, *The Wellcome Archaeological Research
Expedition to the Near East*, I: *Lachish* I: *The Lachish Letters* (1938).
Better translated by W. F. Albright, *Bulletin of the American Schools of
Oriental Research*, No. 70 (1938), pp. 11 ff.; in *Ancient Near Eastern
Texts*, ed. J. B. Pritchard (1950). E. L. Sukenik, *Palestine Exploration
Fund Quarterly Statement*, 1936, pp. 35 ff.; *Palestine Exploration Quarterly*,
1937, pp. 140 f., professes to find the name Yahweh on a sherd from
Samaria of the Hellenistic period, but his reading has not been accepted
by scholars and seems to be quite impossible.

יהוה and on an inscribed pot from Megiddo as יו.[62] Here
we have a phenomenon that is unique in the Semitic world,
a god name appearing in a variety of forms and never once
in its full form in personal names,[63] and that raises immediately the questions, why this should be so and which of the
forms is the earliest. It is to be noted at once that the form
יהוה appears in only two places outside the Old Testament
and it is never found either in or out of the Old Testament
as an element in personal names, and that immediately throws
suspicion upon it. Without going into an elaborate discussion of the problem, the true solution seems to be that יה
(Yah) and יהו (Yahu) are early forms, and יהוה (Yahweh)
a later and perhaps artificial form.[64] The origin of the form
יהוה, or at any rate the Hebrew explanation of it, is to be
found in Ex. 3:13 f.: "Moses said to God, 'In case I go to
the Israelites and say to them, "The God of your fathers
has sent me to you," and they say to me, "What is his name?"'
what am I to say to them?' And God said to Moses, 'I am

[62] For a complete discussion of the variant writings of Yahweh, with
tables, see G. R. Driver, Zeitschrift für die alttestamentliche Wissenschaft,
XLVI (1928), 7 ff. For the occurrence of יו see H. G. May, American
Journal of Semitic Languages, L (1933), 10 ff.

[63] It is true that there is the name יהוה צדקנו "Yahweh is our vindi-
cator," in Jer. 23:6, but this is an artificial, symbolic name after the
order of those in Is. 7:14; 8:3; 9:6; Hos. 1:6, 9, and was never the actual
name of an individual and hence is not written as one word in the Hebrew
text but as two. There are also place names of the same character in Gen.
22:14; Ex. 17:15; Judg. 6:24; Ez. 48:35.

[64] This solution is just the opposite of the popular one; see, e.g., W. F.
Albright, Journal of Biblical Literature, XLIII (1924), 370 ff.; XLIV
(1925), 158 ff.; XLVI (1927), 175 ff.; LXVII (1948), 379 f.; From the
Stone Age to Christianity (1940), p. 197. Albright makes Yahweh, a caus-
ative imperfect, the original form, of which Yahu is the jussive form, further abbreviated to Yah in the postexilic period. However, Yah is found
in such early writings as Ex. 17:16 and particularly Ex. 15:2, cited in Is.
12:2; Ps. 118:14, and hence the original reading. It is true that the word
is found chiefly in the Psalter, but liturgical literature is notoriously
archaizing and tends to preserve the old, and that would seem to be the
case here.

who I am.' Then he said, 'Thus shall you say to the Israelites, "I am" has sent me to you.' " If we change very slightly the wording in verse 14 (viz., *'ahyēh 'ăsher yihyēh* in place of *'ehyēh 'ăsher 'ehyēh*), we get the phrase "I cause to be what comes to pass" in place of "I am who I am," suggesting that "Yahweh" is an abbreviation of an original *Yahwēh-'ăsher-yihwēh*, which could be translated "he causes to be what comes to pass,"[65] i.e., he is the continuous creator of all that daily comes to pass.[66] According to the author of Ex. 3:14, this apparently was the explanation of the divine name and this was the new revelation that came to Moses; and that may possibly be true, because in it we have an old Egyptian liturgic formula that must have been well known to Moses and a conception that is characteristically Egyptian, the idea of a god who continually brings about all that day by day comes to pass, the ever-present creator and guide of all.[67] In that case it was the old god that Moses took over, but the old god in a new dress borrowed from Egypt, and it was an interpretation that could very well have rallied the people to his side. It is precisely this interpretation of God that we have in all the Exodus stories and throughout the rest of the Old Testament, later spiritualized and ethicized, and the name *Yahweh* has accordingly almost completely displaced the older name *Yah* in the biblical text.

On the other hand, it is not at all certain that the author of Ex. 3:14 intended what he says there to indicate the meaning of the word "Yahweh." He apparently did not know the etymology of the word, and in answer to the question of

[65] This translation, however, is possible only by equating the verbs *hwy* and *hyy*.

[66] Cf. the Babylonian personal name, Mushabshi-Marduk, "he who causes to be is Marduk," K. L. Tallqvist, *Assyrian Personal Names* (1914), p. 14.

[67] See W. F. Albright, *Journal of Biblical Literature*, XLIII (1924), 378; *From the Stone Age to Christianity* (1940), pp. 198 f.

Moses he puts into Yahweh's mouth a phrase that is perhaps intentionally vague and noncommittal, "I am who I am." It is to be noted that he does not use the phrase "I am he who is," which would definitely have indicated a derivation of "Yahweh" from the verb "to be," but instead he uses a phrase that is exceedingly vague, identical in every respect with phrases of similar purport elsewhere; e.g., "I am gracious to whom I am gracious and compassionate with whom I am compassionate" (Ex. 33:19); "I, Yahweh, will speak what I will speak" (Ez. 12:25); "I go whither I go" (II Sam. 15:20); "As I am bereaved, I am bereaved" (Gen. 43:14).[68]

The reason, then, that there is such uncertainty about the exact name of the Hebrew god (Yah, Yahu, and Yahweh) and the reason that its explanation is so uncertain and vague may well be because the name was of foreign origin and the Hebrews had accordingly no proper derivation of it in their own language. Indeed D. S. Margoliouth has given good reasons to show that the name was of Arabian origin.[69] There are at least two Hebrew personal names, one element of which is *Yahu* and the other a verb which can only be explained from early Arabic. These are יהואש and יאשיהו, where the root of the verbal form is Arabic or proto-Aramaic אוש, according to Margoliouth,[70] or אוש for the first and Arabic *'asā* for the second, according to Martin Noth.[71] Here clearly are two names which cannot be explained from any Hebrew root, so they must be indigenous to Arabia. They must have been formed in pre-Hebraic times, and that implies that Yahu or Yahweh originated somewhere in Arabia. The

---

[68] Cf. also A. Lods, *Israel* (Eng. trans., 1932), p. 323.

[69] *Relations between Arabs and Israelites prior to the Rise of Islam* (1924), pp. 14, 20 ff., 69. Cf. also A. Vincent, *La religion des Judéo-Araméens d'Éléphantine* (1937), p. 31, n. 3.

[70] *Op. cit.*, p. 14.

[71] *Die israelitischen Personennamen* (1928), p. 212.

name, accordingly, was foreign to the Hebrews and in their attempted explanation of it they connected it with the word *hāyāh*, "to be," just as the Greeks, who did not know the origin and exact meaning of "Zeus," connected the name with ζάω, "to live," whereas it is derived ultimately from Indo-European *dyu*, "to shine." The contention that Yahweh was of Arabian origin is clearly in accord with the Old Testament records, which connect him with the Negeb and with southern sanctuaries like Sinai-Horeb and Kadesh. A further evidence of his Negebite origin is the discovery of the same word, *yhw'*, attached to a place or district in the Negeb in an Egyptian inscription of the time of Ramesses II, early thirteenth century B.C.[72] Moreover, scholars have been almost universally of the opinion that the name can only be explained from Arabic, although they have not been able to agree on the exact derivation. The most probable in our opinion is the one that we have already given, viz., that from the Arabic root *hwy*, "to blow." Even if the word be derived from the root "to be," it can only come from proto-Semitic *hwy*, now found in Aramaic as *hw'*, and not from the Hebrew root "to be," which is *hyy*.[73] In fact, there is not a single derivation of the word "Yahweh" from a native Hebrew root;[74] they are all from foreign roots, most of them

[72] This inscription has not yet been published, but is reported by W. F. Albright, *Journal of Biblical Literature*, LXVII (1948), 380.

[73] Cf. also J. A. Montgomery, *Arabia and the Bible* (1934), p. 169; *Jewish Quarterly Review* (new series), XXV (1934-35), 269. Both Montgomery and Margoliouth point out a number of points where the Hebrew religion would seem to rest on Arabia, and this would be another indication as to where we are to look for the origin of Yahweh.

[74] For the more important derivations, together with his own from *hwy*, "to speak," see R. A. Bowman, *Journal of Near Eastern Studies*, III (1944), 1 ff. See also A. Schleiff, *Zeitschrift der Deutschen Morgenländischen Gesellschaft*, XC (1936), 679-702. The most recent explanation of the name is that by J. Obermann, *Journal of Biblical Literature*, LXVIII (1949), 301-323, who would make the word *yahweh* an Ifil participle, "the

Arabic, indicating quite clearly that Yahweh was a foreign
god, most probably originating in Arabia. He was anything
but a native Hebrew god, and on that particular point practically all scholars are agreed. They agree, too, that he originated in the south. They differ only as to whether he was
of Arabic or Kenite origin, and we favor the first but do
not rule out the other as a possibility.

There is good reason to believe that the Hebrew tribes
before they amalgamated to make the confederacies of Israel
and Judah had each its own tribal god. The early Hebrews,
like their neighbors, thought of the god as a physical member of the tribe, as father, brother, or kinsman; hence the
members of the tribe were actually sons or brothers or kinsmen of the god.[75] Accordingly, each tribe had its own tribal
god. Ever since the time of Robertson Smith[76] this has been
almost universally accepted, although there has naturally

---

sustainer," on the analogy of a similar form in the recently discovered
Phoenician inscription from Karatepe in southern Anatolia. However, it
is anything but certain that the analogous form in the Karatepe inscription is a participle because the Ifil participle should have the preformative
m and so should a form as clearly Piel as *ml'* in line 6 or *'n* in line 18 if
they are participles. The form can only be the infinitive used for the finite
verb, a construction that is very common in Hebrew, which has exact parallels to the Karatepe construction, infinitive plus pronoun, in Eccl. 4:2 and
Esth. 9:1. However, it cannot be an infinitive absolute, which Hebrew
would require, because it is found several times with a pronominal suffix; in
fact, it is not certain that Phoenician had any more than one infinitive,
and not two as in Hebrew, which in that respect would seem to be unique
among the Semitic languages. Cf. further on the Karatepe form A. M.
Honeyman, *Le Muséon*, LXI (1948), 49 f.; C. H. Gordon, *Journal of
Near Eastern Studies*, VIII (1949), 112 f.; J. Obermann, *ibid.*, IX (1950),
94-100. Obermann's contentions are possible, but they do not seem to be
probable.

[75] The evidences for this are the considerable number of personal names
consisting of a god name plus the element *'ab*, "father," *'aḥ*, "brother,"
or *'amm*, "kinsman." Cf. e.g., W. F. Albright, *From the Stone Age to
Christianity* (1940), pp. 185-187.

[76] *Journal of Philology*, IX (1877), 75 ff.

been considerable difference of opinion as to the identity of
the several gods.[77] Some of the tribal names suggest animal or
even totem gods, e.g., Leah (wild cow), Rachel (ewe), and
Caleb (dog). Such names as Dan, Gad, and Asher are at the
same time god names,[78] so that we have here the common
phenomenon, a tribe bearing the name of its eponymous
god.[79] Zebulun looks like a hypocoristicon from Zebul,
which may possibly be a god name, but that is not certain.[80]
Issachar is apparently derived from 'ish śākār, "man" or "men
of Sakar," and Sakar we know was a god.[81] Arguing from
data like these, scholars have concluded that all the Hebrew
tribes must have had tribal gods originally, and before becoming the god of the Hebrews as a whole Yahweh must
first have become the tribal god of one of the tribes that
went into the making of the Hebrew people; and it is our
further task to discover which of these it was that first
adopted him and from being solely a god of nature trans-
formed him into a tribal god.

To answer this question we need to keep several points in
mind: (1) Yahweh unquestionably had his origin in the

[77] See, e.g., H. P. Smith, *American Journal of Semitic Languages*, XXIV
(1907), 34 ff.; W. C. Wood, *Journal of Biblical Literature*, XXXV (1916),
254 ff.; G. A. Barton, *The Religion of Israel* (1928), pp. 53 f.; C. F. Burney, *Israel's Settlement in Canaan* (3rd ed., 1921), pp. 55 f.

[78] Dan was probably a Canaanite deity, while Gad is the name of a god
in Is. 65:11, but whether Asher was a god is not so certain unless the
name is the masculine counterpart of Asherah, as many suppose. The
word appears in the Ras Shamra texts, but not as a god name, as many
nave supposed; see, e.g., C. H. Gordon, *Analecta Orientalia*, 25 (1947),
p. 216, No. 353.

[79] See, e.g., J. Wellhausen, *Skizzen und Vorarbeiten*, III (1887), 4 f.; E.
Meyer, *Die Israeliten und ihre Nachbarstämme* (1906), pp. 297 f.; A. Lods,
Israel (Eng. trans., 1932), pp. 241 ff.; J. A. Montgomery, *Arabia and the
Bible* (1934), p. 12, n. 22.

[80] The word appears in the Ras Shamra texts as the title of a god, but
not as a god name; see Gordon, *op. cit.*, p. 227, No. 633.

[81] See A. Deimel, *Pantheon Babylonicum* (1914), No. 2832.

south. Upon this point all the Old Testament sources are
definitely agreed and likewise modern scholars. Hence the
tribe that adopted him as its tribal god must have been for
some time resident in the south. (2) With the tribe that first
adopted Yahweh we should find the first evidences of his
worship, and these are best to be found in personal names,
since these are always a sure criterion of a people's religion.
(3) Yahweh came in time to be something more than a tribal
god; he became the god of the southern confederacy, and
that extension of his sway must have come co-ordinate with
the extension of the political power of his tribe.[82] As one
tribe conquered another or brought another into alliance
with itself, the sway of its god was correspondingly extended. The god grew in prestige as the tribe grew, and
could grow in no other way in ancient times. (4) From being
a confederate god Yahweh gradually became the god of the
Hebrews as a whole, both north and south, and this could
only have happened as the south under the leadership of its
dominant tribe extended its influence into the north and
finally dominated the north.

Now, the only tribe that can answer all these conditions is
the tribe of Judah. Judah was of course a tribe long resident
in the south, as we know from Gen. 38, and apparently as
much of indigenous stock as it was of Hebrew.[83] Moreover,

[82] This point cannot be too strongly emphasized and is elaborated on pp.
161 ff. below. Cf. also A. W. Shorter, *An Introduction to Egyptian Religion*
(1931), p. 8: "As is well known, in ancient religions the power and popularity of gods were almost always decided by the political position enjoyed
by the places in which they were worshipped." Also J. M. P. Smith,
American Journal of Semitic Languages, XXXII (1916), 264: "A national
god as such can be the god of only one independent, political unit. The
only way for a national god to increase his territorial domain is by conquest or by absorption."

[83] Cf. W. O. E. Oesterley and T. H. Robinson, *A History of Israel*, I
(1932), 63, 100, 169 f.; T. H. Robinson, *Amicitiae Corolla*, ed. H. G.
Wood (1933), pp. 265 ff.; L. Waterman, *American Journal of Semitic
Languages*, LV (1938), 29 ff.

Yahweh names are first found in any number with the Judeans, but that, we have to confess, was not until the time of Samuel, Saul, and David, when Yahwism first became prominent. The only clearly attested, possible Yahweh names for the earlier period are Jochebed (Ex. 6:20; Num. 26:59), Joshua (Ex. 17:9 and elsewhere), Jonathan (Judg. 18:30), Joash (Judg. 6:11), Jotham, (Judg. 9:5 ff.), and Micayehu (Judg. 17:1, 4; abbreviated to Micah, 17:5 ff.), only six in number, and of these Jochebed, Joash, and Jotham are questioned by some and Joshua has to be deleted. According to Num. 13:16, Joshua's original name was Hoshea and it was only later that he was given the name Joshua. It was doubtless when E was absorbed by J and E's traditions were given a Judean, Yahwistic coloring that Hoshea's name was changed. According to Num. 13:16, it was Moses that gave him his new name and Moses was of course a southerner and a Yahweh worshiper. It is as Hoshea that he is known in Num. 13:8 and Deut. 32:44, and in Neh. 8:17 we have the form Jeshua (יֵשׁוּעַ), corresponding to which we have the cuneiform Jashuia, or more correctly Yashuya (ia-šu-ia), in the Tell el-Amarna letters, Jeshua on a Phoenician seal, and the Greek transcription Jesus,[84] all implying that the form Jehoshua or Joshua was a later modification of the name to make Joshua a Yahweh worshiper, even as Joseph was later spelled Jehoseph (Ps. 81:5) to make this a Yahweh name. Of the remaining Yahweh names in the early period two are those of converts to Yahwism, Joash and Micah,[85] and a third name, Jotham, is that of a descendant of Joash. This leaves only one name, Jonathan, definitely a Yahweh

---

[84] Cf. A. T. Olmstead, *History of Palestine and Syria* (1931), p. 201. Another way out of the difficulty created by the name "Joshua" is to retain the association of Joshua with Moses, thus dissociating him from Jericho and leaving the northerners with an unnamed leader; so J. W. Flight, *The Drama of Ancient Israel* (1949), p. 14.

[85] See pp. 145 f. below.

name and the earliest of all, the name of a young man engaged as priest by Micah and explicitly called a Judean,
Judg. 17:7, "a young man from Bethlehem in Judah, belonging to the clan of Judah," and a descendant of Moses according to Judg. 18:30. If we were to admit as genuine the
names that the Chronicler gives in his genealogies of the
various tribes (I Chron. 2 ff.), we would find a goodly number of Yahweh names among all the tribes, but more particularly among the Judeans. Scholars, however, are adverse
to admitting the genuineness of these lists. The fact that we
have so few Yahweh names from the early period may be
surprising, but after all we do not have many clearly attested
names of any kind from that period.

The paucity of Yahweh names before the time of Samuel
and their decided increase from the time of David onward
are evidences that Yahwism spread very slowly among the
Hebrew tribes and only became prominent in the time of
David, and this extension of Yahwism exactly parallels the
growth of the power of Judah. One by one various tribes in
the south fused or were fused with Judah (the Levites,
Kenites, Simeonites, Calebites, Jerahmeelites, and others)
until Judah dominated the south completely. This is manifest in the fact that Judah gave its name to the southern confederacy and it is also very clear from the Old Testament
records themselves. According to Judg. 1:16, the Kenites
early lost their tribal independence and were fused with the
tribe of Judah. Later records locate them in Judean territory
(I Sam. 15:6; 27:10; 30:29), and I Chron. 2:55 definitely
reckons them as an integral part of Judah. Hence if the Kenites were worshipers of Yahweh at the time that Moses married one of their number, as they probably were, it was because they were converts to the Yahweh cult. Their fusion
with Judah meant that by that very fact they had to adopt

the cult of the stronger tribe, and since we know them as Yahweh worshipers, the indication is that Yahweh was the tribal god of Judah when that fusion took place. In exactly the same way the Levites, Simeonites, Calebites, and Jerahmeelites were amalgamated with Judah[86] and so must have adopted its Yahweh religion. Indeed this is stated explicitly for the Levites in Ex. 32:25-29. The spread of a common cult among these several tribes could only have come as they were fused into one by some stronger tribe, and to discover the source of the cult, all we have to do is to discover the tribe that did the fusing, and that of course was Judah.

But Judah was not content simply to dominate the south. It proceeded presently to extend its sphere of influence and its Yahweh cult into the north, until in the time of David it dominated the north as well and Yahweh was made the national god of the united state. From being a god of nature Yahweh had become a tribal god, then a confederate god, and now a national god. As Judah grew in power, so likewise did Yahweh. The two went hand in hand and must belong together, and that is suggested further by the very name of the tribe. Many scholars explain the name "Judah" as a compound of Yahu and some verbal form,[87] but this unfortunately is by no means certain and is not accepted by most scholars. Albright, following a suggestion of Eduard Meyer, would make the name a hypocoristicon of an original *Yĕhûdāh-'ēl*, "Let El be praised,"[88] and this is possible. However, the original could just as well have been *Yĕhûdāh-yah*, "Let Yah (Yahweh) be praised," later abbreviated to *Yĕhûdāh*, and this has the advantage of being supported by the Old Testament explanation of the name in Gen. 29:35. If

---

[86] See pp. 125 ff. below.
[87] So, e.g., O. Procksch, *Die Genesis* (1913), p. 171.
[88] *Journal of Biblical Literature*, XLVI (1927), 170 ff.

correct, that would definitely connect Yahweh with Judah.

It is true, as A. H. Godbey has pointed out,[89] that Yahweh is rather often called the god of Israel in the Old Testament and never once the god of Judah, but "Israel" here is used in its national sense to mean the Hebrew nation as a whole and not simply the northern tribes. As we have already noted,[90] it was the word "Israel" alone that attained this connotation, whereas "Judah" is always used to designate the southern tribes or the region in which they settled. In the Old Testament records, as we have them now in their final, late form, Yahweh is never represented as the god of one group alone, but of the nation as a whole, i.e., of "Israel," and the god of that nation from its beginning, the god of Abraham, Isaac, and Jacob.

Our contention, then, is that Yahweh was originally a storm-god, first known in Arabia. At some early period, for reasons beyond our ken, he was adopted by Judah as its tribal god, and then as Judah absorbed other tribes into itself by conquest or alliance the domain of Yahweh was correspondingly extended. One of the tribes thus early fused with Judah and won to its Yahweh cult was the Kenites, by marrying among whom Moses became a worshiper of Yahweh, if he was not already that.[91] Through Moses the Levites in Egypt were converted to the cult or had their faith confirmed in it (if they were already worshipers), and eventually they amalgamated with Judah and its subject tribes to make a great southern confederacy or amphictyony. According to tradition, the moving spirit in this was Moses, and that undoubtedly was the case. The success of Moses in delivering his people from Egyptian oppression had made

[89] *The Lost Ten Tribes: A Myth* (1930), p. 116.
[90] See p. 46 above.
[91] This will depend upon whether Jochebed was the name of the mother of Moses and whether it actually contains the element "Yahweh."

him and his tribe ardent protagonists of Yahweh; the movement was as much religious as political (hence the term
"amphictyony"); and there is good reason to believe that
Moses' tribesmen, the Levites, became the priestly order of
the Judeans, as we shall have occasion to see in Chapter IV.

A final indication of the close connection between Yahweh and Judah is the fact that wherever the Judeans went
there went Yahweh, so that he was clearly their peculiar
god. Thus when Judah came to dominate all the Hebrew
tribes, as it did in the time of David, then and then only
did Yahweh become the god of all the people. To the northerners, then, Yahwism was a southern cult to begin with,
more specifically a Judean cult, rather recently come to
Israel, and intimately associated with Moses. This to E
marked its beginning, but E as a northerner probably knew
very little about its real origin. As a comparatively late
writer of the prophetic school and hence a supporter of the
Yahweh cult himself, he maintains that after all Yahweh was
not a new god with Moses, but just the old god under a new
name. Thus he would commend Yahweh to his country-
men, not as a southern god, which would be objectionable
to them, but simply as a reinterpretation of their own god
(Ex. 3:6).[92] P's view is similar to this (Ex. 6:3, 8), and
neither view is altogether inconsistent with that of J, as we
have already noted. The difference in viewpoint resulted
simply from a difference in experience. E expresses the point
of view of Israel, where Yahweh was a comparatively unknown god until he was brought to the fore by Levites and
Judeans; whereas J expresses the point of view of Judah,

[92] Similarly, our Old Testament documents in general tend to interpret
the early numina of springs, trees, and the like, and the Canaanite gods of
the high places as manifestations of the god Yahweh; cf., e.g., Gen. 13:18;
21:14 ff., 33; 28:10 ff.; 32:23 ff.; Ex. 4:24 ff.

where Yahweh in contrast was a god long known and his worship immemorial, a peculiarly Judean god.[93]

[93] Similarly G. H. Skipwith, *Jewish Quarterly Review* (old series), XI (1899), 250: "Why is the invocation of Jahveh represented in J, Gen. iv, 26 (J²), as beginning with אנוש; —a name which must have originally signified the first man—while in E, Ex. iii, it is for the first time revealed to Moses? The answer is very simple: J expresses the point of view of Judah, where the worship of Jahveh was in fact immemorial; E that of Ephraim, where tradition could recall its introduction."

CHAPTER FOUR

The Origin of the Hebrew Priesthood

THE origin of priesthood is manifestly to be traced back to the earliest stage of social evolution and is doubtless to be found very close to the beginning of magical and religious practices. There was a time when each individual invoked the god for himself without the help of a mediator,[1] but the idea early developed that certain individuals could get better, easier, and more intimate access to the spirit world than others. These were the first priests in religion. They were shamans, wonder-workers, medicine men, individuals credited with the possession of mana, or spiritual power; or they could be men who lived near sacred places and so were supposedly on more intimate terms than ordinary folk with the spirits residing there.

Then with the elaboration of magical practices and ritual observances the necessity arose for specialists in these matters, men who were trained through long experience, and thus professional priests came into being, and in course of time these tended to organize themselves into priesthoods. Religion had now become too complicated for the ordinary individual and recourse was had to the more experienced practitioners, at least on the more important occasions when the god would

---

[1] Note, e.g., the early Hebrew patriarchs, Adam, Cain, Abel, Noah, Abraham, etc.

be in an exacting mood and the rites more formal, more elaborate, and more magical, such occasions as the full moon, the new moon, the new year, and the like. On ordinary occasions, for the ordinary conduct of affairs, the head of the family would function for the family, and the larger group would look to their patriarchs or elders for religious guidance, and particularly to the chief of the patriarchs as the one possessed of most experience in such matters.

It would seem that the first form of political organization with ancient peoples was the tribe, and with most this presently became a city-state as the tribe settled on the land. Since there is always the tendency to centralize authority in one individual and exalt him to a position of pre-eminence over all others and see in him a man possessed of mana,[2] the sheikh of the tribe and later the king of the city-state became naturally the chief priest of the state religion, standing to the state as the father stood to the family. As the state grew larger and became more complex in its character and organization, as it naturally must in the course of time, the duties of the king became so many and so varied that he had perforce to delegate some of these to deputies to act in his stead. Certain of his religious duties he accordingly committed to others, and in this we have the beginning of professional state priests, who at first functioned, not on their own account, but in the name of the king.[3] Presently these grew in numbers and tended to organize themselves into priesthoods, and the office became more or less hereditary in consequence. Thus state priesthoods came into being, and these almost immediately came

[2] Cf. A. Lods, *Israel* (Eng. trans., 1932), pp. 303 f.; J. G. Frazer, *The Golden Bough*, I (3rd ed., 1911), 83 ff.

[3] This is best seen in ancient Egypt, where in both the liturgies and on the bas-reliefs the offerings are represented as coming from the king himself, when as a matter of fact they were presented by a priest acting as deputy for the king; see, e.g., A. Erman, *A Handbook of Egyptian Religion* (Eng. trans., 1907), pp. 52 ff.

into conflict with the popular priesthoods, the functionaries of the popular religion. The latter tended to disappear in face of the greater wealth and authority of the state priesthoods, but they might survive for a long time, if not to the very end, as they did in Rome,[4] or they might be absorbed into the state religion, as they usually were.

As far as the matter can be stated in brief and general terms, this seems to have been the way that the priesthood with most peoples anciently developed. And yet there were some manifest exceptions, at least in some particulars, as, for instance, in the case of the Magi of the Iranians, the Druids of the Celts, and possibly the Brahmans of India. These seem to have been clan or tribal in their origin, and in the case of the Magi at least, it would appear that they were a tribe who, defeated in an effort to obtain political power, eventually made up in religious prestige what they failed to obtain politically. May this not be suggestive of the origin of the Levitical priesthood with the Hebrews?

That the Levites were originally a tribe is the unequivocal testimony of the Old Testament narratives. A tendency among scholars is to suppose that they were from the beginning a priestly caste and not a tribe, and that the term "Levite" denotes, not tribal connection, but profession.[5] But is this in accord with the evidences in the case? Our earliest source of information is Gen. 49:5-7, dated by all

---

[4] Ancient priesthoods like the Fetiales, the Sodales Titienses, the Fratres Arvales, the Salii, and the Luperci all but disappeared in Rome, but were revived or confirmed by Augustus; see, e.g., W. W. Fowler, *Religious Experience of the Roman People* (1911), pp. 434 ff.

[5] The stock reference in support of this is Ex. 4:14, where Aaron in contradistinction from Moses is called "the Levite," i.e., the priest, but this verse is universally regarded as late. The whole verse, or at any rate the phrase "the Levite," comes from a period when the Aaronites were winning the ascendancy in the priestly profession, so that Aaron was the Levite *par excellence.*

scholars no later than the early Monarchy and by John
Skinner early in the period of the Judges.[6] According to this,
Levi is not only a tribe, but a purely secular one at that. Even
in the much later poem, Deut. 33:8-11, he still figures as a
tribe, although now entrusted with priestly functions. In the
early Old Testament narratives many individuals not of the
tribe of Levi are recorded as bearing the title of priest or as
performing priestly functions (see, e.g., Judg. 6:26 f.; 13:19;
17:5; I Sam. 7:1; II Sam. 6:3 f.; 8:18; 20:26; I Kings 4:5;
18:30 ff.), but these are nowhere called Levites, as would be
the case if the term "Levite" denoted official rather than
tribal status. Furthermore, if "Levite" began as a professional term and was synonymous with "priest," we would
unquestionably have such expressions as "Levites of Yahweh,"
"his Levites," and "my Levites," whereas these are never
found.[7] All the pentateuchal sources, J, E, D, and P, are quite
unanimous in their testimony that the term in the first
instance was tribal (see, e.g., Gen. 29:34, J; Gen. 34, J+E;
Ex. 2:1, E; Deut. 10:8; 18:1-8, D; Gen. 35:23, P), and there
would seem to be no good reason to doubt their testimony.[8]

As a secular tribe, the Levites from all appearances had
the serpent god, Nahash[9] or Nehushtan (a hypocoristicon),
as their tribal god. This was first argued by G. H. Skipwith,[10]

[6] *International Critical Commentary on Genesis* (1910), pp. 510 f.

[7] The expression "our Levites" is found once in the Old Testament, in
a very late writing, Neh. 9:38, by which time the term "Levite" had long
since lost its original meaning and was quite distinct from the term
"priest," as the verse clearly indicates in reading "our nobles, our Levites,
and our priests."

[8] Cf. G. B. Gray, *Sacrifice in the Old Testament* (1925), pp. 240 ff.;
C. F. Burney, *The Book of Judges* (2nd ed., 1920), pp. 436 ff.

[9] Cf. a similar god name in the Babylonian pantheon, Nahish; A. Deimel,
Pantheon Babylonicum (1914), No. 2256.

[10] "The Name of Levi," *Jewish Quarterly Review* (old series), XI (1899),
264 f.

and later adopted by Eduard Meyer and B. Luther[11] with no acknowledgment whatever to Skipwith. The argument in each case is essentially the same. The setting up of the serpent in the desert as a god of healing (cf. Asklepios) is ascribed to the Levite Moses (Num. 21:5-9, E; II Kings 18:4), and the pole (*nēs*) on which he set up the serpent (Num. 21:9) is doubtless to be identified with the rod or pole that appears in the name of the altar, *Yahweh-nissi* ("Yahweh is my rod"), erected by Moses in celebration of the victory over the Amalekites through the use of the magic wand of Yahweh (Ex. 17:8-16, E). It was this wand which, when cast on the ground, turned into a serpent (Ex. 4:2-5, J), and with which, according to E (Ex. 4:17), Moses was to work wonders, and did so, in Egypt (Ex. 7:15, 17, 19 f.), at the crossing of the Red Sea (Ex. 14:16), in making water come forth from the rock (Ex. 17:5 f.; cf. Num. 20:7-13), and against the Amalekites (Ex. 17:9). According to J (Ex. 15:25), it was a stick (usually translated "tree") with which Moses made the water sweet at Marah, but this is simply another form of the magic rod. In P it is noteworthy that the rod is no longer Moses', but Aaron's (Ex. 7:9, 10, 12; 8:5, 16 f.), and this would further indicate its Levitical origin; for Aaron in the later period was the "Levite" *par excellence* (Num. 16-18). A further connection between Levi and the serpent cult is to be found in the probable connection between the name "Levi" and the dragon god Leviathan,[12] both being derived apparently from *lāwāh* = Arabic *lawā*, "to twist, coil," and לוי, "Levite," is manifestly a hypocoristicon from an original לוי-אל, "God coils," or the ending may be gentilic, to designate class, as in the case of נכרי, "foreigner," and

[11] *Die Israeliten und ihre Nachbarstämme* (1906), p. 116 (Luther); pp. 426 f. (Meyer).

[12] Skipwith, *op. cit.*, p. 264, contrasts לְוָנָה לֵוִי, לֹוָה לְוָנָן and שָׁמַ, נְחֻשׁ, נְחֹשֶׁת, נְחֻשְׁתָּן. Cf. also Meyer, *op. cit.*, p. 426.

חפשי, "free person." Finally, the presence of serpent names among the Levites points indubitably in the same direction, although these, it must be confessed, are few in number, due doubtless to the fact that serpent names, like animal names in general, came to be suppressed as out of accord with later religious ideas. The father-in-law of Moses is given the name Hobab, probably "serpent," by J (Num. 10:29). Even P preserves the name of Aaron's brother-in-law as Nahshon, "serpent" (Ex. 6:23), and with the Chronicler we have Naás, "serpent," in the Septuagint as the name of a Levite (I Chron. 26:4), and Shuppim, "horned snakes" (I Chron. 26:16), as the name of another Levite, but the text here is uncertain. We know from the excavations that the serpent cult was quite prevalent in Palestine,[13] and its popularity must have been due in part to the Levites.

Our sources all agree that the once-secular tribe of Levi came in course of time to be invested with priestly functions. As to how that came about the traditions differ, and it is a matter veiled in deepest mystery, but it has its parallel in the history of the Magi. Here was a tribe that made a temporarily successful bid for political power under Gaumata, but defeated finally in that effort, they resorted to religion to recoup their fortune and eventually came to monopolize the priestly office to the exclusion of the earlier *athravan* and *zaotar*, who had been limited to no particular class.[14] Along similar lines

[13] See the extensive literature cited by J. Pedersen, *Israel: Its Life and Culture*, III-IV (1947), 711, n. 2 to p. 452; also W. C. Graham and H. G. May, *Culture and Conscience* (1936), pp. 81-89; W. F. Albright, *The Archaeology of Palestine and the Bible* (1932), pp. 87 f.; *Archaeology and the Religion of Israel* (1942), p. 189, n. 51; K. Galling, *Biblisches Reallexikon* (1937), pp. 458 f.; C. C. McCown, *The Ladder of Progress in Palestine* (1943), pp. 58, 74, 89 f., 151, 162 f., 270; *Tell en-Naṣbeh* (1947), p. 247.

[14] See J. H. Moulton, *Early Zoroastrianism* (1913), Lectures VI and VII.

the Levites would seem to have developed. That they made an early bid for political power is the natural inference from Gen. 34 and 49:5-7. That the incident was exactly as recorded in Gen. 34 is very doubtful. Both Levi and Simeon, who also is involved in the incident, were southern tribes, and it is surprising to find them so far north as Shechem, unless perhaps we have in the story the record of an early attack by two southern tribes on the northerners, the first of a long series of conflicts between north and south. Moreover, the Shechemites clearly did not suffer the destruction depicted in the story, because they continued to flourish down to the time of Abimelech, as we know from Judg. 9. It would seem better with Eduard Meyer[15] to suppose that the story originated near the Simeonite territory in the south, probably Kadesh, and was transferred to Shechem because of certain points of affinity with the Abimelech episode, or it may have been confused with an incident recorded in the Tell el-Amarna letters, the alliance of Shechem with the invading Habiru.[16] We have already noted the tendency for traditions to be transferred from one place to another. It is the sort of thing that has gone on in the world ever since the time when traditions and sagas were first formed. That Simeon and Levi are classed together in the saga is doubtless due to common traditions, to common southern origin, and possibly also to an apparently old tradition that they were the *only* sons of Leah.[17]

If the story in Gen. 34, then, has any historical foundation, and it probably has, it would seem to indicate that Simeon and Levi together made some drastic attempt to secure political power, probably in some conspiracy against the growing

[15] *Op. cit.,* pp. 422 ff.
[16] See J. A. Knudtzon, *Die el-Amarna-Tafeln* (1915), No. 289.
[17] Cf. Meyer, *op. cit.,* pp. 286, 426 f.

dominance of Judah in the southern confederacy.[18] Defeated in that project, the two tribes were rather severely handled and all but wiped out of existence, as reflected in the curse of Gen. 49:7:

> Cursed be their anger, for it is fierce,
> And their wrath, for it is cruel!
> I will disperse them throughout Jacob,
> And scatter them throughout Israel.

What remained of them came in course of time to be absorbed into Judah, their probable conqueror. That Judah was a mixed tribe which drew by conquest and other means many elements to itself is a well-established fact,[19] manifest from the very beginning of the tribe, as attested by such passages as Gen. 49:8-12 and 38:1 ff. Simeon, we know, was one of these elements (Josh. 19:1, 9)[20] and Levi was clearly another. Like Simeon, Levi was unquestionably of southern origin. This is shown unmistakably by the connection with Massah

---

[18] Hence the rather mild censure of Gen. 34:30 and the reason for the later comparative insignificance of these tribes politically. In Gen. 49:5-7 this censure has been magnified into a curse, a reflection probably of the spirit of antipathy against the rising power of the Levites. It was in this period, viz., that of the Judges and early Monarchy, as noted below, that the Levites were struggling for religious ascendancy among rival priesthoods, particularly in the north. Another reason for the curse may be that the lines come from a northern poet who is voicing the old-time antipathy of the north against the south. Later writers, more favorably inclined toward the Levites, extol Simeon and Levi for their act of destruction (see, e.g., Jth. 9:2; Jub. 30:4, 18; Test. of Levi 5:2 ff.; cf. R. H. Charles, *The Book of Jubilees* [1902], p. 179; *Testament of the Twelve Patriarchs* [1908], p. 22). In Deut. 33:8-11, written probably in the reign of Jeroboam II (so most scholars believe), when the Levites had all but won religious ascendancy in both north and south, Levi is very naturally blessed and his enemies (rival priesthoods) cursed.

[19] Cf., e.g., C. F. Burney, *The Book of Judges* (2nd ed., 1920), pp. 45 f.; W. O. E. Oesterley and T. H. Robinson, *A History of Israel*, I (1932), 63, 93, 100, 169 f.

[20] Cf. Burney, *op. cit.*, p. 4; S. R. Driver, *International Critical Commentary on Deuteronomy* (1895), p. 395.

and Meribah (Deut. 33:8), and by many other references in the Old Testament connecting Levi with the south (e.g., Ex. 32:26-29; Judg. 17:7; 19:1). The traditions and genealogies of the Levites associate them with the south, and their names are connected with sites in the south and with names found elsewhere among southern groups.[21] As a southern tribe, then, Levi was closely contiguous to Judah, and the evidences would further indicate that it was conquered by, or became attached to, the stronger tribe of Judah, even as happened with Simeon. This is suggested by the Old Testament itself in deriving the word "Levi" from *lāwāh*, "to join, be joined" (Gen. 29:34), and the story of how they joined the Yahweh cult and hence its tribe Judah is recorded in Ex. 32:25-29. Similarly, the plain interpretation of the genuinely old story in Judg. 17 f., attached to the Book of Judges, is that the Levite there mentioned was, as the text clearly states, "a young man from Bethlehem in Judah, belonging to the clan of Judah" (Judg. 17:7). This would indicate that the Levites by the time of the story had become amalgamated with the Judeans, unless we interpret "Levite" here as meaning profession and not tribe, as some scholars do.[22] To do this, however, is to violate the plain meaning of the text and is out of accord with references to Levi elsewhere. Just as Caleb came to be regarded as belonging to the tribe of Judah although in origin quite distinct from it,[23] so it was with Levi.

The tribe of Simeon so completely merged with Judah that in time it disappeared altogether, but this was not the case

[21] Cf. Eduard Meyer, *Die Israeliten und ihre Nachbarstämme* (1906), pp. 83, 120; S. A. Cook, *Critical Notes on Old Testament History* (1907), pp. 84 ff.; *Jewish Quarterly Review* (old series), XIX (1907), 169 ff.

[22] E.g., G. F. Moore, *International Critical Commentary on Judges* (1895), p. 383.

[23] Cf. Burney, *op. cit.*, p. 12.

with the Levites. They saved themselves from complete absorption and ultimate extinction as a tribe by championing the cause of the stronger tribe, particularly their Yahweh cult, and of this there is more than a hint in Deut. 33:8-10:

> Give thy Thummim to Levi,[24]
> And thy Urim to the man devoted to thee;
> Whom thou didst test at Massah,
> With whom thou didst contend at the waters of Meribah;
> Who said of his father and mother,
> "I no longer recognize them";
> And disowned his brothers,
> And disavowed his own children;
> But he has kept thy injunctions,
> And guarded thy covenant.
> He communicates thy ordinances to Jacob,
> And thy law to Israel;
> He provides the savor of sacrifices for thy nostrils,
> And holocausts on thy altars.

That is, the Levites renounced all earthly aspirations and all considerations based on earthly relationship to become the priests of Yahweh. And this, too, is the statement of Ex. 32:25-29, where Moses says to the Levites in verse 29, "You have installed yourselves today as priests to Yahweh, each at the cost of his kith and kin [*lit.*, his son and his kinsman], that he may bestow a blessing on you today."[25] And in this capacity, as priests, they must have been welcomed by the Judeans. As we have already noted, the tribal god of the Levites was in all probability the serpent god, and with the serpent there has always been associated a certain occult mantic power, as is indicated with the Hebrews by the word for serpent, *nāḥāsh*, which differs only in vocalization from

[24] So Greek; Hebrew omits "give to Levi."
[25] So Greek and Syriac; Hebrew reads the imperative for "you have installed yourselves"; it inserts "for" before "each" and "and" before "that he may bestow."

the word for divination, *nāḥash*, both being derived from the same root. Hence the early Levites were manifestly regarded as medicine men or shamans by the surrounding tribes, and now in a time of need that fame stood them in good stead and they became priests, because that is precisely what the Hebrew word for priest, *kôhēn*, implies, identical with the Arabic *kāhin*, "soothsayer, medium, shaman," one who acts as a medium between god and man and between man and god.[26] It is a peculiar fact that among ancient peoples the religious functionaries of neighboring tribes were held in greater awe and repute than their own.[27] Indeed it seems to have been a universal belief among early peoples that the secret powers of strangers were greater than those of well-known persons, and strangers were accordingly always looked upon with awe and a certain amount of fear, even as they still are among backward people, e.g., the Arabs of the desert or the peasants in Italy, whose dread of the evil eye of strangers is most acute. For that reason Muhammad as a *kāhin*, or shaman, was invited by the citizens of Yathrib to leave his native city, Mecca, where he was unappreciated, and become *kāhin* to Yathrib, and that he did, much to his and their advantage. In some regions whole tribes have been regarded as powerful wizards and their services have been sought by neighboring tribes,[28] and one could cite among others the Druids, "the very knowing ones," as they were

[26] It is to be noted that I do not derive Hebrew *kôhēn* from Arabic *kāhin*, as W. F. Albright assumes, *From the Stone Age to Christianity* (1940), p. 314, n. 31; I simply say that the two words are identical philologically. The frequent occurrence of the same word, *khn*, with the meaning "priest," in the Ras Shamra texts gives credence to the suggestion of G. B. Gray, *Sacrifice in the Old Testament* (1925), p. 183, that the word was of Canaanite origin. Cf. also A. Haldar, *Associations of Cult Prophets among the Ancient Semites* (1945), pp. 162 ff.

[27] Cf., e.g., in the Old Testament, II Kings 5:1 ff.; 8:7 ff.

[28] See E. B. Tylor, *Primitive Culture*, I (6th ed., 1920), 113 ff.

called, and a non-Celtic tribe who attained their priestly position with the Celts through their supposed possession of unusual magic knowledge.[29] Hence it was probably in some such way as this that the Levites from being a purely secular tribe became the priestly order of another tribe and so saved themselves from the extinction that was the lot of Simeon. Among the ancient Arabs the priesthood was largely in the hands of special families that did not belong to the tribe among whom they exercised their office.[30] Indeed there is strong probability that some of these were Levites, who migrating southward into Arabia became priests to certain Arabs there, as their brethren whom they left behind became priests to the Judeans.[31] This would seem to be the best, if not the only, way to account for the word *lawi'u*, identical with the Hebrew *lēwî* (Levi), as the term for priest in the Minean inscriptions of the Persian period from al-'Ula (ancient Dedan) in north Arabia.[32] The word seems to mean literally "one pledged for a debt or vow," just as Samuel

[29] See J. A. MacCulloch, *The Religion of the Ancient Celts* (1911), pp. 293 ff. Similarly, J. H. Moulton, *Early Zoroastrianism* (1913), Lectures VI and VII, maintains that the Magi, who became the priestly order of the Persians, were a non-Aryan tribe.

[30] See J. Wellhausen, *Reste arabischen Heidentums* (2nd ed., 1897), pp. 130 ff. Similarly, among the Wahhabis in Arabia today the ecclesiastical hierarchy consists of the descendants of the founder of the sect, a man of alien origin; see H. St. J. B. Philby, *The Heart of Arabia*, I (1922), 297. In Egypt the Merabit tribe are the religionists of the Saadi and their dependents, although originally their masters; see Austin Kennett, *Bedouin Justice* (1925), pp. 24 ff.

[31] Similarly, L. H. Gray, *Expository Times*, XXV (1909), 257, and D. B. Spooner, *Journal of the Royal Asiatic Society*, 1915, pp. 63 ff., 405 ff., believe that there are evidences that not all the Magi remained in Persia, but that some of them migrated early to India.

[32] See Eduard Meyer, *Die Israeliten und ihre Nachbarstämme* (1906), pp. 88 f., 428; G. B. Gray, *Sacrifice in the Old Testament* (1925), pp. 242 ff.; H. Grimme, *Le Muséon*, XXXVII (1924), 169 ff.; W. F. Albright, *Archaeology and the Religion of Israel* (1942), p. 204, n. 42. Rather than derive *lawi'u* from *lēwî* Albright would derive *lēwî* from an original *lawiyu* through Minean *lawi'u*, but we prefer to follow Gray, *op. cit.*, p. 247.

was vowed by his mother to Yahweh at Shiloh (I Sam. 1:11).
Unlike the Hebrews, the Mineans used the word in the
feminine, *lawi'atu*, and they also used such an expression as
"his *lawi'atu*." This would indicate that the term was native
to the Hebrew language and borrowed at al-'Ula, the language to which it was native naturally exercising a greater
restraint on its correct usage.[33] Likewise there may be some
connection between *lēwî* and Arabic *weli*, "saint," as D. S.
Margoliouth has suggested.[34] So largely did the Levites take
to the priestly profession and so completely in the end did
they monopolize it that the term "Levite" came to be identical with "priest" in all the countries in which they settled,
exactly as *magus* in Persia replaced the older *athravan* and
zaotar as the term for "priest," when the incoming Magi came
to appropriate the priestly profession.[35]

In losing their political existence the Levites of necessity
gave up most of their own tribal religion, the serpent cult,
as is shown by the fact that in al-'Ula they were priests of the
god Wadd, the chief deity of that district, whereas in Judah
they were priests of the Judean god Yahweh. And yet there
are evidences that they did not leave their own religion
completely behind, but grafted some of it on to the Yahweh
cult.[36] It always happens when two peoples unite that the
religion of the united peoples partakes something of the
character of the earlier religion of each. It is only so that we
can account for the fact that the serpent cult became so

[33] Cf. Gray, *op. cit.*, p. 247.

[34] Quoted from a private communication by C. F. Burney, *The Book of
Judges* (2nd ed., 1920), p. 437, note. The transposition of consonants is a
common phenomenon among the Semitic languages, of which Burney gives
two examples: Hebrew *ṣāwā*=Arabic *waṣā* and Hebrew *ḥāwā*=Arabic
waḥā.

[35] See J. H. Moulton, *Early Zoroastrianism* (1913), p. 194.

[36] Similarly, Moulton, *op. cit.*, Lectures VI and VII, maintains that
Ahura Mazda was not originally the god of the Magi, but in becoming
priests to the Persians the Magi adopted the Zoroastrian faith, at the same
time grafting on it certain peculiar beliefs and practices of their own.

closely knit with the Yahweh cult and continued right down to the time of Hezekiah to be an integral part of it and was only eradicated under the vigorous polemic of the prophets against idolatry (II Kings, 18:4, "He [i.e., Hezekiah] broke in pieces the bronze serpent that Moses had made; for as late as those days the Israelites had been offering sacrifices to it, and it was called Nehushtan"). The presence of "serpent" as an element in certain Hebrew personal names[37] is another indication of the impact of the serpent cult on the Hebrew religion, as are likewise the name of the altar erected by Moses, *Yahweh-nissi*, "Yahweh is my rod" (Ex. 17:15; cf. the magic wand of Ex. 4:2-5), and the ascription to Yahweh of the art of healing (Ex. 15:26; 23:25). The "serpent" (*sārāph*) of Num. 21:8 appears again in the "seraphim" of Is. 6:2, 6 (cf. also Is. 14:29; 30:6; Deut. 8:15); and still another evidence of the serpent cult may be found in the "serpent's stone" of I Kings 1:9, and in the "dragon's spring" of Neh. 2:13.[38] To put the matter beyond all dispute we have the evidence of excavations in Palestine, which show the presence of the serpent cult from early times down to the late period.[39]

That there were priests before the Levites is unquestioned. The statement that Rebekah[40] "went off to consult Yahweh"

[37] For a list of these see W. C. Wood, *Journal of Biblical Literature*, XXXV (1916), 242, n. 20; M. Noth, *Die israelitischen Personennamen* (1928), p. 230.

[38] Cf. W. R. Smith, *Religion of the Semites* (3rd ed., 1927), p. 172, n. 3.

[39] See note 13 above.

[40] By some strange trick of the pen I wrote "Rachel" here in the first edition and great was my consternation somewhat later to see the whole context, scribal error and all, quoted almost verbatim by a well-known scholar in a well-known journal, but fortunately for me the source of the quotation was not given. The incident goes to show that some scholars are not averse to plagiarism and supposedly critically minded scholars are not so critically minded after all; like sheep they tend to follow blindly in one another's track, even when that track leads to error.

in Gen. 25:22 f. (J) suggests an oracle and an interpreter, like the Arab *kāhin*,[41] and likewise does the same expression in Ex. 33:7 (E) and elsewhere. Similarly, the early laws prescribing that certain cases be brought before God for settlement (e.g., Ex. 21:6; 22:8, 9, 11, E) suggest an oracle or a priest at a sanctuary to interpret the will of God; as do also "the terebinth of the oracle-giver" (Gen. 12:6, J) and "the terebinth of the soothsayers" (Judg. 9:37). In fact the Hebrew word for "law," *tôrāh*, carries this same import, because "message" or "oracle" is clearly its root meaning.[42] It is very evident, then, that there were priests, and probably priesthoods as well, long before the Levites entered the profession, and it was a long-drawn-out and bitterly contested struggle among the rival priesthoods before the Levites finally attained the priestly monopoly; for there is plenty of evidence that there were priests who were not Levites down to a time not long antedating the Deuteronomic Code,[43] and between these and the Levites there was the fiercest kind of rivalry.[44] Some indeed seem to have been admitted to the Levitical order who were not of the tribe of Levi, as, for instance, Samuel, of the tribe of Ephraim (I Sam. 1). Similarly, the Brahmans in India up to the sixth century B.C., although fast

[41] Cf. A. Dillmann, *Genesis*, II (Eng. trans., 1897), 194; J. Wellhausen, *Reste arabischen Heidentums* (2nd ed., 1897), pp. 134 ff.

[42] It used to be derived from a root meaning "to cast (lots)," but W. F. Albright, *Journal of Biblical Literature*, XLVI (1927), 178 ff., challenges this derivation, although he does not deny the connection with Akkadian *têrtu*, the meaning of which is "oracle," a message sent from deity. For a complete discussion with conservative results see Gunnar Östborn, *Tōrā in the Old Testament: A Semantic Study* (1946).

[43] See, e.g., W. von Baudissin, *Dictionary of the Bible*, ed. James Hastings, IV (1902), 70 ff.; G. B. Gray, *Sacrifice in the Old Testament* (1925), pp. 253 ff.

[44] The sagas which reflect the progressive stages in the conflict of priestly prerogatives are well discussed by S. A. Cook, *Jewish Quarterly Review* (old series), XVIII (1906), 749 ff.

becoming a separate hereditary caste, were not absolutely closed by the rule of heredity, nor was the practice of priestly functions absolutely restricted to members of the Brahman class, but between them and others there was continued rivalry, as was of course natural.[45] With all peoples in all times religion has been a source of contention and strife, as rival groups of religionists have fought for special privileges and exclusive prerogatives. These the Levites obtained rather early in the south, as was to be expected. The south was dominated by the powerful tribe of Judah, and the Levites were their protégés. As the Magi in Persia became the protagonists of the Zoroastrian faith, although probably not originally professing it, so it was with the Levites. They became the sponsors and missionaries of the Judean faith, the Yahweh cult, and not simply in the south, but presently in the north as well. Here for political as well as religious reasons they naturally met with opposition. And yet even here they were not entirely unwelcome, at least in some quarters, probably because of their fame as shamans and priests and the ancient belief, already noted, that the occult powers of strangers are greater than those of familiar persons. It was for this reason doubtless that Micah welcomed the coming of a Levite to be priest for him in place of his son (Judg. 17),[46] and that Yahwism got a hold in the north at all in the early period.

The greatest religious opponents that the Levites met in their propaganda in the north were the Baal priests, but *baal* here, or more correctly *ba'al*, is not to be understood as referring to the Canaanite god of agriculture, but rather to

---

[45] See A. B. Keith, *Encyclopaedia of Religion and Ethics*, ed. James Hastings, X (1924), 313.

[46] On the other hand, he may already have been a Yahweh worshiper, as his name would suggest, or this may have been the name that he took after his conversion.

the bull-god.[47] Unquestionably *ba'al* in many instances does refer to some Canaanite or other non-Israelite deity, but there is every reason to believe that in many cases, particularly in the early period, the reference is to the Israelite bull-god. As the south had its dominant tribe and accordingly its dominant cult and priesthood, so likewise had the north. In the north, however, the domination came more slowly and was not so complete, because the tribes there were more scattered and less a racial unit, and geographical and other conditions made political unity much more difficult to achieve.

Leroy Waterman would make the bull cult in early Israel a Canaanite cult which the Israelites took over on their entry into Canaan,[48] but of this there is no indication anywhere in the Old Testament. Like so many other scholars, he would seem to err in assuming that the Israelites of the north entered Canaan as worshipers of Yahweh, and after their entry grafted the bull cult, along with others, on to their own and then came to identify Yahweh with the bull, as well as with other baals. But of this there is not a particle of evidence. The facts are rather that a particular tribe of Israel entered Canaan as worshipers of the bull-god.[49] As this tribe came more or less to dominate its neighbors and thus constitute a confederacy, the bull naturally came to be the confederate god, but grafted on it were of course certain elements from

[47] In the Old Testament the bull is often called a calf (*'egel*) because the sacred bull in the Near East was regularly represented as a young bull about three years old; see W. F. Albright, *From the Stone Age to Christianity* (1940), p. 332, n. 33, and the literature there cited.

[48] *American Journal of Semitic Languages*, XXXI (1915), 231 ff.

[49] The bull cult does not necessarily presuppose agriculture, as Waterman maintains, *op. cit.*, p. 231; for the wild bull, at least, was known to nomads from the beginning and domesticated cattle from a very early time. Furthermore, the Hebrews entered Canaan as a seminomadic rather than a nomadic people; see W. F. Albright, *Archaeology and the Religion of Israel* (1942), pp. 99-102.

the other less victorious cults. Then, as the confederacy was won to Yahwism in the time of David, Yahweh came to be the national god, but it was little more than the god name that was changed. The old forms remained, the old theology, and much of the old paraphernalia, but reinterpreted to suit new ideas and a new situation. This is the process that has gone on in all religions throughout the world, and there is every reason to believe that the Israelite religion was no exception to the rule. Hence it would appear that we must look to some one of the Israelite tribes for the origin of the bull cult, and not to the Canaanites.

It is noteworthy and significant that every reference to the bull cult in the Old Testament locates it in Israel, and never once connects it with the south. The place that is particularly prominent in the cult is the sanctuary at Bethel, and R. H. Kennett is unquestionably right in finding in Ex. 32 an old Israelite saga recounting its origin, and in connecting the saga with Bethel rather than with Kadesh as it now stands.[50] Exodus 32 is universally recognized as being composite in character, but critics have never agreed as to the details of its analysis. It is clear, however, that the story in its original form was complimentary to Aaron.[51] As Moses was the founder of the Levitical priesthood, so Aaron was the eponym of the Ephraimite priesthood and the traditional founder of the bull cult of the north.[52] Aaron never once appears in the J

[50] "The Origin of the Aaronite Priesthood," *Journal of Theological Studies*, VI (1905), 161 ff.

[51] See R. Smend, *Die Erzählung des Hexateuchs auf ihre Quellen untersucht*, (1912), pp. lxix, 204.

[52] Cf. J. Pedersen, *Israel: Its Life and Culture*, III-IV (1947), 192, who speaks of Aaron as "an early Israelite progenitor of priests," and agrees "that Aaron, in the narrative of the golden calf, represents the North Israelitish cultus to which, as we know, the calf belonged." Cf. also W. C. Graham and H. G. May, *Culture and Conscience* (1936), p. 163; A. Haldar, *Associations of Cult Prophets among the Ancient Semites* (1945), p. 95.

document,[53] and in E he plays a minor role, acting merely as a sort of adjunct to Moses (cf., e.g., Ex. 5:1, 4), and he is clearly a supernumerary who was later introduced into the narrative as Israelite and Judean sagas became fused with the union of the two peoples.[54] It is only in the episode of the golden calf that Aaron acts on his own account and not as a pale reflection of Moses. As Kennett says,[55] "The golden calf is his; he demands the materials of which it is made; he fashions it; and he presents it to the people, and dedicates it. Certainly if any of the recorded acts of Aaron be historical, the episode of the golden calf can best claim to be so considered." Hence Aaron would seem to have been an integral and original part of the saga as it was at first current in Israel. Between that time and the rendering of the episode as we have it now in Ex. 32, the story went through many redactions, as stories long told always do. First there was the original tale attributing the origin of the bull-god to Aaron. As Yahwism came to dominate the north, the golden calf was interpreted as simply another form of Yahweh.[56] Then in a later period, when prophetic propaganda brought idolatrous practices into disrepute, the story was brought into conjunction with the act of Jeroboam I in re-establishing the bull cult (I Kings 12:28-33) after its partial eclipse during the Judean domination of the north in the two previous reigns, those of David and Solomon, and the tale was retold in much the form in which we have it now in verses 1-6, 15-24, 30-35. In view of the prominence that the Aaronites had attained in the priesthood by that time the blame for making the image was quite naturally shifted from Aaron and was loaded on the people

[53] So practically all scholars since J. Wellhausen, *Prolegomena to the History of Israel* (Eng. trans., 1885), pp. 139 f.
[54] Cf. R. H. Kennett, *Journal of Theological Studies*, VI (1905), 162 ff.
[55] *Ibid.*, p. 165.
[56] See p. 171 below.

(vv. 21-24, 30 ff.) and they were made to bear the penalty (v. 35; cf. Deut. 9:12, 16, 21). When the story came into Judean hands and received from them a Judean rendering, there was joined to it the old southern story of the consecration of the Levites to the Yahweh cult (vv. 25-29), very much to the credit of the Levites and the discredit of the Aaronites. Here again is reflected something of the old-time jealousy between north and south, accentuated now by the friction between the Zadokites of Jerusalem and the Aaronites of the northern sanctuaries that followed in the wake of Josiah's reformation.[57]

It would seem, then, that the bull cult was native to Israel, as originally the cult of some one of the northern tribes, and all the evidences for the identification of that tribe point to Joseph, the outstanding tribe of the north. In what is probably the oldest writing that has anything to say about Joseph, "The Blessing of Jacob," Gen. 49, we read in verses 22-26:

> Joseph is a young bull,
> A young bull at a spring,
> A wild-ass at Shur.[58]
> Shooting at him in enmity,
> The archers fiercely assailed him;
> But their bow was broken[59] by the Eternal,
> And their arms and hands trembled
> At the might of the Bull of Jacob,[60]

[57] See T. J. Meek, "Aaronites and Zadokites," *American Journal of Semitic Languages*, XLV (1929), 149-166.

[58] For this rendering of verse 22 cf. A. B. Ehrlich, *Randglossen zur hebräischen Bibel*, I (1908), 250 f. Cf. also H. Zimmern, *Zeitschrift für Assyriologie*, VII (1892), 164 ff.; H. Gressmann, *Die Schriften des Alten Testaments*, ed. H. Gunkel *et al.*, I, 2 (1922), pp. 173, 180.

[59] So Greek; Hebrew, "their bow remained," which makes no sense here.

[60] As is generally recognized, the vocalization *'abbîr*, "mighty one," is clearly an artificial one for *'ābîr*, "bull," and grew out of the later antipathy to the bull cult.

At the name of the Shepherd of the Israel-Stone,
At your father's God, who helps you,
And God Almighty,[61] who blesses you
With the blessings of the heavens above,
The blessings of the abyss couching below;
The blessings of breast and of womb,
The blessings of fatherhood, yea of man and child;[62]
The blessings of the ancient mountains,[63]
The dainties of the eternal hills—
May these rest on the head of Joseph,
On the brow of him who was cursed by his brothers!

Here we have a direct statement of Joseph's connection with the bull cult at Bethel, or at Shechem, if we follow Luther's suggestion that the "Israel-Stone" of verse 24 is that mentioned in Josh. 24:26 f. as the religious rendezvous of Israel in early times.[64] Similarly, in a later poem, "The Blessing of Moses," Deut. 33, we have a reminiscence of the same thing in verse 17a:

As the first-born of his Bull, may majesty be his,
And may his horns be the horns of a wild-ox,
With which to butt the nations,
And drive[65] them to the ends of the earth!

Just as peoples the world over speak of themselves as the children of their god and as the Judeans thought of themselves as the children of Yahweh, so Joseph is here spoken of

[61] So Hebrew MSS and Versions; Hebrew, "and with (?) the Almighty," which makes no sense here.

[62] The Hebrew here, "the blessings of your father excel above," is senseless and must be corrupt. The emendation followed is that of H. Gunkel, *Genesis übersetzt und erklärt* (5th ed., 1922), p. 487.

[63] So Greek; Hebrew is unintelligible.

[64] See Eduard Meyer, *Die Israeliten und ihre Nachbarstämme* (1906), p. 284, n. 1.

[65] Reading *wayyaddah* for *yahdāw*, as sense and parallelism demand. The emendation requires only a rearrangement of the consonants.

as the first-born of his god, the bull-god.[66] The comparison, too, with the wild-ox is significant, because the word is identical with the cuneiform *rêmu*, which is often used as an appellative of deity.[67] In Balaam's oracles the god of Israel is once again compared with the wild-ox, Num. 23:22 = 24:8:

> God who brought them out of Egypt
> Is like the horns of a wild-ox for them.

It surely cannot be without significance that the association between the bull and Israel is so frequent in the Old Testament and that the term *'ābîr*, "bull" (later vocalized *'abbîr*, "mighty one," when the bull cult fell into disrepute), as an appellative of deity, is used *only* of the god of Jacob (Gen. 49:24; Is. 49:26; 60:16; Ps. 132:2, 5) or of Israel (Is. 1:24), and never once of the god of Judah.

In view of all these evidences it would not seem too extravagant to say that the tribal god of Joseph, or Ephraim, or whatever we care to name the dominant tribe in the north, was the bull-god and his priests were the Aaronites. In that case it was in the name of this god that Joshua made the covenant at Shechem and established the beginning of the northern amphictyony.[68] As this confederacy established its sway in the north, bull worship became the dominant cult among the Israelite tribes, as Yahwism did in the south, and it was found at their more important sanctuaries, Bethel, Shechem, Shiloh, Gilgal, etc. The Shiloh pilgrimage (Judg. 21:19 ff.; I Sam. 1:3, 21; 2:19), like the Shechem festival (Judg. 9:27),[69] suggests an institution originally connected with the bull cult (cf. Ex. 32: 6, 19); and Hosea tells us that

[66] On this see further Meyer, *op. cit.*, pp. 284 f.; J. A. Montgomery, *Arabia and the Bible* (1934), p. 12, n. 22.

[67] See, e.g., Morris Jastrow, Jr., *Aspects of Religious Belief and Practice in Babylonia and Assyria* (1911), pp. 74 ff.

[68] See p. 26 above.

[69] Cf. J. Morgenstern, *Jewish Quarterly Review* (new series), VIII (1917), 31 ff.; *Journal of Biblical Literature*, LXVIII (1949), 5 ff.

the cult was continued at Gilgal even down to his day, if we adopt the Vulgate reading of 12:11, "In Gilgal they sacrifice to bulls (*lĕshôrîm*)." The cult accordingly spread throughout the north and in the process absorbed certain elements from other cults, particularly from the old Canaanite fertility cult of the god Adad (known in the Old Testament as Hadad),[70] with which it had many points in common. In fact, when the Israelites settled on the land and became agriculturists, the bull cult definitely became a fertility cult, as is evident from the passage in Gen. 49 (vv. 25 f.) which we have already quoted, and part of the liturgy of that cult seems to have survived in the Song of Songs, as I have tried to show elsewhere.[71] That the bull cult of the Old Testament is to be identified with the Adad cult there can be no reasonable doubt. The bull was the regular symbol of Adad, and both the later bull cult and that of Adad were fertility cults. Adad interchanges with Baal in personal names in the Tell el-Amarna period,[72] and in the Ras Shamra texts Baal is clearly Adad,[73] all of which shows that Baal was a common title of

[70] According to W. F. Albright, *From the Stone Age to Christianity* (1940), p. 186, Hadad was the principal deity of the pre-Mosaic Hebrews in Palestine, and these according to our thesis were the Israelites.

[71] See "Canticles and the Tammuz Cult," *American Journal of Semitic Languages*, XXXIX (1922), 1-14; "Babylonian Parallels to the Song of Songs," *Journal of Biblical Literature*, XLIII (1924), 245-252; "The Song of Songs and the Fertility Cult," in *The Song of Songs: A Symposium*, ed. W. H. Schoff (1924); "The Song of Songs," in *The Interpreter's Bible*, shortly to be published. Cf. also S. Minocchi, *Le Perle della Bibbia: Il Cantico dei Cantici e l'Ecclesiaste* (1924); W. O. E. Oesterley, *The Song of Songs* (1936); W. Wittekindt, *Das Hohe Lied und seine Beziehungen zur Istarkult* (1925); Max Haller, *Handbuch zum Alten Testament*, ed. Otto Eissfeldt, Erste Reihe, 18 (1940). For a brief and temperate statement of the place of the fertility cult with the Hebrews see R. B. Y. Scott, *The Relevance of the Prophets* (1944), pp. 184-189. For a fuller statement, completely documented, see B. A. Brooks, *Journal of Biblical Literature*, LX (1941), 227-253.

[72] See *Cambridge Ancient History*, II (1924), 348.

[73] See, e.g., R. Dussaud, *Revue de l'histoire des religions*, CV (1932), 255 ff.; CXIII (1936), 5 ff.

Adad, as it was of the bull-god. Baal is an inclusive term as used in the Old Testament, applying to alien gods in general, but it is usually intended to mean the god of the bull or fertility cult, and so we have the frequent combination of Baal with Ashtart (biblical Ashtoreth) and Asherah (see Judg. 2:13; 3:7; 10:6; I Sam. 7:4; 12:10; I Kings 18:19; II Kings 23:4), both of whom are definitely known to be fertility goddesses. Both from the Old Testament itself and from the excavations in Palestine we know that this cult gained a tremendous hold on the Hebrew people, particularly those in the north.[74] Nothing is found in such abundance in the Palestinian excavations as the evidences of the cult. In every important excavation Astarte figurines and plaques have been found. It is true that none from the Late Bronze or Early Iron Age have been discovered in central Palestine, at Bethel, Gibeah, Shiloh, or Tell en-Naṣbeh,[75] in contrast with their frequency in the later periods and in surrounding areas, but this is simply due to the fact that central Palestine had less contact with the Canaanites and the transition to a thoroughgoing fertility cult was slower. Another evidence for the spread and growing popularity of the bull cult is the increasing number of Baal names down to the time of David,[76] when Yahwism became the official religion and Baal names consequently came into disfavor.

[74] See, e.g., the present writer, *American Journal of Semitic Languages*, XXXIX (1922), 3 ff.; E. G. Kraeling, *Journal of Biblical Literature*, XLVII (1928), 133 ff.; H. G. May and R. M. Engberg, *Material Remains of the Megiddo Cult* (1935), *passim*; W. C. Graham and H. G. May, *Culture and Conscience* (1936), pp. 159 ff.; Elihu Grant and G. E. Wright, *Ain Shems Excavations*, V (1939), 155 ff.; W. F. Albright, *From the Stone Age to Christianity* (1940), pp. 237 f.; J. Pedersen, *Israel: Its Life and Culture*, III-IV (1947), 719, n. 2 to p. 510; J. B. Pritchard, *Palestinian Figurines* (1943).

[75] See W. F. Albright, *Archaeology and the Religion of Israel* (1942), p. 114; C. C. McCown, *Tell en-Naṣbeh* (1947), p. 246.

[76] See G. B. Gray, *Studies in Hebrew Proper Names* (1896), pp. 120 ff.

The thesis that Baalism was the official religion of the north in the period before David might seem to run counter to the evidence of the early poem of *ca.* 1075 B.C.[77] in Judg. 5, the Song to Deborah, but this is not so. Nelson Glueck would seem to have shown quite conclusively that verses 3 to 5 are a late, editorial expansion of the original poem.[78] His most telling argument is that verses 4 f. make Edom extend west of the Arabah, whereas we know positively from both biblical and archaeological evidence that this westward expansion of Edom did not take place until late exilic times at the very earliest.[79] In answer to this it is not sufficient to say with Leroy Waterman[80] that there might well have been an Edomite nomadic or seminomadic occupation in the early period west of the Arabah, which of course would have left no physical remains for archaeologists to discover. Nor is it sufficient to say with J. Pedersen,[81] followed by W. F. Albright,[82] that the exact location of the holy mount of Yahweh was a matter of indifference to his worshipers, so that its location in Judg. 5 is not to be examined too minutely. However, whether verses 3 to 5 are an editorial expansion or not, the poem as it stood originally could well have had no reference at all to Yahweh, but only to the storm-god of the north, Baal or Adad. In that case we would have here, as with several of the Psalms, another instance of the adaptation to the Yahweh religion of a poem originally unconnected with Yahweh. Just as Ps. 29, for example, was clearly an ancient hymn to the storm-god, Baal, made over into a Yahweh

[77] For this date see R. M. Engberg, *Bulletin of the American Schools of Oriental Research*, No. 78 (1940), pp. 4-7; W. F. Albright, *ibid.*, pp. 7-9.

[78] *Journal of the American Oriental Society*, LVI (1936), 462-471.

[79] See Nelson Glueck, *Hebrew Union College Annual*, XI (1936), 141-156.

[80] *Journal of Biblical Literature*, LVI (1937), 255.

[81] *Op. cit.*, pp. 198 f.

[82] *From the Stone Age to Christianity* (1940), p. 199.

hymn,[83] so it probably was in the case of Judg. 5, which has many parallels with Canaanite (both north and south) in language, imagery, and literary technique.[84] However, even though we grant that the poem stood originally in pretty much its present form, there is still nothing in it to indicate that Yahwism was the official religion of the northerners, but quite the contrary. It is clear from the poem that Yahweh was not at home in Israel. It was not his land as yet. On the contrary, he had to come on a long journey from the south and on a special occasion to help his devotees, of whom the Kenite, Jael, of verse 24 was one and the author of the poem another. There is no question but that the poem was written, or more likely rewritten, by a worshiper of Yahweh who would make his god the god of all the people. The storm, which won the victory for the Israelites by turning the plain of Esdraelon into a quagmire of mud that made the chariots of the Canaanites worse than useless, was interpreted as the direct intervention of the storm-god, Yahweh, and a demonstration of his power. To the Israelites, then, the poet would commend this all-powerful god, and at the end of the poem we have his ardent prayer, reflecting the contest between Yahwism and the rival cults:

> Thus may all thy enemies perish, O Yahweh,
> But let thy devotees be like the rising of the sun in his might!

It is clear from our records that the bull cult did not hold the field for long uncontested; for presently there came

---

[83] See H. L. Ginsberg, *The Ugarit Texts* (Hebrew, 1936), pp. 129-131; W. F. Albright, in *Old Testament Commentary*, ed. H. C. Alleman and E. E. Flack (1948), pp. 157 f.; T. H. Gaster, *Jewish Quarterly Review* (new series), XXXVII (1946), 55 ff.; Frank M. Cross, Jr., *Bulletin of the American Schools of Oriental Research*, No. 117 (1950), pp. 19-21.

[84] See H. L. Ginsberg, *Orientalia*, V (1936), 180 f.; W. F. Albright, *Bulletin of the American Schools of Oriental Research*, No. 62 (1936). pp. 29-31.

Kenites, Levites, and prophets from the south as missionaries of Yahwism. Some scholars have contended that Yahweh was not known in Israel at all until the time of Deborah, but this can only be maintained by such a drastic treatment of the Old Testament text as to be untenable. However, the practical absence of Yahweh names in the north down to the time of David, a fact that we have already noted, would indicate that the Yahweh cult was not very largely known until the Judean domination of Israel by David. The only clearly attested Yahweh names in Israel before the time of Samuel are Joash, Gideon's father (Judg. 6:29), and Micah (Judg. 17). Micah was probably a convert to Yahwism, and so may have changed his name after he became a Yahweh worshiper, even as Amenophis IV of Egypt changed his name to Akhenaten after he became an Aten worshiper. That Gideon's father should have borne a Yahweh name is more surprising, but it is not absolutely certain that his name, Joash, does contain the Yahweh element and this some scholars have denied. Gideon himself, according to the saga, was a champion of Yahwism,[85] and it is very clear that the story in Judg. 6:25-32 has to do with his destruction of the sanctuary of Baal or the bull-god at Orphah. That the god was a popular one in the community is shown by the stealthy device to which Gideon had to resort in order to carry out his project and the intense indignation of his fellow townsmen when they discovered his sacrilegious act. In the crisis that followed Joash felt impelled to rally to his son's support and hence to the support of his god Yahweh as against his own god, who had shown his impotence in allowing his sanctuary to be destroyed by Gideon. As an outcome of the episode Gideon's name was changed to Jerubbaal (v. 32), and there is much to suggest that Joash's own name came from the

[85] Cf. I. G. Matthews, *The Religious Pilgrimage of Israel* (1947), pp. 87 f.

same incident, provided it is a Yahweh name meaning, as generally interpreted, "Yahweh is strong" or "Yahweh has bestowed." When we come nearer to the time of David, Yahweh names increase somewhat in number. In the two Books of Samuel there are about a dozen. Of these only four are names of northerners, viz., Joel and Abijah, sons of Samuel (I Sam. 8:2); Jonathan, Saul's son (I Sam. 13:2); and Micah, his great-grandson (II Sam. 9:12). Samuel, we know, was a champion of Yahwism and some would make him a Levite, even as the Chronicler does (I Chron. 6:28, 33). Saul was one of his converts to Yahwism and in his early enthusiasm gave his first-born son a Yahweh name, Jonathan, "Yahweh has given," but later years showed him very fickle in that faith.

It was actually not until the time of David that Yahwism became at all widespread in either north or south. Whatever may be the facts lying behind the stories of David's early relations with Saul,[86] there can be no question that David was the founder of the southern kingdom, at first under Philistine suzerainty, and this was a keen rival of the northern kingdom and the two were often in conflict. In this conflict the south had the open support of the Yahweh prophets and Levites already established in the north, and this of course antagonized Saul (I Sam. 19:18 ff.; 22:11 ff.). Disappointed in Saul, the prophets and Levites naturally turned to David and were the more ready to support him in that he was from the south, the home of Yahwism, and like them he was a zealous champion of the cause of Yahweh. The petty kingdom of Ishbaal that survived the death of Saul succumbed quickly to the growing power and prestige of David; and David, now king of the united states of Judah and Israel, proceeded to

---

[86] For discussion see S. A. Cook, "Saul and David," *Jewish Quarterly Review* (old series), XIX (1907), 363 ff.

throw off the Philistine yoke and make himself king in fact as well as in name. With that glorious victory to its credit Yahwism reached the height of its power and this is reflected in the rapid increase of Yahweh names, particularly among the upper classes,[87] who responded more readily to the new cult than did the more conservatively minded lower classes. David established a national sanctuary for Yahweh at the new capital, Jerusalem, and the ark was brought from Baale-Judah or Kirjath-jearim and deposited there (II Sam. 6). Yahwism was made the official religion of the united state, and to secure it in that place the priests were organized under the Levite, Abiathar, as chief priest, and he and Zadok, together with other leading priests, were made members of the royal court at Jerusalem (II Sam. 8: 17). Thus were the Levites ensconced in a position of supreme priestly authority in the religion and there came a temporary eclipse of the bull cult and its Aaronite priesthood. This of course did not mean the suppression of the bull cult nor of any other; it simply meant that Yahwism was now the state religion and Yahweh the national god. In their local sanctuaries the people could and did worship what gods they would, but all affairs of state were under the aegis of the state god, Yahweh, and state religious services were in the hands of his priests, the Levites, now tending more and more to become a closed sacerdotal order, and once again we make comparison with the Druids, Brahmans, and Magi, with whom the Levites in their origin and early development had so many points in common.[88]

[87] See G. B. Gray, *Studies in Hebrew Proper Names* (1896), pp. 255 ff.
[88] For an account of the later history of the priesthood see the present writer, "Aaronites and Zadokites," *American Journal of Semitic Languages*, XLV (1929), 149-166.

CHAPTER FIVE

The Origin of Hebrew Prophecy

PROPHETS and priests have a common origin. We have
already noted that the Hebrew priests, like those of other
peoples, were in the first instance shamans and owed their
priestly office to their supposed possession of mantic power.
The ancient Arab priests gave oracles, and likewise did the
Hebrew priests.[1] All the early references to them (e.g., Judg.
18:5 f.; I Sam. 14:18, 36 ff.; 23:9 ff.; 30:7 ff.; Deut. 33:8)
indicate this as their most important function; but as time
went on and the cultus became more elaborate, and a shrine,
idol, and other paraphernalia came to be provided, new duties
arose: caring for the shrine and its equipment, and officiating
in the cultus. At the same time the priestly office tended to
become professional, and in becoming professional it tended
to become hereditary. Now, duties like caring for the shrine
and officiating in the cultus are the sort of thing that can
become vested interests; they can be handed down from one
generation to another until they become the monopoly of a
particular class; and this is precisely what happened with the
Hebrew priests, as it did with all others. But soothsaying,
the ability to have the ecstatic experiences that brings a man
into direct contact with deity and makes him a shaman, this is
altogether dependent upon predisposition and temperament,

---

[1] Cf. A. Bentzen, *Introduction to the Old Testament,* I (1948), 185 ff.;
A. R. Johnson, *The Cultic Prophet in Ancient Israel* (1944), pp. 10 f.

and is not heritable. One man might have this ability, but it would not follow at all that his son would necessarily have it. Accordingly, as the priests became a professional and hereditary class, this earlier and more important function was lost to the profession, except as it could be preserved along merely mechanical lines, through the casting of lots, the consultation of the teraphim and the ephod, and the observation of certain phenomena; and even these methods ceased in time. But though shamanism died out in the priesthood, the man of vision could not disappear. As the priests functioned less and less along this line and less and less satisfactorily, the need for the direct appeal to deity was met more and more outside the profession, but rather naturally in a circle closely allied to it. It was thus that the Hebrew prophets came into being. In time they grew to such numbers and prominence that they got into the records and we read of their exploits in the stories of the later judges.

The early Hebrew prophets, like others,[2] were intimately associated with the priesthood and were found at the priestly sanctuaries, as we see from references like I Sam. 10:5, II Kings 2:3, 5; 4:38. Many grew up within priestly circles. Samuel, for instance, was brought by his parents to Shiloh to be trained for the priesthood and became a priest (I Sam. 1:24 ff.), but presently threw in his lot with the prophets. It was their type of mind that was more akin to his own, and among them he became a most influential leader (I Sam. 19:20). In the later period, Jeremiah may have been of priestly descent,[3] and Ezekiel throughout his lifetime remained more priest than prophet. But prophecy, whether

[2] See, e.g., J. M. P. Smith, *The Prophet and his Problems* (1914), pp. 3-35; A. Haldar, *Associations of Cult Prophets among the Ancient Semites* (1945); J. Pedersen, in *Studies in Old Testament Prophecy*, ed. H. H. Rowley (1950), pp. 127-142; N. W. Porteous, *ibid.*, pp. 144 ff.

[3] On the other hand, Jeremiah may not have been a priest at all; see T. J. Meek, *The Expositor*, Eighth Series, XXV (1923), 215-222.

within or without priestly circles, represented the more primitive, more spontaneous, more ecstatic, and less professionalized expression of the religious consciousness. It represented the break in the religious ranks that must inevitably come with the institutionalization of religion and its professionalizing.

The early Hebrew prophets were clearly oracles of the shamanistic type. The very words for prophet in Hebrew indicate this. The oldest word is *rô'ēh*, "seer," from the root *rā'āh*, meaning "to see." This was the title given to Samuel and the early prophets in general.[4] Another word almost identical with this is *ḥôzēh*,[5] from the root *ḥāzāh*, "to see," or more properly "to see" or "experience ecstatically." Both these words indicate that the prophet to the Hebrews was possessed of the power to see things hidden from the eyes of ordinary folk. The third word for prophet is the one that became the most popular of all and almost wholly replaced the older term *rô'ēh*. It is *nābî'*, from a root not found in Hebrew, but found in Akkadian as *nabû*, "to call, to call out, to speak."[6] It accordingly means "speaker, spokesman (of God),"[7] and is correctly translated in the Septuagint by the

[4] See, e.g., I Sam. 9:18 f.; I Chron. 9:22; 26:28; II Chron. 16:7, 10.

[5] See, e.g., II Sam. 24:11; II Kings 17:13; I Chron. 21:9; 25:5; 29:29; II Chron. 9:29; 12:15; 19:2; 29:25, 30; 33:18 f.; 35:15; Amos 7:12; Mic. 3:7; Is. 29:10; 30:10. For an attempt to differentiate between *rô'ēh* and *ḥôzēh* see Johnson, *op. cit.*, pp. 13 ff., but cf. H. H. Rowley, *Harvard Theological Review*, XXXVIII (1945), 8 ff. The words correspond to *barû* in Akkadian.

[6] This root rather strangely is not found in Hebrew, but it is common in Akkadian. The noun, *munambû*, from this root in Akkadian, was applied to a class of priests who recited the lamentation liturgy. The root is also found in Arabic and the noun derived from it, *munābi*, as used by the Ruwala Arabs today, means "spokesman" see A. Musil, *The Manners and Customs of the Ruwala Bedouins* (1928), pp. 400 f.

[7] W. F. Albright, *From the Stone Age to Christianity* (1940), challenges this interpretation on the ground that the etymological meaning of the word is "one who is called," but etymology alone is rarely a safe guide to the meaning of a word and must always be checked by its usage. In this

Greek προφήτης, a noun derived from the preposition πρό, "for, in behalf of," and the verb φημί, "to speak." Hence the prophet of the *nābî'* type was strictly not a "foreteller," as is popularly supposed, but a "forthteller, preacher," and this was the meaning of "prophet" in English until after the time of Queen Elizabeth, when for some reason the term came to be equated with foretelling, predicting. For example, a book by Jeremy Taylor published in 1647, entitled *The Liberty of Prophesying*, is not what the present connotation of the words would lead one to think; it is a book on freedom of speech—in modern language, "The Freedom of Preaching." Accordingly, the strict meaning of the word "prophet" in English and its meaning in the original Greek and Hebrew is "speaker, spokesman"; and this is made absolutely certain by such a passage as Ex. 7:1, where Yahweh says to Moses: "See, I make you a god to Pharaoh, and your brother Aaron shall serve as your spokesman (your *nābî'*)." Note also Ex. 4:16: "He [Aaron] shall speak for you to the people; he shall serve as a mouthpiece for you, and you shall act the part of god to him [*lit.*, he shall be to you for a mouth, and you shall be to him for a god]."[8] That is, the prophet was a spokesman, the mouthpiece of God; "man of God" he is often called;[9] he was an oracle possessed by the spirit of God. This experience was expressed by various terms: "Yahweh put his spirit upon," "poured his spirit upon," or "the spirit of God (or Yahweh) was upon," "rested upon," "came upon," "fell

---

instance it so happens that there is at least one occurrence which makes the meaning of the word absolutely certain in Hebrew and that is Ex. 7:1, which is quoted below. See further T. J. Meek, *Journal of Biblical Literature*, LXI (1942), 40 f. Cf. also Johnson, *op. cit.*, p. 24, n. 8.

[8] Cf. Deut. 18:18; Jer. 15:19; Is. 1:20.

[9] For the prophet as an extension of the personality of Yahweh see A. R. Johnson, *The One and the Many in the Israelite Conception of God* (1942), particularly pp. 36 ff.

upon," "entered into," "spoke by," or "the power [*lit.*, hand] of Yahweh was upon," "came upon," "fell upon" such and such a man,[10] and under the influence of that possession he expressed himself in religious ecstasy (see, e.g., I Sam. 10:5-12; 19:18-24; II Kings 9:11), sometimes so wild and uncontrolled that the prophet came to be classed with the madman and is twice called a madman (II Kings 9:11; Jer. 29:26). The reaction was often so violent as to lead to acts almost insane, as, for example, in the case of Saul, so that on one occasion, as recorded in I Sam. 19:24, "even he stripped off his clothes and even he prophesied before Samuel, and falling down, lay naked all that day and all night."[11] The onlookers were surprised that Saul should have succumbed to the experience, but they were not surprised at its manifestations. As a matter of fact there is a close relationship between prophecy and insanity. The kind of temperament that lends itself to psychic experiences, to automatisms, may result in genius or it may become psychopathic and lead to melancholia and outright insanity, as it did, for example, in the case of Saul.

The prophetic experience came spontaneously, unanticipated and uninvited, and took the man completely out of himself. It was a mystic experience, completely transforming in its character, as indicated by Samuel's words to Saul in I Sam. 10:6: "The spirit of Yahweh shall rush upon you and you shall prophesy along with them [the prophets], and you shall be changed into another man." Sometimes the experience came even though undesired or resisted, as, for example, in the case of Balaam, Num. 24:15 f. (cf. 24:3 f.):[12]

[10] See, e.g., Num. 11:25 f., 29; 24:2; I Sam. 10:6, 10; 11:6; 16:13; 19:20, 23; II Sam. 23:2; I Kings 18:46; II Kings 2:9, 15 f.; 3:15; II Chron. 24:20; Ez. 1:3; 2:2; 3:14; 8:1; 11:5; 33:22; 37:1; Is. 61:1; Joel 2:28 f.

[11] Cf. David's stripping himself of his clothes in his ecstatic dance in front of the ark on its way to Jerusalem, II Sam. 6:14 ff.

[12] Cf. also the case of Saul, I Sam. 10:5 ff.; 19:23 f. For extrabiblical

The oracle of Balaam, the son of Beor,
The oracle of the man whose eye is true,
The oracle of him who hears the words of God,
And is acquainted with the knowledge of the Most High,
Who has a vision of the Almighty,
Prostrate, but with eyes open.

Here, it is to be noted, the experience was so overwhelming that it left the prophet exhausted, completely the tool and mouthpiece of the God who had laid hold of him, and his vision was no dream that came with shut eyes and sleep, but a real, ineffable experience of the mind. It reminds one of the revelations that came to Muhammad in his early career, or those of Gautama, or the ecstasies of the Sufis or Dervishes, or the mystic experiences of St. Teresa, who thus describes one of them: "I was in prayer one day—it was the feast of the glorious St. Peter—when I saw Christ close by me, or, to speak more correctly, felt Him; for I saw nothing with the eyes of the body, nothing with the eyes of the soul. He seemed to be close beside me; and I saw, too, as I believe, that it was He who was speaking to me."[13] The prophets were mystics,[14] and like the mystics they experienced the feeling of transport, of transcendence over things material. They felt at times that they had broken through all sensuous barriers and had come into the veritable presence of God himself, to speak directly with him and he with them; and so carried away were they by the experience, so surcharged by its rapturous ecstasy, that they felt impelled

---

and modern examples of the same phenomenon see A. Lods, *Israel* (Eng. trans., 1932), p. 444. In his composition of *The Messiah* Handel believed in all sincerity that he was divinely inspired, even as the Hebrew prophets did.

[13] Quoted by Evelyn Underhill, *Mysticism* (3rd ed., 1912), p. 341.

[14] See, e.g., H. W. Hines, "The Prophet as Mystic," *American Journal of Semitic Languages*, XL (1923), 37-71; W. F. Lofthouse, "Thus Hath Jahveh Said," *ibid.*, pp. 231-251; T. H. Robinson, "The Ecstatic Element in Old Testament Prophecy," *The Expositor*, Eighth Series, XXI (1921), 217-238; *Prophecy and the Prophets in Ancient Israel* (1923).

to give utterance to it in prophetic oracles, regularly introduced by the phrase "Thus said Yahweh" or "Thus showed
Yahweh" in a vision, and regularly validated at the conclusion as "the word of Yahweh" or "the oracle of Yahweh." It was not the prophet who was speaking in the
oracle, but Yahweh who was speaking through him, and
the prophet's words, be it noted, were only uttered *after*
his mystic experience and as a result of that experience.
Hence his frequent use of the perfect of certainty; to him
the future had become the past because of his projection
into the future. Like oracles in general the prophet's words
were usually set forth in metrical form. This might seem
strange to us, but mystics are of a temperament akin to that
of poets, and poetry in any case flows easily from Eastern
lips. The ecstatic experiences were ordinarily of short dura-
tion, and hence the verses were short, direct, authoritative,
and only slightly argumentative. Their authority was not
argument, but God, and they were not long-drawn-out,
logically arranged sermons, but oracles, full of conviction,
surcharged with the white heat of emotion.[15] As Amos put
it (3:8), "The Lord Yahweh has spoken; who will not
prophesy?"

The prophets were of a highly sensitive and imaginative

[15] Earlier commentators did not recognize this fact at all, and later
commentators have done little better. Most of them deal with the
prophetic literature as if it consisted of scholarly essays, highly argumentative and carefully reasoned through to logical conclusions. But such
subtleties of reasoning are the creation of the exegete. They are in no way
characteristic of prophetic literature, nor for that matter of any class of
Oriental literature. The Oriental mind does not work that way. On the
other hand, one must not err by going to the opposite extreme and deny
to the prophets all intellectual acumen, making them solely creatures of
inspiration or intuition. Most of them had keen minds as well as sensitive
souls; they were as keen as they were sensitive. Cf. also A. Bentzen, *Introduction to the Old Testament*, I (1948), 195, 204; J. Pedersen, *Israel:
Its Life and Culture*, I-II (1926), 123 f.

temperament, or to put it psychologically, their subliminal mental processes were developed to a high degree. Their subconscious self was more active than it is with most people, with the result that they were exceedingly sensitive, hypersensitive, to stimuli in their environment, so sensitive in fact that they responded quickly and strongly to anything unusual in the environment. Prophecy was limited to a particular type of mind, but within that circle it found ready response and was contagious. The sight of a prophet or a group of prophets prophesying immediately found response with any others of like temperament in the vicinity and they too prophesied (I Sam. 10:10; 19:20, 23 f.).

This ecstatic type of prophet was common throughout the ancient Semitic world, and some scholars have gone so far as to maintain that the type was adopted by the Hebrews from the Canaanites, who in turn are supposed to have got it from Asia Minor as the movement swept through that region toward the end of the second millennium into Greece on one side and into Syria and Palestine on the other.[16] The parade example for this type of prophet is the one who intervened with the king of Byblos on behalf of Wenamun, the envoy from Egypt,[17] but his ecstaticism was after the order of that of the Baal prophets, described so vividly in I Kings 18:26-29. It was akin to the Dionysian frenzy that characterized the movement in Asia Minor, but there was little that was extreme about the activities of the Hebrew prophets. They may to some slight degree have been influenced by the movement from Syria, but only slightly

[16] See, e.g., E. A. Leslie, *Old Testament Religion in the Light of Its Canaanite Background* (1936), 116-118; A. Lods, *Israel* (Eng. trans., 1932), p. 444; G. Hölscher, *Die Profeten* (1914), pp. 140 ff.; J. Pedersen, *Israel: Its Life and Culture*, III-IV (1947), 111, 115 f., 125, 142; A. Haldar, *Associations of Cult Prophets among the Ancient Semites* (1945), p. 110, n. 3.

[17] The story of Wenamun has been most recently translated by J. A. Wilson, in *Ancient Near Eastern Texts*, ed. J. B. Pritchard (1950).

so. There is no question but that the early prophets were
ecstatics, corresponding in a way to the *maḫḫû* of the
Babylonians,[18] but their ecstaticism was seldom, if ever, of
the frenzied type and was never orgiastic. Neither was there
any effort to attain oneness with God, as in the Dionysian
cult and the mystery religions. The Hebrew type of
prophecy was less ecstatic and more rational, and it had its
own roots in Palestine and grew out of the needs of the day.
An experience so universal as prophecy need owe nothing
to other civilizations.

Hebrew prophecy arose in a time of stress and strain,
which was its necessary condition, as it is of mysticism in
general. "In fact," as Hines has put it,[19] "one might make
bold to say that all of Israel's great religious advances came
out of times of stress and suffering and pain, from the
sojourn in Egypt to the struggles of the Maccabees. Pain
is the great stimulator of religious experience." Moses
might well be regarded as a prophet (cf. Deut. 18:15; Hos.
12:14), and Deborah apparently was.[20] Both Moses and
Deborah appeared in times of stress, and to both the people
were accustomed to resort for oracles of counsel and
direction (Ex. 18:15 f.; Judg. 4:5).

A definite prophetic movement, however, of the new
type, the *nābî'* or preacher type, did not develop until the
Philistine conquest, when the land was ground under the
heel of a foreign foe, and that fact had much to do, not
only with inaugurating this new kind of prophecy peculiar
to the Hebrew people, but with stimulating its development and molding its character. The movement became
political as well as religious, and its propaganda was as
much the one as the other. The Hebrew prophets, like

[18] See Haldar, *op. cit.*, pp. 21 ff.
[19] *American Journal of Semitic Languages*, XL (1923), 59.
[20] See, e.g., Elihu Grant, *American Journal of Semitic Languages*,
XXXVI (1920), 295 ff.

prophets in general,[21] were the partisans of a single deity, but more intensely so than any others. Those that we read of in the early Old Testament records were partisans of the god Yahweh, and as zealous champions of him they opposed anything and everything that was alien to his cult; that is, they were as jealous as they were zealous.[22] With them the seer of the earlier period and the ordinary type of prophet in the ancient world, became the *nābî'*, the preacher, the propagandist. As we read in I Sam. 9:9: "He who is now called a *nābî'* was previously called a *rô'ēh* [a seer]." Intensely emotional, easily excitable, and given to fanaticism as these prophets of the new type were, the tragedy of the day found ready response in their hearts and they went up and down the country preaching a politico-religious crusade against the heathen. They were firebrands of war[23] and were the means ultimately of rousing the people to the white heat of revolt, and in this they advanced tremendously the cause of their god Yahweh.

By the time of Samuel Yahwism had evidently obtained a firm hold in the north as a result of Levitical and prophetic propaganda. Many of the sanctuaries had become centers of the new cult. Shiloh, for instance, at one time evidently a center of the bull cult,[24] was early converted to Yahwism, probably by Eli, a Levite (I Sam. 2:27 f.), who was

[21] Cf. Grant, *ibid.*, XXXIX (1923), 264; Haldar, *op. cit.*, p. 29.

[22] It is of interest to note that "zealous" and "jealous" come from the same root; see H. L. Creager, *Lutheran Church Quarterly*, VII (1934), 271-282; W. F. Albright, *From the Stone Age to Christianity* (1940), p. 236.

[23] So likewise in the later period; see I Kings 20:13, 22, 28, 35-42; 22:6, 10-12; II Kings 3:11-20; 6:8-23; 13:14-19; 14:25. Cf. also II Kings 2:12; 13:14, where Elijah and Elisha are called "the chariots of Israel and its horsemen."

[24] Cf. B. Stade, *Zeitschrift für die alttestamentliche Wissenschaft*, III (1883), 10. The Shiloh pilgrimage (Judg. 21:19 ff.; I Sam. 1:3, 21; 2:19), like the Shechem festival (Judg. 9:27), suggests an institution originally connected with the bull cult (cf. Ex. 32:6, 19).

able to establish his family there as "priests to Yahweh" (I Sam. 1:3). The phrase "to Yahweh" is quite unnecessary here and was doubtless inserted to distinguish the new priesthood from the old and to indicate that the priests of the old bull cult had been replaced by Yahweh priests. Similarly, in I Sam. 14:3 Eli himself is called "the priest of Yahweh in Shiloh," with which one may compare the designation of the Philistine priests in I Sam. 5:5, "the priests of Dagon." According to the traditions, the sacred ark of Yahweh played an important role in the spread of the cult in the north, and this was for long settled at Shiloh. To Shiloh Samuel came as a young boy to train for the priesthood of the new faith, but identified himself with its more vigorous advocates, the prophets, and in time he grew out of sympathy with the priests. An indication of this is to be seen in the fact that after the destruction of Shiloh the priests moved to Nob (I Sam. 22:11; cf. 14:3), whereas Samuel returned to his home at Ramah (I Sam. 7:17) and is henceforth found in the company of the prophets. In this we have the beginning of a cleavage between him and his party, the prophets, and the Levitical priests, and in him prophecy is seen in the process of splitting away from the priesthood to give a more spiritual and less mechanical and ritualistic turn to religion. But prophets and priests in their separate and different ways continued to extend the sway of the Yahweh cult.

According to our earliest and most reliable source (I Sam. 9:1-10:16), Samuel was the prime mover in the establishment of Saul as king. He was no doubt prompted in this by religious as well as political considerations. If the Hebrews were ever to throw off the yoke of the Philistines, it could only be as they were organized politically, and to do this in the name of Yahweh would give an added impetus to the Yahweh cult. Saul had come early under Samuel's notice and apparently through his influence had become a convert to the new faith (I Sam. 10:1-13),[25] much to the surprise of his friends; cf. I Sam. 10:12; 19:24, where they are represented as exclaiming, "Is Saul also among the prophets?" It was under the guiding hand of prophecy, therefore, that the first kingdom, such as it was, came into existence; but it was a disappointment to all concerned. The revolt against the Philistines was not the success anticipated, and Saul, like many a new convert, was fickle in his allegiance to Yahwism and the prophetic party. In his first enthusiasm he gave his first-born son a Yahweh name, Jonathan, but the early enthusiasm waned, and with his fourth son he reverted to the bull cult, giving him the name of Ish-baal, "man [i.e., worshiper] of Baal." Like many another suddenly raised to power, he took his prerogatives too seriously and too jealously.[26] He looked upon religious functionaries as subordinate officials whom he could appoint, control, and depose at will. The result was that he had not been king very long before he quarreled and broke with Samuel and the prophets (I Sam. 13:8-15; 15:1 ff.; 18:18 ff.), with the mediums and wizards (I Sam. 28:3, 9),[27] and with the priests of Nob (I Sam. 22:11 ff.). His break with the prophets and his massacre of the priests of Nob were serious blows to Yahwism in the north, and succor now could only come from the south.

[25] Cf. also I Sam. 14:49, where Saul is represented as building his first altar to Yahweh, clearly as a recent convert.

[26] A part of the prerogative of any ancient monarch was participation in religious functions. For Hebrew kings see, e.g., I Sam. 13:9; II Sam. 6:14, 17 f.; 8:18; I Kings 8:5, 62 ff.; 9:25; 12:33.

[27] This has generally been regarded as unhistorical (cf., e.g., Karl Budde, Die Bücher Samuel [1902], p. 178), but there could have been no possible motive for a redactor to attribute such an act to one whom he esteemed so lightly as Saul.

Samuel, as an Ephraimite,[28] had naturally hoped to see
a union of the Hebrew people achieved under a northern
king, but his hopes and his efforts in that direction ended
in dismal failure. It was then that he turned to David, and
David more than fulfilled his highest aspirations. We have
already noted that David made Yahwism the official religion
of the united state, established the sanctuary in the new
capital, Jerusalem, and made the Levites the official priesthood of the cult, attaching the leading priests to his court
in Jerusalem.[29] Similar prestige was given to prophecy in
that the leading prophets, Gad and Nathan (Samuel by this
time being dead), were admitted to the royal court (II Sam.
24:11 ff.; I Kings 1). The work of David as patron of the
Yahweh religion was continued by his son and successor,
Solomon, but with less vigor. Solomon was more tolerant
of other cults (I Kings 11:1-10), and certain features of
the old bull cult were absorbed into the Yahwism of his
day, the evidences of which are to be seen in the presence
of the bronze bulls and cherubim in his temple and the
two colossal cherubim of olive wood within the holy of
holies.[30]

The north rather naturally did not take kindly to southern
domination. There were revolts even in the time of David,
as we read in II Sam. 15:20. The feeling of bitterness grew
in intensity throughout the reign of Solomon until on his
death Israel seceded under the leadership of Jeroboam, and
all the tedious work of Levites, prophets, and kings in the
attempted conversion of the north to Yahwism seemed un-

[28] The Chronicler (I Chron. 6:13, 18), as we might expect, makes him a
Levite. So also do others, e.g. R. B. Girdlestone, *The Expositor*, Fifth
Series, X (1899), 385 ff., and A. van Hoonacker, *Le sacerdoce Lévitique*
(1889), pp. 265 f., but without good reason, we believe.

[29] See p. 147 above.

[30] See Leroy Waterman, *American Journal of Semitic Languages*, XXXI
(1915), 249 ff.

done at a single stroke. Jeroboam broke with the south religiously as well as politically, and re-established the bull cult as the official religion of the north (I Kings 12:26 ff.; II Chron. 11:15; 13:8). Political revolt in ancient times always meant religious cleavage, just as political conquest or submission always meant religious conquest. A good illustration of this in Hebrew history is the fact that when Ahaz made an alliance with Assyria and acknowledged the suzerainty of Tiglath-pileser he immediately took the altar of Yahweh from its place of honor in the temple and re- placed it by one of the Assyrian cult (II Kings 16:10-16), thus degrading Yahweh to the position of a minor deity, as in fact he had become according to the current phi- losophy of the day.[31] Scholars recognize the principle as working everywhere else,[32] but for some peculiar reason they made Israel's revolt an exception. They persist in saying that the bulls or calves which Jeroboam set up at Dan and Bethel as symbols of the national god of Israel were images of Yahweh,[33] despite Jeroboam's explicit state-

[31] Cf. A. T. Olmstead, *History of Palestine and Syria* (1931), p. 452.

[32] See, e.g., D. Nielsen, *Journal of the Palestine Oriental Society*, VII (1927), 207 f.: "In Arabian antiquity religion and nation are inseparable; the making of a nation is the origin of a new national god, the god of the people." So also W. O. E. Oesterley and T. H. Robinson, *A History of Israel*, I (1932), 277: "Jeroboam saw clearly that a merely political severance of the two districts [Israel and Judah] was inadequate to main- tain the independence of the north; as always in the ancient east, there must also be a religious basis for the new regime." Then they go on to make the strange, contradictory statement that Jeroboam "had no intention whatever of abandoning the national God, Yahweh; that would have been inconceivable." But according to the current philosophy of the day Jeroboam had to do this very thing in order to create a new nation inde- pendent of Judah. To have retained the Judean god, Yahweh, would have meant subservience to Judah.

[33] Contrary to most scholars, W. F. Albright, *From the Stone Age to Christianity* (1940), pp. 203, 229 f., follows K. Th. Obbink, *Zeitschrift für die alttestamentliche Wissenschaft*, XLVII (1929), 264-274, in main- taining that Jeroboam's bulls were no images at all, but constituted the

ment to the contrary (I Kings 12:28): "You have gone up to Jerusalem long enough. Behold your god, O Israel!" One might just as well say that the image of their old god Rē, which the Egyptians restored on the breakdown of Akhenaten's reform shortly after his death, was now not an image of Rē at all, but one of the ousted god Aten. The cult that Jeroboam established could not have been an importation from without, but must have been something genuinely national, symbolic of the new state that was born. Even so conservative a scholar as Jacob Hoschander recognizes this when he says,[34] "In former days the Israelites themselves worshipped the Baalim in the images of bulls. Thus the introduction of the Bull-worship [by Jeroboam] was not an innovation but a restoration of the former mode of worship.[35] There was only one difference between the past and present practices. Formerly the image of a bull was the representation of Baal or the Baalim, while now it

___

pedestal upon which the god Yahweh was enthroned, but this would seem to be a very farfetched and most unnatural interpretation as against the plain reading of the biblical text. It is true that ancient Near Eastern iconography often represents deity as standing on the back of an animal or as sitting on a throne borne by animals, but how the biblical writer could have confused the god with his support is not easy to see. If the bulls were a pedestal only, there would be no more occasion to condemn them than there was to condemn the cherubim on which Yahweh was enthroned in the Jerusalem temple. I fail to follow Albright when he says on page 230 that the cherubim, being mythical animals, served to enhance the majesty of Yahweh, while the young bulls of Bethel and Dan could only debase his cult. Furthermore, Albright's assertion on page 229 that the gods were never represented among the Canaanites, Arameans, and Hittites in animal form does not accord with his statement on page 201 that "Near-Eastern gods shifted in disconcerting fashion from astral form to zoomorphic, dendromorphic and composite manifestations," nor is it borne out by the excavations.

[34] The Priests and Prophets (1938), p. 13.

[35] Similarly W. F. Albright, op. cit., p. 230, says that Jeroboam may well have been harking back to early Israelite traditional practice when he made the golden calves, and that he assuredly was.

became the representation of Jahveh." However, it is quite impossible that the cult introduced by Jeroboam could have been Yahwism under another form, for that would have made it Judean; it must have been genuinely Israelite and hence anti-Yahwistic, and in that all sources without exception agree.

According to I Kings 11:29-39, Jeroboam's revolt was instigated by the northern prophet Ahijah, a native of Shiloh. The present narrative is probably an expansion of the original story[36] and was clearly introduced in order to present a moral lesson. Solomon was not to escape the consequences of his sins, but in expiation of them his line was to lose a part of the kingdom. It is not certain, accordingly, that the narrative has any basis in fact. A. T. Olmstead would seem to have demonstrated quite conclusively that for the earliest and most authentic account of Jeroboam's revolt we have to go to the Lucianic recension of the Greek version, which must closely approximate the original Septuagint text, and hence the original Hebrew.[37] According to this account, Ahijah was in no way responsible for the revolt, but heaped the bitterest kind of denunciation upon the head of Jeroboam as the revolt was about to start. Instead of being favorably inclined toward Jeroboam, he was quite the opposite. Hence it is surprising to read in the Hebrew version of the revolt that it was instigated by the prophet Ahijah, and yet that is possible. From the very beginning the prophets were intensely nationalistic; so it is not difficult

[36] See, e.g., J. M. P. Smith, *The Prophets and their Times* (1925), p. 30, n. 3.
[37] "Source Study and the Biblical Text," *American Journal of Semitic Languages*, XXX (1913), 1 ff.; "The Earliest Book of Kings," *ibid.*, XXXI (1915), 169 ff. The differences between the Hebrew and Greek versions are best seen from the parallel summary of the two presented by C. F. Burney, *Notes on the Hebrew Text of the Book of Kings* (1903), pp. 163-166.

to understand that a northern prophet like Ahijah would be ready to support any movement toward independence in Israel, particularly when Solomon was so disliked in the north and was so displeasing to the prophets because of his introduction of foreign cults. However, no matter how much Ahijah may have favored the revolt in the first place, he assuredly could not accept the disestablishment of Yahwism and when Jeroboam took this further step, both the Hebrew and Greek accounts agree that Ahijah immediately broke with him and condemned his actions in no uncertain terms, as recorded in I Kings 14:7-16, where Jeroboam is explicitly accused of apostasy and the establishment of the fertility cult, the cult of Ashtart. In fact, so alien was the new cult to Yahwism that many of the Israelites who remained loyal to Yahweh felt impelled to leave Israel and settle in Judah, as we read in II Chron. 11:13-16 and I Kings 12:17. According to the Septuagint, Jeroboam's mother was a harlot (γυνὴ πόρνη), which may mean that she was a sacred prostitute connected with the fertility cult. The name that she gave her son suggests this, meaning as it does "May 'Amm bring about increase," 'Amm here being a fertility god apparently.[38] Further, it is to be noted that Jeroboam's son, Abijah, was born to him in Egypt,[39] i.e., before he became king of Israel and re-established the bull cult. Hence there is nothing remarkable in the fact that Jeroboam gave a Yahweh name to his son. Ever since the time of David the Israelites had more and more been using Yahweh names,[40] thereby reflecting the gradual adoption of the Yahweh religion. If Jeroboam had given a Yahweh name to his son after the revolt, it would have been surpris-

[38] See D. Nielsen, *Der dreieinige Gott*, I (1927), 77 ff.; *Handbuch der altarabischen Altertumskunde*, I (1927), *passim*; G. A. Barton, *Semitic and Hamitic Origins* (1934), pp. 208 ff.

[39] So according to the Septuagint.

[40] See G. B. Gray, *Studies in Hebrew Proper Names* (1896), pp. 158 ff.

ing; but as a matter of fact he did not, for his other son was named Nadab (I Kings 14:20).

Irrespective of whether Jeroboam's revolt was backed by the prophets or not, it was the natural outcome of the hostility between north and south and the consequent aspiration of the north for independence. Nevertheless, it had religious results as well, and for this reason it was particularly reprehensible in the eyes of the Deuteronomic redactor of the Book of Kings. Over and over again Jeroboam is denounced as "the man who made Israel sin" (e.g., I Kings 12:30; 13:34; 14:16; 15:26, 30, 34; 16:26; 22:52; II Kings 3:3; 10:29, 31; 13:2, 6; 14:24; 15:9, 18, 24, 28; 17:21 f.; 23:15), and his sin was that he dared to establish in Israel a god other than Yahweh, with distinctive priests, sanctuaries, and cult paraphernalia (I Kings 14:9). It is explicitly stated that Jeroboam ousted the Levites, the priests of Yahweh, from their official position as the state priesthood (I Kings 12:31 f.; 13:33; II Chron. 11:14; 13:9), and in their place he installed "whomsoever he wished" as priests מקצות העם, "from the ends of the people" (I Kings 12:31; 13:33). With the data available it is impossible to determine with certainty what this term means, perhaps "from all sorts of people."[41] "Hosea (10:5) called them kĕmārîm, a word that is applied exclusively in the Old Testament to idolatrous priests (cf. II Kings 23:5; Zeph. 1:4).[42] Hence it is very clear that they were not Yahweh priests, and if our contention

---

[41] So Leroy Waterman translates in The Bible: An American Translation (1948). A. B. Ehrlich, Randglossen zur hebräischen Bibel, VII (1914), 247, argues that the phrase means "from the best [Vornehmen] of the people," but it is exceedingly doubtful whether the author of Kings intended a meaning so complimentary; cf., e.g., I Kings 13:33b.

[42] According to J. Hoschander, The Priests and Prophets (1938), pp. 1 ff., the kĕmārîm were Canaanite priests of the Baal cult who were employed in the Yahweh cult; i.e., they represent the syncretism between Baalism and Yahwism, the worship of Yahweh with Baal rites. According to W. F. Albright, From the Stone Age to Christianity (1940), pp. 178, 325, n. 46, they were eunuch priests of the fertility cult, or galli.

is correct that the Aaronites constituted the priesthood of the bull-god,[43] it was they that were restored to power as the state priesthood. Sanctuaries to the bull-god were established at Bethel and Dan (I Kings 12:29), and probably at other places as well.[44] Scholars are quite generally agreed that Bethel in pre-Davidic times was a sanctuary of the bull cult and was never a permanent Yahweh center, if ever it was one at all;[45] so Jeroboam's act meant simply the re-establishment of the old cult. Dan, however, was early a center of the Yahweh religion (Judg. 18), but that it now gave way to the bull cult is evident from the statement in I Kings 12:29. Even as late as Josephus we have mention of "the temple of the golden cow" at Dan, as if its ruins at least were still visible at that late day.[46] According to the brief description of the altar at Bethel that we have in II Kings 23:15, it was clearly not an altar to Yahweh, but manifestly one to the bull-god, with its fertility-cult object, the Asherah, or sacred pole (cf. I Kings 14:15), and as such it was cursed by the Yahweh prophet from Judah, as recorded in I Kings 13:1 ff.[47] Neither was the feast that Jeroboam instituted a Yahweh feast, but one that "he invented on his own initiative" (I Kings 12:33), to be observed on the full moon of the eighth month, and hence

[43] See pp. 136 ff. above.

[44] B. Stade, *Zeitschrift für die alttestamentliche Wissenschaft*, III (1883), 10, claims that there is evidence in Hosea for the presence of bull images at all the important sanctuaries in Israel. Cf. Hos. 8:5 f.; 10:5; 12:12; 13:2, and similar passages. See also H. G. May, "The Fertility Cult in Hosea," *American Journal of Semitic Languages*, XLVIII (1931), 73 ff.

[45] See, e.g., W. O. E. Oesterley and T. H. Robinson, *A History of Israel*, I (1932), 278. There is also good ground for the belief that Bethel, the god of Israel according to Jer. 48:13, like the god Adad, was a bull god; see J. P. Hyatt, *Journal of the American Oriental Society*, LIX (1939), 93 ff.

[46] Josephus, *Wars*, iv, 1, 1.

[47] If it had been an altar to Yahweh, there would have been no occasion whatsoever for the prophet of Yahweh to curse it.

clearly a feast connected with the fertility cult, since the eighth month marked the beginning of the rainy or growing season.[48] It is significant in any case that Jeroboam chose for his festival a time different from that of the Jerusalem festival, thereby asserting the religious independence of the north; i.e., his revolt was as much religious as it was political, and H. P. Smith is clearly wrong in saying that "at the time of the revolt there was no consciousness of anti-religious motive on the part of the northern tribes."[49] Without religious independence political independence was absolutely unthinkable in ancient times, and it was no mere prejudice or bias, as scholars maintain,[50] but the actual facts of the case, that made the pro-Judean redactor of Kings and the Chronicler condemn the revolt as an act of religious apostasy.[51]

All our sources, then, agree that Jeroboam disestablished the Yahweh cult in Israel and replaced it by the bull cult, and this is strikingly borne out by the fact that personal names compounded with "bull" or "calf" and "Baal" markedly increase in Israel from this time onward; they

[48] So also Hoschander, *op. cit.*, pp. 31 f.

[49] *Old Testament History* (1903), p. 180. Cf. also J. Morgenstern, *Amos Studies*, I (1941), 146-160, who maintains that Jeroboam did nothing more than establish a new national shrine for the Northern Kingdom and the implication of sinfulness on his part is wholly due to the Deuteronomic and Priestly redaction of the text of I Kings 12:32 f. On page 217, however, Morgenstern concedes that "the cult which obtained in all the sanctuaries, both large and small, was that of the old, Canaanite, agricultural religion, but thinly disguised as Yahweh worship"; in other words, a "syncretistic agricultural religion, with its festivals and rites and other institutions designed to ensure and promote fertility and an adequate food supply."

[50] See, e.g., W. O. E. Oesterley and T. H. Robinson, *A History of Israel*, I (1932), 278, n. 3.

[51] A similar act by Athaliah in Judah is interpreted by A. T. Olmstead, *History of Palestine and Syria* (1931), p. 400, as an act of apostasy; so it is all the more surprising that he should not interpret Jeroboam's act in the same way.

even survive into the reign of Jeroboam II, as shown by the ostraca from Samaria,[52] in which we have ten Baal names out of a total of less than sixty.[53] Just as there was an increasing use of Baal names in the period of independence before David, when the north had its own cult, and these suddenly ceased and were replaced by Yahweh names when David made Yahwism the national religion of the whole land, so now we have a revival of the use of Baal names, reflecting the revival of the bull cult, the national cult of Israel. When finally Omri was able to establish a dynasty in Israel and made Samaria his capital, he doubtless had the example of David in mind, and like David he must have planned to erect a temple there to the national god of Israel so as to make it the religious as well as the political center of his people.[54] However, he died before he had time to accomplish this and it was left to his son Ahab to erect the temple, and it is significant that the temple which he did erect in Samaria was not one to Yahweh (there never was a temple to Yahweh in Samaria), but one to the god Baal (I Kings 16:32 f.). Significant, too, is the fact that Ahab's successor on the throne, his son Ahaziah, despite the fact that he bore a Yahweh name, appealed for relief when hurt by a fall, not to Yahweh, but to Baal (Baal-zebub, according to II Kings 1:2). Furthermore, it is to be noted that Ahab's daughter, Athaliah, whose marriage to Jehoram, king of Judah, sealed the alliance of Israel with Judah (II Kings 8:18; II Chron. 18:1; 21:6),

[52] These ostraca used to be dated in the reign of Ahab, but more recent research would put them in the reign of Jeroboam II; see W. F. Albright, *Archaeology and the Religion of Israel* (1942), pp. 41, 160, 214, n. 41.

[53] Since these are names of adults, they must have been given their bearers some time before Jeroboam II and hence reflect conditions of a time earlier than his.

[54] Cf. H. Parzen, *Harvard Theological Review*, XXXIII (1940), 71: "In antiquity the seat of political power and the principal sanctuary, symbolic of the official religion, were never separated."

brought her Baal religion with her to Judah (cf. II Kings
11:18) despite the fact that she, too, bore a Yahweh name.
It is clear, then, that Baalism was the national religion of
Israel from Jeroboam I to Athaliah, and it must have been
introduced by Jeroboam with his disestablishment of Yahwism.

The disestablishment of Yahwism, however, did not mean
that the cult entirely disappeared from Israel. It ceased
simply to be the favored state cult, but it still continued
as a private cult. Not all the people returned to the old
religion, but many naturally clung to the new faith, to such
a degree indeed that even in the dark days of Ahab's reign
it could still be said that seven thousand were "the knees
that had not bowed to Baal" (I Kings 19:18), and even
Ahab's own major-domo, Obadiah, was a faithful follower
of Yahweh (I Kings 18:4). Intolerance in religion was not
a characteristic of ancient peoples, and was only introduced
into Israel by the prophets, although there was of course
rivalry among the several cults for preferment. The days
that followed Jeroboam's revolt must have witnessed the
contest of several rival cults, and to add to their number
Ahab introduced the cult of the Tyrian baal, Melkart, when
he married Jezebel, and thus sealed an alliance with Tyre
(I Kings 16:31 ff.), but after all this was simply a variant
form of his own Baal cult. Ahab, like the ancients in general,
believed that in religious matters as in others there was safety
in numbers, and so he was the worshiper of many gods,
including the god Yahweh. Now that friendly relations
once more obtained between Israel and Judah, cemented by
intermarriage between the royal houses, it was natural that
there should have been a more friendly attitude toward the
Judean god, and this is reflected in the fact that Ahab gave
his children Yahweh names (Ahaziah, Jehoram, and Athal-

iah), but that did not make them worshipers of Yahweh, because they were all worshipers of Baal. Ahab's action was a gesture of good-will toward a neighboring state that he would make his ally. But apart from that, there was nothing more remarkable in Ahab's action than in those of Egyptian, Babylonian, Assyrian, and other Semitic kings, who were often accustomed to give their children names in which gods other than their several state gods appeared as an element; e.g., Sennacherib, although king of Assyria, whose state god was Ashur, had as an element in his name the god Sin, a god of alien origin, and even the great religious reformer, Akhenaten of Egypt, gave names to his two youngest daughters in which the ancient god Rē was an element, Nefer-nefru-Rē and Setep-en-Rē, and even in his hymns to Aten he still retained the ancient royal title, "the son of Rē."[55] The bone of contention between the prophet Elijah and Ahab was not the denial of Yahweh as god, but the denial of supremacy to Yahweh and the worship of other gods along with Yahweh, as witness Elijah's words to Ahab when he accused him of being the troubler of Israel: "I have not troubled Israel, but you and your father's house, by forsaking the commands of Yahweh and by running after the Baals" (I Kings 18:18); or again his words of explanation to Yahweh when he fled in terror to Horeb and Yahweh asked him what he was doing there: "I am but jealous for Yahweh, God of hosts; for the Israelites have forsaken the covenant with thee, in that they have thrown down thy altars and slain thy prophets, so that I alone am left, and they seek to take my life" (I Kings 19:10, 14). Elijah was jealous for the primacy of Yahweh and was intolerant of the precedence given to Baal or the bull-god and to Jezebel's newly imported god, the "Asherah" of I Kings 18:19 (cf. also II

[55] See E. A. W. Budge, *Tutānkhamen* (1923), pp. 92, 116.

Kings 3:13), and as a result he found himself bitterly opposed to the prophets of these gods, who of course were just as sincere champions of their respective gods as he was of his. The issue, however, was more definitely with the prophets of the bull-god; for it is to be noted that, although Elijah's challenge was issued to "the four hundred and fifty prophets of the Baal and the four hundred prophets of the Asherah who ate at Jezebel's table" (I Kings 18:19), the contest on Carmel was with the former alone, since they and their god occupied the place that Elijah would have for himself and his god. The polemic of Elijah was vigorously continued by Elisha and a few others until in the end came its culmination in the revolution of Jehu, fomented by the Yahweh prophets and directed particularly against the Baal cult. As a result Baalism was overthrown, and Yahwism was once more established as the official religion of the north (II Kings 10:18 ff.). But the change was not so great after all. Old customs, old forms, and old institutions die hard. The interpretation and application may change, but the substance remains. Hence the Yahweh cult in the north came to be little more than the old bull cult under a new name, as the redactor of Kings well saw (II Kings 10:29 ff.) and as the writings of Hosea make only too apparent. It has always been as easy as it is natural for the vested interests to transfer their allegiance from the losing to the winning side, and in making the transfer they carry much of the old over to the new. The result is fusion of the two, and so it was in the case of Yahwism and Baalism, but that fusion took place not in the time of Jeroboam, as generally understood, but much later. It had its beginnings in the popular mind from the time that Yahwism and Baalism first came into contact, long before the days of Jeroboam, but it found its way into the theology of the state only after the revolution of Jehu, when Yahwism displaced Baalism and then absorbed it.

In this long-drawn-out contest between Yahwism and the bull cult not all the prophets of Yahweh were the vigorous propagandists that Elijah, Micaiah, and Elisha were. Most of them seem to have been much more tolerant toward other cults. Prophecy was becoming more and more professionalized, and less aggressive. One mark of this growing professionalism was the use of mechanical means to induce the prophetic ecstasy. In I Sam. 10:5 we read of a band of prophets coming down from a high place with lyre, tambourine, flute, and harp before them and prophesying, but there is no statement that the music here was anything other than the accompaniment of the prophetic state and its natural emotional outlet (cf. I Chron. 25:1). There is no doubt, however, that music would help to bring on that state, and by the time of Elisha it was definitely so used, as we read in II Kings 3:15: "Elisha said, 'Now then, procure a minstrel for me.' And as soon as the minstrel played, the power of Yahweh came upon him," and he proceeded to prophesy. It was inevitable that the prophets, like most mystics, should in course of time develop a technique, making use of mechanical means like music, dancing, shouting, and intoxicating drinks,[56] and that of course would tend to professionalize the office. Another mark of growing professionalism was the fact that some of the later prophets bore some kind of mark to indicate their calling. In I Kings 20:38 a prophet is represented as disguising himself from Ahab by putting a bandage about his head, upon removing which he was immediately recognized as belonging to the prophetic order (v. 41), indicating that the bandage must have covered some brand on the forehead or some peculiar tonsure that

[56] See, e.g., I Kings 18:26 ff.; Is. 28:7 f.; IV Esd. 14:40; and cf. the various Dervish orders today.

was the distinguishing mark of the prophet. That the custom was a prevalent one is attested by Zech. 13:4-6, where the professional prophet is accused of wearing a hairy mantle to deceive the people and of having distinguishing brands or scars on his chest.[57]

It was inevitable of course that the prophets should become professional. Their common cause and common temperament naturally drew them together, and from the very beginning we note the tendency for them to congregate in bands (I Sam. 10:5 ff.; 19:20). As time went on, this tendency increased and they became definitely organized groups. We read of one of these groups as living together in a communal way at Bethel (II Kings 2:3), another at Jericho (II Kings 2:5, 7, 15), and another at Gilgal (II Kings 4:38), and in II Kings 6:1-7 another group is represented as enlarging their living quarters. Just as the Baal prophets went about in bands of four hundred or four hundred and fifty (I Kings 18:19), so likewise did the Yahweh prophets. When Ahab summoned them for consultation, they came in a body four hundred strong and pronounced their oracle as one voice (I Kings 22:6). They were a gregarious folk, living and working together, because through the contagion of numbers the ecstatic state was more easily induced.

From the very beginning the prophets naturally expected a fee for their services when asked to act as oracles or diviners (I Sam. 9:8; I Kings 14:2 ff.; II Kings 8:8 ff.), but apparently only when acting in that capacity; for we read that Elisha absolutely refused any fee when he cured Naaman of leprosy (II Kings 5:16), and his servant, who secretly took the fee, was stricken with the leprosy cured in Naaman (vv. 26 f.).[58] When acting as champions of Yahweh

[57] "Chest," as the interpretation of the Hebrew expression used here, is based on its occurrence in Ugaritic; lit., "between the hands."
[58] Cf. the incident recorded in I Kings 13:7 f.

the prophets would have no occasion or opportunity to collect fees, but they would when acting as oracles. It was inevitable, then, that certain prophets would take to divination as being the more lucrative field of labor, and in the end prophecy as a whole became definitely commercialized, so much so that it was simply taken for granted that a prophet made his living from his profession, as is very evident from the words of Amaziah to Amos (ch. 7:12): "O seer, go away, off with you to the land of Judah, and there earn your living by prophesying there."[59]

Thus did prophecy become commercialized and professionalized. It went the way of the priesthood, and for that matter of all institutions. It lost its original spontaneous, inspired character and became in time as professional as the priesthood against which it was originally a protest. As a result a new crisis developed within Yahwism. But after all it was this new religious crisis that brought forth a new and a better champion of Yahweh in the person of a new type of prophet, and prophecy had as it were a second birth. As earlier prophecy had been a protest against the professionalization of the sacred office of interpreter of Yahweh, so the new type came into being as a movement of the same order, and found itself more bitterly arrayed against the professional order of prophecy than the earlier prophets had ever been arrayed against the priests (Amos 7:12; Mic. 3:5, 11; Jer. 23:9 ff.; 26:7 ff.; 28:1 ff.; Ez. 13:1 ff.; Zech. 13:2 ff.). The issues now were clearer and men had advanced in ethical and religious discernment. The transition to the new type of prophet was in the persons of Elijah, Elisha, and Micaiah, particularly the last-named. They were not of the general run of prophets of their day; they were more individualistic

---

[59] For this translation see the present writer, *Journal of Biblical Literature*, LXIV (1945), 8.

and were seldom found with the prophetic bands, and
Micaiah at least was definitely out of accord with their views
and attitude. When summoned for consultation by Ahab,
he pronounced an oracle diametrically opposed to that of the
four hundred professional prophets (I Kings 22:5 ff.), and
just here we see the difference between the new type of
prophet and the professional, or cultic, prophet of the day.
The latter was making his religion a business, and he was
running his business as one would run a grocery store, viz.,
to please his clients,[60] because to the degree that they were
pleased, to that degree he would prosper. The new type of
prophet, on the other hand, was in no way concerned with
the likes or dislikes of his audience. He spoke only what the
inspiration of the moment impelled him to speak, what
Yahweh spoke to him (I Kings 22:14). His oracles were
not the kind that people would ask for or expect to pay for.
The professional prophet was a diviner, foretelling the
future for a fee (cf. Mic. 3:11); he was the seer of the earlier
day, the *rō'ēh* and *ḥōzēh*. The new type of prophet was a
revival of the *nābî'* type in its original form, the champion
of Yahweh, and it found its first full expression in Amos,
who repudiated utterly any connection with the prophetic
order of his day (ch. 7:14 f.): "I am not a prophet; I am not
a member of the prophetic order [*lit.*, a son of a prophet],[61]
but I am a herdsman and a dresser of sycamores, and

---

[60] Cf. Mic. 3:5: "Thus says Yahweh regarding the prophets who lead
my people astray, who, having something to bite with their teeth, preach
prosperity, but against him who does not give them something to eat,
they declare war." Cf. also Mic. 3:11*a*:

> Her [Israel's] chiefs pronounce judgments for a bribe,
> And her priests declare oracles at a price,
> And her prophets divine for money.

[61] "Son" here is used in the common Semitic idiom meaning "one belonging to the class, prophet," just as "son of man" means "one belonging
to the class, man." See, e.g., J. M. P. Smith, *The Prophets and Their Times*
(2nd ed., W. A. Irwin, 1941), pp. 1 f.

Yahweh took me from following the flock and Yahweh said to me, 'Go, prophesy to my people Israel.' " Here Amos asserted that prophesying was not his profession; that was something else. He was a herdsman,[62] but called by Yahweh to deliver his message to Israel and win them back to him. Amos and his spiritual successors, the great ethical prophets, were champions of Yahweh and all that he stood for. They were not concerned in predicting future events as such, but they were tremendously concerned in the present and its reformation. Hence what predictions they made were seldom categorical, but usually conditional, intended as warnings to their audience of the inevitable consequences of their evil doing: "If you do so and so, so and so shall be the consequences." In their labors, then, in contrast with the professional prophets, they were successful to the degree that their predictions did not come true; but alas for the Hebrew people, the warnings of the prophets all too often fell on deaf ears and the people went their stubborn way. "Foolish and senseless people," Jeremiah called them (ch. 5:21); "eyes they have, but they see not; ears they have, but they hear not."

Some years ago there was a tendency among scholars to exaggerate the ecstaticism of the prophets.[63] In contrast, the tendency of late has been to play down their ecstaticism.[64]

[62] J. Morgenstern, *Amos Studies*, I (1941), 19 f., emends "herdsman" here to "shepherd," and this may be right. A. Haldar, *Associations of Cult Prophets among the Ancient Semites* (1945), p. 112, interprets both "herdsman" and "shepherd" as cultic terms, but this is surely farfetched and fanciful.

[63] See, e.g., G. Hölscher, *Die Profeten* (1914), who started the movement.

[64] See, e.g., W. A. Irwin, in J. M. P. Smith, *The Prophets and Their Times* (2nd ed., 1941), pp. x, 12 ff.; S. Mowinckel, "Ecstatic Experience and Rational Elaboration in Old Testament Prophecy," *Acta Orientalia*, XIII (1935), 264-291; H. H. Rowley, *Harvard Theological Review*, XXXVIII (1945), 4 ff.

It is acknowledged that the early prophets were given to ecstatic experiences, but not the canonical prophets, not even Ezekiel.[65] What used to be interpreted as ecstasy has come to be interpreted as a literary device. It is apparent that the later prophets were not given to ecstaticism to the degree that the earlier prophets were and it was of a milder sort.[66] It is difficult, too, to decide in their writings what is real experience and what is merely form and style. Nevertheless, it seems impossible to escape the conclusion that they did have experiences of an ecstatic, or perhaps more correctly, a mystic character.[67] Jeremiah felt impelled throughout his lifetime by a force outside himself, against which he was utterly powerless (Jer. 1:4 ff.; 20:7 ff.), and Amos had to leave his sheep to prophesy in a strange land (ch. 7:14). It is possible that Habakkuk's argument with Yahweh is presented in the form of visions as a literary device, comparable to that in Egyptian and Babylonian literature,[68] but Isaiah's

[65] See, e.g., W. A. Irwin, The Problem of Ezekiel (1943), pp. 333 f.

[66] For a discussion of ecstasy as applied to the prophets see, e.g., A. Guillaume, Prophecy and Divination (1938), pp. 290 ff., supplemented by A. R. Johnson, The Cultic Prophets of Israel (1944), p. 19, n. 16; also H. Th. Obbink, "The Forms of Prophetism," Hebrew Union College Annual, XIV (1939), 23-28; A. Bentzen, Introduction to the Old Testament, I (1948), 194 ff., who makes the interesting suggestion that it was only a single word or phrase that came flashing to the prophet in a moment of inspiration and this became the text of a sermon worked out in his calmer moments.

[67] Cf. Haldar, op. cit., pp. 115 ff.

[68] In an Egyptian poem the author presents his reflections on whether life is worth living under the guise of a conversation between himself and his own soul; translated by J. A. Wilson, in Ancient Near Eastern Texts, ed. J. B. Pritchard (1950); discussed most recently by the same author, in H. Frankford et al., The Intellectual Adventure of Ancient Man (1946), pp. 102 ff. Similarly, a Babylonian poet discusses the same problem under the guise of a conversation between himself and his slave; translated by R. H. Pfeiffer, in Ancient Near Eastern Texts (1950); discussed most recently by T. Jacobsen, in The Intellectual Adventure of Ancient Man (1946), pp. 216-219.

call (ch. 6) surely came to him by way of a vision,[69] and the visions of Amos (chs. 7:1-9; 8:1-9:4) must be something more than a literary device. Hence it is not altogether correct to say with W. A. Irwin[70] that "the psychology of the canonical prophets was a normal religious psychology." The prophets were not ordinary folk,[71] as witness the actions of Isaiah in going naked and barefoot for three years (Is. 20:1-6), or those of Jeremiah in wearing an iron yoke (Jer. 28:12-14),[72] or many of the strange doings of Ezekiel. The prophets were religious geniuses and cannot be explained by the psychology of the ordinary man. Everyone recognizes that they were the spiritual heirs of the earlier prophets and so they must have had much in common with them. In fact, it is our contention that they were a revival of the nābî' type of prophet in his original form as champion of Yahweh.

In recent years a good deal has been made of the fact that priests and prophets belonged together at the sanctuary and both groups were cultic functionaries.[73] This was definitely true of the earlier prophets and was pointed out as long ago as 1895 by W. Robertson Smith,[74] and it has long been the contention of the present writer, but it is questionable whether many of the canonical prophets were cult officials,

[69] A very recent discussion of Is. 6 is that by Ivan Engnell, *The Call of Isaiah: An Exegetical and Comparative Study* (1949).

[70] *Op. cit.*, p. 14.

[71] Cf. Rowley, *op. cit.*, pp. 26 ff.

[72] Cf. the actions of the ecstatic prophet, Zedekiah, in wearing a pair of iron horns (I Kings 22:11; I Chron. 18:10).

[73] See, e.g., S. Mowinckel, *Psalmenstudien III: Kultprophetie und prophetische Psalmen* (1923); A. C. Welch, *Prophet and Priest in Ancient Israel* (1936); A. R. Johnson, *The Cultic Prophet in Ancient Israel* (1944); A. Haldar, *Associations of Cult Prophets among the Ancient Semites* (1945); J. Pedersen, in *Studies in Old Testament Prophecy*, ed. H. H. Rowley (1950), pp. 130 ff.; N. W. Porteous, *ibid.*, pp. 143 ff.

[74] *The Prophets of Israel* (2nd ed., 1895), p. 85.

despite the opinion of modern scholars to the contrary.[75] Ezekiel, as a priest, officiated in the cult in Jerusalem, but when he was deported to Babylonia he immediately lost his cultic status. If Jeremiah belonged to a priestly family, which is doubtful,[76] we have no record of his officiating in any way in the cult, but instead we have frequent references to the intense hostility between him and the priests. He was repudiated by them (Jer. 18:18; 20:1 ff.; 26:7 ff.), and in no uncertain terms he repudiated them and all their devices (Jer. 1:18; 2:8; 3:16; 4:9; 5:30 f.; 6:13; 7:1-28; 8:8 ff.; 13:13 f.; 14:18; 19:1 ff.; 20:1 ff.; 23:11, 33 f.; 26:1 ff.; 34:18 ff.). It has sometimes been said that Isaiah was in the temple as a cult official when he had the vision of his call (ch. 6),[77] but because he had a vision of Yahweh in the temple it does not follow that he was a functionary there or that he was in the temple; he could have had such a vision anywhere and in any capacity. When Hezekiah wished to consult Isaiah (Is. 37:2), there is no indication that he sent his messengers to the temple or that Isaiah was to be found there. Also, Isaiah, like the other canonical prophets, is rarely represented as being consulted (only in Is. 37:2); instead, he is regularly represented as pressing his message on others. Even the prophetess Huldah, to whom Josiah sent a deputation for consultation, was not to be found in the temple, but in the newer quarter of the city (II Kings 22:12-15). Amos assuredly had nothing to do with the cult,

[75] It is striking to note how many of the most recent commentaries on the canonical prophets take the ground that they were cult functionaries; see, e.g., G. Gerleman, *Zephanja textkritisch und literarisch untersucht* (1942); P. Humbert, *Problèmes du livre d'Habacuc* (1944); A. H. Edelkoort, *De profeet Zacharia* (1945); A. Haldar, *Studies in the Book of Nahum* (1947).

[76] See the present writer, *The Expositor*, Eighth Series, XXV (1923), 215-222.

[77] Cf. Ivan Engnell, *The Call of Isaiah: An Exegetical and Comparative Study* (1949), pp. 27 ff.; S. Mowinckel, *Profeten Jesaja* (1925), pp. 15 ff.

nor is there any indication that Hosea belonged to the cultic personnel, even though we interpret the woman that he married as a religious prostitute connected with the cult. It would seem impossible to explain the hostility between the priests and the canonical prophets and the severe criticism of the cultus by the prophets, if they themselves officiated in that cultus. There were of course prophets who did, but between them and the canonical prophets there was the bitterest enmity (Hos. 9:7; Is. 28:7; Mic. 3:5, 11; Jer. 14:14; 23:9 ff., 32; 29:21; Ez. 13:17 ff.). The postexilic canonical prophets may have had some place in the cultus,[78] but not so the pre-exilic. Those who did have a place in the cultus were the professional prophets, the consultative specialists, who are often coupled with the priests (Hos. 4:4 f.; Is. 28:7; Mic. 3:11; Zeph. 3:3 f.; Jer. 2:8; 4:9; 5:31; 6:13; 8:1, 10; 13:13; 14:18; 23:11; 26:7, 16; 29:1; Lam. 2:20; 4:13) and like them derived their livelihood from their official connection with the cultus, as the canonical prophets did not. If Waterman and others are correct in interpreting the prophetic denunciation of the cultus (e.g., Amos 5:21-25; Hos. 6:6; Is. 1:11-17; Mic. 6:6-8; Jer. 6:19 f.; 7:21-23) literally, as absolute repudiation[79] and not as hyperbole, then the prophets could not have been cultic functionaries at all.

We have already noted the opinion of some scholars that the earlier type of Hebrew prophecy was an importation from without. Likewise there have been scholars who main-

[78] E.g., Haggai and Zechariah were rather clearly attached to the Jerusalem cultus; see A. Jepsen, *Nabi* (1934), pp. 227 ff.; A. R. Johnson, *op. cit.*, pp. 55 f.

[79] See Leroy Waterman, *Journal of Biblical Literature*, LXIV (1945), 297-307. For a contrary view of the prophetic attitude toward the cultus see H. H. Rowley, *Bulletin of the John Rylands Library*, XXIX (1946), 326-358. For an exhaustive study of recent views regarding the prophets see H. H. Rowley, "The Nature of Prophecy in the Light of Recent Study," *Harvard Theological Review*, XXXVIII (1945), 1-38; *The Re-Discovery of the Old Testament* (1945), pp. 133-160.

tain that the later type owes not a little to alien prophecy, not so much to Babylonian as to Egyptian prophecy,[80] and that there is real dependence upon Egypt in both literary technique and content of thought. As long ago as 1906 Eduard Meyer posited a considerable dependence of the Hebrew prophets upon Egyptian seers,[81] and later writers in the field,[82] although more conservative in their conclusions, have been quite as fully persuaded of the fact that there was some dependence. One outstanding characteristic of Egyptian prophecy, as McCown, Gressmann, and Bentzen have indicated,[83] is the peculiar combination of threat and promise, and this finds its reflection in the Hebrew prophets. Some scholars would make all the passages of hope in the early prophets spurious;[84] but Egyptian parallels would lead us to believe that, unless there are strong evidences to the contrary, there is just as good reason for accepting the genuineness of the promises as of the threats.[85] A good illustration is Deut. 32, where, in a poem undeniably a unit, there is a sudden transition at verse 26 from the severest denunciation of Israel to the glorious promise of the following verses. Another remarkable likeness between the Egyptians and the Hebrews is the fact that it is in the prophetic writings of these alone of the ancient Semitic

[80] H. Gressmann, however, claims considerable dependence upon Babylonia in his posthumous work, *The Tower of Babel* (1928); so also A. Haldar, *Associations of Cult Prophets among the Ancient Semites* (1945).

[81] *Die Israeliten und ihre Nachbarstämme* (1906), pp. 451 ff.

[82] E.g., J. M. P. Smith, *American Journal of Semitic Languages*, XXXV (1918), 1 ff.; C. C. McCown, *Harvard Theological Review*, XVIII (1925), 357 ff.; H. Gressmann, *Journal of Theological Studies*, XXVII (1926), 241 ff.; J. H. Breasted, *The Dawn of Conscience* (1933), pp. 363 ff.; cf. also A. Bentzen, *Introduction to the Old Testament*, I (1948), 258 f.

[83] See the references in the preceding note.

[84] See, e.g., Kemper Fullerton, *Journal of Biblical Literature*, XLI (1922), 1 ff.

[85] Cf. C. C. McCown, *The Promise of His Coming* (1921), pp. 81 ff.

world that there is a passion for the regeneration of the
social order. This is the reason for the threats and promises
of the prophets; by their threats and promises they sought
to bring about a new order, which in both countries came
eventually to be conceived of in terms of the Messianic era.
The fact that the ideals and aspirations of the Hebrew
prophets far surpassed those of the Egyptian might suggest
that they took up the ideas of their predecessors and carried
them further. But after all the two could have been quite
independent of each other and there is nothing to prove that
Hebrew prophecy owed much to that of other lands. It
began like theirs, but it developed further and took on new
form with each new birth. It had its own independent
beginnings and, though influenced perhaps to some degree
by foreign contacts,[86] it had its own peculiar development.
Those who argue the contrary confuse posteriority with
dependence. Before posteriority can indicate dependence
there must be actual proof of direct or indirect borrowing
and the lack of local stimuli. In the case of prophecy no
proof of borrowing has been furnished, but of posteriority only, and we have shown how Hebrew prophecy
grew up in its own way in its own environment with all
the necessary stimuli locally present. The prophets were
men of their time, for their time, but also above their time.
They were the product of their day and the spokesmen of
its needs, but because they were religious geniuses they rose
above their time to become the challengers of a new world
order. What little they may have borrowed they made

[86] One of course cannot deny all foreign influence because it is very
manifest that in certain fields the Hebrews were much influenced by their
neighbors; see, e.g., the present writer, "The Interpenetration of Cultures
as Illustrated by the Character of the Old Testament Literature," *Journal
of Religion*, VII (1927), 244-262; *Readings in Sociology*, ed. W. D. Wallis
and M. M. Willey (1930), pp. 81-86.

forever their own. What foreign influence there may have been was peripheral and not central so that even Gressmann has to admit, "If anywhere, the originality of Israel attains to its most striking expression in prophecy."[87] In any case, "higher than the Tower of Babel towered Mount Zion."[88]

[87] *The Tower of Babel* (1928), p. 39.

[88] Gressmann, *op. cit.*, p. 92; cf. W. F. Albright, *The Archaeology of Palestine* (1949), p. 219: "Though the Old Testament contains a synthesis of the best that had been contributed by the ancient East, it was transmuted by Hebrew religious insight into a work which rises mountain-high above even the highest hills of Egypt and Mesopotamia, and which is permeated through and through with the elusive fragrance of Palestine."

CHAPTER SIX

The Origin of Hebrew Monotheism

AMONG all peoples everywhere there has always been a tendency toward monotheism, ever growing a bit stronger than the movement toward polytheism,[1] but with no people in ancient times did that tendency attain such full expression as it did with the Hebrews, and the question immediately arises, whence and how came that monotheism? It is a question difficult to answer and one to which various solutions have been offered. According to some, the origin of Hebrew monotheism is not to be found with the Hebrews themselves, but is to be traced back to some alien people. *A priori* there is nothing to indicate that the Hebrews could not have borrowed their monotheism from abroad, although it used to be said that the Hebrews owed their uniqueness to the fact that God had separated them from the rest of the world and had given to them an interpretation of himself that he had denied to others, as if one "could isolate a people and treat it as a unique phenomenon in history, as a flower that bloomed solitary in some divine or magic garden, without striking roots in the common earth, without breathing the common air, without expanding in the com-

---

[1] Cf. S. A. Cook, in W. Robertson Smith, *The Religion of the Semites* (3rd ed., 1927), pp. 526 ff.; *The Old Testament: A Reinterpretation* (1936), pp. 142 ff.

mon sunshine." These words were spoken by Sir James Frazer in reference to the Greek people,[2] but they apply equally well to the Hebrews. If history has taught us anything, it has taught us this: that nations never lived in watertight compartments, in splendid isolation one from the other; and least of all did the Hebrew nation, situated as they were on the great highroad between east and west. With alien caravans and armies constantly passing through their very midst, they could not have remained aloof from the world even had they so desired. Instead of developing their unique characteristics because of isolation from the world, it was actually because of contact with it. Nations are like individuals. That nation develops most which borrows most. The most original of peoples appropriates most, drinking deeply from the common heritage of mankind. It was just because the Hebrew people lived in such intimate contact with the world and borrowed so largely from others, thus adding the attainments of others to their own, that they so far outdistanced their contemporaries in real cultural development.

Immediately upon opening the covers of a Hebrew Bible, the reader sees evidences of borrowing by the Hebrews. The very languages in which it is written were not their own. Part of it is written in Aramaic (Dan. 2:4b-7:28; Ezra 4:8-6:18; 7:12-26; Jer. 10:11), and the rest of it in a language that we call Hebrew, but this was not the language with which the Hebrews came into the country; it was the language of the people of Palestine that they conquered and with whom they amalgamated. The Hebrews by their own confession were a mixed people and of composite origin. The original stock may have been Aramean, as Deut. 26:5

[2] Preface to M. P. Nilsson, *A History of Greek Religion* (Eng. trans., 1925), p. 2.

asserts, "A nomad Aramean was my father." In their early home in Mesopotamia and in their migrations into Palestine they seem to have fused to some extent with various "Hittite" groups (Hurrians and others), and in Palestine they gradually absorbed the native Canaanite-Amorite population, even as the Old Testament asserts over and over again (cf., e.g., Gen. 38:1 ff.; Josh. 9:3-27; Judg. 1:21, 27-35; 2:2; 3:5 f.). Hence Ezekiel in 16:3, 45 could say of Jerusalem: "Your origin and nativity are of the land of Canaan; your father was an Amorite, and your mother a Hittite." Long before the Hebrews arrived in Palestine the country had come under the control of Egypt. Then about the twenty-second century there came hordes of Amorites, as evidenced by the many Amorite personal names of the time preserved in the execration texts,[3] and Palestine thereafter came gradually within the Babylonian orbit of culture. From *ca.* 1720 to *ca.* 1560 B.C. the Hyksos were in control and then came the conquests of Tuthmosis III in the fifteenth century which brought the Egyptians back to the country. These held sway in the land for several centuries and left an indelible impression upon the land and its people, as the excavations have made only too manifest.[4] Moreover, a part of the Hebrew people spent some little time in Egypt and must unquestionably have brought Egyptian culture and Egyptian blood back with them, which in course of

[3] Published by K. Sethe, *Die Ächtung feindlicher Fürsten, Völker und Dinge auf altägyptischen Tongefässscherben des Mittleren Reiches* (1926); G. Posener, *Princes et pays d'Asie et de Nubie* (1940); *La Chronique d'Égypte*, No. 27 (1939), pp. 39-46; *Mélanges Syriens offerts à M. R. Dussaud*, I (1939), 313-317.

[4] There has not been a single extensive excavation in Palestine that does not show the influence of Egyptian culture in the way of scarabs, seals, inscriptions, and the like; see, e.g., the seals published by the present writer, *Bulletin of the American Schools of Oriental Research*, No. 90 (1943), pp. 24-27.

time they communicated in some measure at least to their compatriots in Palestine. Hence the Hebrews from the beginning were open to all sorts of alien influences, and in their ethnic composition they were a conglomerate of many different stocks, all of which is apparent in their cultural remains as revealed by the excavations and in their language.

Like most languages of progressive peoples, Hebrew is full of loan-words from other languages,[5] some of which came in at the very beginning and others in the course of the centuries of foreign contacts. Hebrew, for example, has two words for the personal pronoun "I," one 'ānôkî, identical with the Assyro-Babylonian or Akkadian anākū and the Egyptian 'nk, and the other 'ănî, identical with the Arabic 'anā. Similarly it has two words for "god," 'ēl and 'ĕlôhîm, the first reflecting the Akkadian ilu, and the second the Arabic 'ilāh. The word for "palace," hêkāl, is a loan-word from Sumerian by way of Akkadian. In Akkadian it is ekallu, and in Sumerian é-gal, literally, "great house." One of the words for "river," yĕ'ôr, is an Egyptian loan-word, while another, nāhār, is identical with the Akkadian nâru and the Arabic nahr. One of the verbs "to see," rā'āh, corresponds to the Arabic ra'ā, while another, hāzāh, is the Aramaic hāzā. Even the common word sûs, "horse," was derived from the Indo-Iranian aśwas through "Hittite" contact. These are only a few of the dozens of examples that might be given to illustrate the composite character of the Hebrew language, sure evidence that the people who used it were a borrowing people, and so the Hebrews might well have borrowed their monotheistic conception of God from abroad instead of developing it themselves. And this is precisely what many

[5] Cf. H. Bauer, *Zur Frage der Sprachmischung im Hebräischen* (1924); H. Bauer und P. Leander, *Historische Grammatik der hebräischen Sprache* (1922), pp. 19-22; R. Marcus, *Journal of Biblical Literature*, LX (1941), 141 ff.

scholars have maintained, some urging that it was Babylonian in origin and others that it was Egyptian, and these
claims it is our task to investigate.

A number of the older Assyriologists like Radau, Delitzsch, and Winckler were accustomed to make the assertion
that the Babylonians were at heart monotheists and to them
the Hebrews were indebted for their monotheism and for
nearly everything else as well. A statement so sweeping as
this would not merit serious consideration if it were not for
the fact that it received the support of the late Professor
Stephen Langdon, the noted Assyriologist of Oxford University, whose views have been given wide publicity by Sir
Charles Marston.[6] Langdon maintains that the Babylonians,
or more correctly the Sumerians who preceded them and
from whom they got most of their culture, were originally
monotheists, being worshipers of the one god An, later
semiticized as Anu(m).[7] His argument is that An is the only
Sumerian deity whose logogram, originally the picture of
a star, is never preceded by the determinative for deity,[8]
that logogram itself being the determinative used with all
other god names. Hence the Sumerians wrote [d]Enlil, [d]Enki,
&c., but never [d]An.[9] From this he argues that An, the sky-
god, was originally the only god that the Sumerians had and
then, as they fell away from monotheism into polytheism,
they thought of the several new gods as simply forms or
aspects or manifestations of An, and so in writing their
names they used the logogram for An as the determinative

[6] *The Bible Comes True* (1937), and other writings.

[7] See, e.g., his *Semitic Mythology* (1931), pp. 89, 93.

[8] Correct accordingly the statement of W. F. Albright, *Journal of
Biblical Literature*, LIV (1935), 195, n. 73, that the name of Anum is
sometimes written with the determinative.

[9] The superscript *d* is the abbreviation used by Assyriologists for *dingir*,
the Sumerian word for "god," here used as a determinative.

of deity.[10] The same argument was used many years ago by M.-J. Lagrange[11] and more recently by Langdon himself,[12] in the effort to prove that the Semites as a whole were originally monotheists, having as their one god El, also interpreted as a sky-god. From being a proper name originally, it is argued, El came to be used as a common noun to mean god in general, and hence the several gods as they were introduced were regarded as forms or manifestations of the original El and so each in turn was called an El. The same argument might be used to prove that the Greeks were originally monotheists, because Zeus (=Vedic Dyaush) is derived from the root dyu, "to shine," which is likewise the root of the regular Indo-European word for "god," deivos (=Avestan daeva, Sanskrit devas, Latin deus), literally "shiner,"[13] so that Zeus, like the Sumerian An and the Semitic El, was a sky-god. Similarly, James Legge, followed by John Ross, has argued that the Chinese were monotheists to begin with,[14] and some have gone so far as to claim that man wherever found was originally monotheistic and that monotheism accordingly antedates polytheism.[15] But, as W. L. Wardle has well said,[16] "the way in which God has led the stumbling feet of humanity along the path towards the goal of every other science makes it antecedently probable that in theology,

[10] Op. cit., p. 93.

[11] Études sur les religions sémitiques (2nd ed., 1905), pp. 70 ff.

[12] Op. cit., pp. 65 ff., 93.

[13] See, e.g., M. P. Nilsson, Archiv für Religionsgeschichte, XXXV (1938), 156 ff.; M. Bloomfield, The Religion of the Veda (1908), pp. 108-110.

[14] James Legge, The Religion of China (1881); John Ross, The Ancient Religion of China (1909).

[15] See especially Wilhelm Schmidt, Der Ursprung der Gottesidee (6 vols., 1926-1937); The Origin and Growth of Religion (Eng. trans., 1931); High Gods in North America (Eng. trans., 1933); Primitive Revelation (Eng. trans., 1939).

[16] Israel and Babylon (3rd ed., 1925), pp. 107 f.

too, man started at the beginning rather than at the end."
All modern anthropologists of standing[17] are absolutely con-
vinced that monotheism could not have antedated polytheism
and they can find no evidence whatsoever for the fall of man
from a pristine state of perfect knowledge and moral perfec-
tion.

Langdon in his arguments fails to take account of two
facts: (1) when the Semites and Sumerians began to write,
they had by that time advanced far along the road to knowledge, and theology was already hard at work on the riddle of
the universe, and (2) the Sumerians and Babylonians did not
at first use the determinative before god names, the usage
being only gradually introduced for the easier identification
of the names as god names.[18] We have already expressed our
belief that the earliest form of religion was naturism, out of
which animism developed in course of time,[19] and this is
the common belief among scholars today,[20] and is borne out
by our knowledge of the ancient Sumerians and all other
early peoples. When the Sumerians first appear on the pages
of history, they are worshipers of many gods, nature and
ancestor gods, and not of one god alone, and on this point
Langdon[21] and all others are agreed. Out of the early welter

[17] The only exceptions are the Roman Catholic anthropologist, Wilhelm
Schmidt, and his few followers. For a searching criticism of their thesis
see the present writer, *The Review of Religion*, IV (1940), 286 ff.; see
also S. A. Cook, *Journal of Theological Studies*, XXXIII (1932), 1 ff.; R.
Pettazzoni, *Revue de l'histoire des religions*, LXXXVIII (1923), 193-229;
Archiv für Religionsgeschichte, XXIX (1931), 108-129, 209-243; N. Söder-
blom, *Das Werden des Gottesglaubens* (1916).
[18] In the inscriptions down to the time of the Third Dynasty of Ur
most of the god names are written without the determinative.
[19] See pp. 85 ff. above.
[20] See, e.g., H. Frankfort, *Ancient Egyptian Religion* (1948), pp. 4 ff.;
H. Frankfort *et al.*, *The Intellectual Adventure of Ancient Man* (1946);
G. F. Moore, *The Birth and Growth of Religion* (1923); H. J. D. Astley,
Biblical Anthropology (1929).
[21] See, e.g., *op. cit.*, pp. 88 ff.

of gods, goddesses, and spirits the Sumerian theologians tried to develop some kind of order, and so in the Creation Myth they traced all the gods back to the father god An, since he was the sky-god and hence god over all, above all, the god *par excellence*. What was more natural, then, than that the sign which represented the sky-god, when a system of writing came to be invented, should be used as the logogram of god in general and the determinative for deity, when a determinative came to be written before god names; and what was more natural than that El, the sky-god of the Semites, or Zeus, the sky-god of the Indo-Europeans, should likewise come to be the designation of god in general? Instead of seeing in the phenomenon a reminiscence of earlier, prehistoric mono-theism, we are rather to see in it the work of early theologians trying to bring cosmos out of chaos, order out of disorder. In exactly the same way in a later period we see the word "Ishtar" going through precisely the same process. To begin with it was the personal name of the one goddess who was not the pale reflection of a male consort, but a goddess in her own right, the goddess *par excellence*. Because of this the word came in course of time to mean goddess in general, as well as Ishtar in particular, and was often used in the plural. Similarly, the word "Enlil" was originally the name of a Sumerian deity, at one time head of the Sumerian pantheon, but in the later period it came to mean nothing more than "lord," a synonym and frequent alternative of *bêlu*, "lord," and as such it could be used of any god, more particularly of Marduk as the head or "Enlil" of the Babylonian pantheon.[22]

To his earlier argument Langdon more recently added

[22] Thus it is used, for example, in the Royal Inscriptions of the Neo-Babylonian Period.

another.[23] This runs as follows. The Sumerian religion in its latest development contains about 5,000 gods; the inscriptions of ca. 3000 B.C. (better ca. 2700 B.C.) from Tell Farah (ancient Shuruppak)[24] show only 750; the 300 tablets from Kish (strictly Jemdet Nasr)[25] mention only three gods (An, the sky-god, Enki, the earth-god, and Utu,[26] the sun-god); while the 575 tablets from Uruk,[27] which he dates ca. 4000 B.C. (fully 500 years too early), contain the names of only two deities (An, the sky-god, and Inanna, the mother goddess). In this statement, however, Langdon is no more accurate than he usually is. In the Jemdet Nasr texts there are more gods than three; he himself speaks of four a little later in his article; in the introduction to the publication of his own texts from Jemdet Nasr[28] he lists the names of five gods: An, Enlil, Enki, Utu, and Lamma, with the last rather doubtful; and in some additional texts[29] he has discovered still another god, Shara, to make six in all according to his own count; while Falkenstein in the study of his Jemdet Nasr texts indicates the probability of a seventh, Shume, in the personal name En-dingir-shu-me (var., En-shu-me),[30] and still another god, Enlu, is manifestly to be found in the personal name En-lu-ti.[31] Since the archaic texts from Jemdet

---

[23] "Monotheism as the Predecessor of Polytheism in Sumerian Religion," *Evangelical Quarterly* for April, 1937; reprinted in full by Sir Charles Marston, *The Bible Comes Alive* (1937), pp. 259-274.

[24] Langdon makes no mention of the somewhat older texts from Ur published by E. Burrows, *Archaic Texts* (1935). There are 425 texts in this collection, containing the names of fifty gods at most.

[25] Published by S. Langdon, *Oxford Editions of Cuneiform Texts*, VII (1928).

[26] Langdon gives the name of this god as "Babbar," the older reading of the name.

[27] Published by A. Falkenstein, *Die archäische Texte aus Uruk* (1936).

[28] *Op. cit.*, p. vii.

[29] Published in the *Journal of the Royal Asiatic Society*, 1931, pp. 837 ff.

[30] *Op. cit.*, p. 36, n. 1.

[31] Falkenstein, *op. cit.*, No. 626, ii, 1.

Nasr and Uruk are as yet imperfectly understood and the god names are written without determinatives, there are doubtless a number of god names in them as yet unrecognized. With the larger understanding of the texts, and with the publication of additional texts of the same kind, the list of gods will unquestionably be extended, but the fact remains that we can never expect the number to be large. Hence Langdon has some right on his side when he says that the numerous pantheon of the late Sumerian period "dwindles down to four and then only two deities," proving, so he holds, that earlier there must have been one god alone, the sky-god An. To the layman this argument is most impressive and convincing, and particularly so when Langdon goes on to say that "if there really was a larger pantheon at the dawn of history, these numerous tablets, which are all temple records, would have mentioned them." But just there is the weakness of his whole argument. The argument *e silentio* is always a precarious one, and particularly so in the present instance. It is true that the tablets are probably temple records, but they are in no sense religious. With the ancient Sumerians the temple was the center of business, and all the archaic texts from Uruk and Jemdet Nasr, with the exception of a few word-lists, are account tablets, listing the quantities of various items (bread, barley, beer, sheep, land, etc.) administered by the temple in its capacity as business agent. In such tablets in the early period, or in any other period, there is seldom any occasion to mention the gods and hence they rarely appear. Following out Langdon's line of reasoning, we would have to say that the Old Akkadians of Nuzi had no gods at all, because none of their many tablets so far excavated[32] names a single deity. And yet it is utterly

[32] Published by the present writer, *Old Akkadian, Sumerian, and Cappadocian Texts from Nuzi* (1935).

ridiculous to say that they had none,[33] but no more ridiculous than to say that the Sumerians had only four gods in the Jemdet Nasr period and only two in the Uruk period. Outside of texts definitely religious (myths, hymns, prayers, liturgies, and the like), the gods of a people are seldom mentioned, and when their names do occur in account tablets they are found almost exclusively as elements in proper names, but it so happens that there are practically no proper names in the Jemdet Nasr texts, while the earlier texts from Uruk consist only of itemized lists of articles or lists of words. The further back we go the fewer are the religious texts, with none from the archaic period; and the earlier the text the fewer are the proper names. Hence the diminution in god names is not at all a reflection of the religious ideas of the Sumerians and has a vastly different explanation from that so glibly presented by Langdon, the perversion of which was due to his preconceived notion and theological bias that man was originally monotheistic. The ancient Sumerians might have been worshipers of only one god or a million gods, but neither situation could possibly be reflected in the kind of texts that have been preserved to us from that early period.

However, no matter what may have been the first form of religion with man, when we come to know him in history he is everywhere far removed from monotheism, and on this point all scholars are agreed. It is true, however, that to early man the tribal god was the sole object of worship and allegiance when the tribe approached god *as a tribe*, but that did not preclude belief in the efficacy of other gods or the worship by the tribe as families or as individuals of other gods and spirits. Hence the Greeks, although looking up to Zeus as father god and great High God, when they really wanted

---

[33] Although no gods are named in the texts, god names appear frequently as elements in the personal names appearing in the texts.

something important as individuals, turned each to his local deity, or as a tribe to the tribal god, as, for example, the Dorians looked to Apollo and not to Zeus for guidance and succor as a tribe, and the Athenians to Athena.[34] In the same way the god of chief importance to the early Sumerians, the god of everyday worship, was the tutelary god of the city-state, Nanna of Ur, Enki of Eridu, Enlil of Nippur, and so on. And likewise it was with the later Babylonians and Assyrians. Hence the hymns and prayers to the local gods might often be so worded as to suggest that the god addressed alone was god, as, for example, Adad-nerari III's praise of Nabu,[35] "Trust thou in Nabu, and trust thou in no other god," or a hymn to Nanna from a copy in the library of Ashurbanipal,[36] in which such expressions as the following occur:

> Lord, ruler of the gods, who in heaven and earth alone is exalted!
>
> Father Nanna, who has become absolute sovereign, ruler of the gods!

[34] Cf. the present writer, *The Review of Religion*, IV (1940), 288 f.: "What man has always wanted, and still insists on having, is a god to meet his immediate needs, a god near at hand, a local god. When a Muslim finds himself in very great trouble, it is not to almighty Allah that he appeals, but to the local Weli, even as the Catholic in similar circumstances prays to his patron saint or the Virgin Mary. When modern man finds it so difficult to reach out beyond his environment and find satisfaction in a great High God, it must have been quite impossible to primitive man. With all peoples everywhere it has been to the friendly little spirits, near at hand and approachable, that man has looked for protection, and not to the great gods of the Pantheon or to the great High God when there was one. The great gods were never of much use in daily life, but belonged to the cultus of the state. They were too far away to be trusted by the common people, or to be meaningful or useful."

[35] H. Rawlinson, *Cuneiform Inscriptions of Western Asia*, I (1861), 35, No. 2, l. 12.

[36] Rawlinson, *op. cit.*, IV (1875), 9; translated by E. Ebeling, in *Altorientalische Texte*, ed. H. Gressmann (2nd ed., 1926), pp. 241 ff.

In heaven, who is exalted? Thou alone art exalted!
On earth, who is exalted? Thou alone art exalted!

O Lord, for dominion in heaven, for rule upon earth, thou
hast among the gods, thy brothers, no rival!
Exalted king of kings, whose command none rivals, whom
no one resembles in divinity!

This is nothing other than flattery, an appeal to the vanity
of the god,[37] like the addresses of a young man to his lady-
loves, declaring to each in turn that she alone is his love. It
is the sort of thing that is very common in all polytheistic
literature, for example, in the early Vedic and Egyptian
hymns,[38] and it is not an evidence of monotheism, because the
same worshiper will make the same extravagant addresses to
each of the gods in turn. Each god in turn is, as it were, sole
god. Regardless of strict propriety, ancient peoples the whole
world over came to attribute practically every power to
every god. Every god had become, so to speak, any god, so
that there gradually arose the idea of one god who was all
the gods, a kind of pantheistic monism. In Canaan this found
expression in the fact that the plural of "god," *ilāni* in the
Tell el-Amarna letters, *'ēlîm* in the Phoenician inscriptions,
and *'ĕlôhîm* in the Old Testament, came to designate the
totality of the gods, and so could mean "god" as well as
"gods," but all these plurals are instances of a common
Semitic idiom, the intensive plural or the plural of majesty,
and carry no deep theological implications whatever.

This movement toward monotheism was furthered by the
fact that different communities sometimes chanced to hit on

[37] So also G. A. Barton, *Journal of the American Oriental Society*, LV
(1935), 481.

[38] For the Vedic hymns see, e.g., E. W. Hopkins, *The Religions of
India* (1902), pp. 138 ff.; for the Egyptian see, e.g., T. E. Peet, in *Cambridge Ancient History*, II (1931), 206: " 'Sole god beside whom there is
none other' proves nothing, this being used quite impartially of various
deities in polytheistic Egypt."

the same god for their local deity or gave him the same name; e.g., in early Egypt Horus was the local god of several different nomes; among the Hittites different communities called their local god Teshub; and in Mesopotamia Ishtar was the local deity of various cities. It was furthered, too, by the fact that the minor gods of the pantheon, in order to share in the chief god's glory, came to be interpreted by the priests and theologians as forms or manifestations of the chief god. This was monotheism by syncretism, the only kind of monotheism that the Babylonians ever attained. It was henotheism, identical with the henotheism of India. As the city-state of Babylonia gradually extended its sway over other city-states, the gods of the conquered states became subservient to Marduk, the god of Babylon, until the establishment of the great Babylonian Empire by Hammurabi along much of the Fertile Crescent from the Persian Gulf to the far west made all the gods subservient to him and he reigned supreme over the pantheon, so much so that Marduk came eventually to be all the gods. The other gods came to be conceived of as but forms or manifestations of him, and this presently found expression in various religious texts, the most famous of which [39] reads as follows:

> Tu(?) is Marduk of planting;
> Lugal-a-ki-la(?) is Marduk of the deep;
> Ninurta is Marduk of might;
> Nergal is Marduk of war;
> Zababa is Marduk of battle;
> Enlil is Marduk of lordship and government;
> Nabu is Marduk of accounting;
> Sin is Marduk as luminary of the night;
> Shamash is Marduk of justice;

[39] Published in *Cuneiform Texts from Babylonian Tablets in the British Museum*, XXIV (1908), Pl. 50, No. 47406; discussed by T. Jacobsen, in *The Intellectual Adventure of Ancient Man* (1946), pp. 133 f.

Adad is Marduk of rain;
Tishpak is Marduk of armies;
Gal(?) is Marduk of strength(?);
Shuqamunu is Marduk of wickerwork.

In this text all the important gods, even foreign gods like Tishpak and Shuqamunu, are equated with Marduk, being regarded as Marduk functioning in different capacities, but this at best is only an approximation to monotheism,[40] and we have priesthoods of other gods making similar claims for their gods.[41]

In another text, a hymn to Ninurta found in the excavations at Ashur,[42] but ultimately of Babylonian origin, all the important deities are identified successively with the parts of the body of Ninurta; e.g., Shamash is his face, Enlil and Ninlil are his two eyes, Gula and Belit-ilani are the protecting goddesses of his two eyes, Ishtar of the Stars is his chin, Anu and Antum are his lips, Ea and Damkina are his ears—and so on throughout all the parts of his body. It is noteworthy that goddesses are included here, as they were not in the preceding list, which leads Albright to say that "this incorporation of all the gods and goddesses in one all-embracing deity is monotheistic to the extent that it eliminates all but one god from ultimate theological reality."[43] But does it? The text does not represent a denial of the individual deities listed so much as it attempts to weave them into a theological system. Not a single god is eliminated from the cultus, any

[40] G. F. Moore, *History of Religions*, I (1913), 242, calls it "a liturgical glorification of Marduk."
[41] See, e.g., R. W. Rogers, *Cuneiform Parallels to the Old Testament* (1912), pp. 190 ff.
[42] Published by E. Ebeling, *Keilschrifttexte aus Assur religiösen Inhalts*, II, 3 (1922), No. 102; translated by E. Ebeling, in *Altorientalische Texte*, ed. H. Gressmann (2nd ed., 1926), pp. 250 f.; discussed by Jacobsen, *op. cit.*, p. 133.
[43] *From the Stone Age to Christianity* (1940), p. 165.

more than Tanit was eliminated from the Carthaginian pantheon and cultus when she was called "the face of Baal." These texts are no more monotheistic than modern Hinduism, which makes the many Indian gods forms or manifestations of the one god Vishnu (so according to one sect) or of the one god Śiva (so according to the other sect). In fact, they are less monotheistic than that, because the movement in Babylonia was not nearly so thoroughgoing, and there is no evidence whatsoever that the local cults were absorbed into the state cult and lost their separate identity. The old gods were not dethroned; if they were changed at all, they were simply reinterpreted as manifestations of Marduk or some other god, but their separate cults remained. Hammurabi, for instance, paid chief homage to Marduk as god omnipotent, the state god of his empire, but that did not prevent him from worshiping other gods and building temples to them.[44] At no point in their history did the Babylonians or the Assyrians rise to the truly monotheistic conception of god that the Hebrews did, so that Hebrew monotheism could scarcely have been derived from them.

No reputable scholar of modern times, so far as I know, has argued that the early Egyptians were monotheists, although religion with them was no whit different from what it was with the early Semites or Sumerians or Babylonians, for whom monotheism has been claimed. Apparently the Egyptologists have been rather more rational in their interpretation of early religion than the Semitists. When the Egyptians first appear in the light of history, they are settled in city-states, or nomes, as the Greeks later called them. As elsewhere, each city-state or nome had its own particular god, but that of course did not exclude the wor-

---

[44] See, e.g., the Prologue and Epilogue to his Code, translated by the present writer, in *Ancient Near Eastern Texts*, ed. J. B. Pritchard (1950).

ship of other gods. As A. Wiedemann long ago said,[45] "The
nome god was simply regarded in general as the tutelary lord
who had the first claim upon the inhabitants in all specifically
important matters, and, above all, when their common interests were concerned." Amid the rivalry and conflict among
the nomes there gradually arose one in the Delta region of
sufficient strength to dominate the other nomes and make the
united state of Lower Egypt, with the sky-god Horus as
the national god. A similar union was achieved in Upper
Egypt, with Seth as the national god, and then, as Lower and
Upper Egypt came to be united into a single kingdom, Horus
was exalted to the position of national god of the united state.
A reflection of that exalted position is to be found in the fact
that in hieratic the falcon (the hieroglyph for Horus) on the
standard came to be the determinative for deity, exactly as in
Sumer the sign for the sky-god An became the determinative
for deity there. Amid the early dynasties there was much
political and religious rivalry, particularly between the priesthood of Rē, with its center at Heliopolis, and that of Ptah,
with its center at Memphis—a rivalry identical with that
which we have already noted in the case of the Hebrew
priesthoods.[46] By the end of the Fourth Dynasty and the
beginning of the Fifth the party supporting the sun-god Rē
attained the ascendancy and Rē displaced Horus as the
national god of Egypt, which position he held almost continuously throughout the rest of Egyptian history. Even
when a new city-state got control of Egypt, as it did in the
Middle Kingdom, and Thebes became the capital, Amun,
the god of Thebes, did not oust Rē, as Rē had previously ousted Horus, but instead he coalesced with him

[45] *Dictionary of the Bible*, ed. James Hastings, V (1904), 183a. Cf. also
G. Steindorff and K. C. Seele, *When Egypt Ruled the East* (1942), pp.
132 ff.
[46] See pp. 126 n., 133, 138, 146 above.

under the hyphenated title of Amon-Rē. To such a degree had the priesthood of Rē advanced the prestige of their god and to such a degree had the sun-god won his way into the hearts of the people that the priesthood of Amun realized that it was to their own and their god's advantage not to attempt to displace Rē by Amun, but to identify their god Amun with Rē so that Amun came to be regarded as simply another form of Rē. It was the same tendency that we have seen elsewhere, but in Egypt there was this difference: it was the conquering god and not the conquered that fused with the other, but after all it was a fusion in name only, because the two cults remained quite distinct and the two priesthoods long continued to be rivals of each other, with the Amun priesthood in the saddle and growing ever stronger as Thebes rose to new power with the expulsion of the Hyksos, with whom Seth had been the chief god. From this time onward we note an ever-increasing tendency to identify all the gods with Amon-Rē until in the end they had been pretty much absorbed into one god as the manifestations of that one god. This was henotheism after the order of Indian henotheism; it represented a strong tendency in the direction of monotheism, but it was not monotheism.

From the beginning the Egyptians, like other ancient peoples, had a great High God and in course of time they came to distinguish between God and god, as is manifest, for example, in the declaration of the deceased before the forty-two gods in Chapter 125 of the Book of the Dead: "I have not cursed God," in contrast with "I have not contemned the god of my city." There is also in the Wisdom Literature a concept of deity which so closely approximates the idea of God that some scholars would see in it an influence in the development of Hebrew monotheism, but the concept here is simply one that includes the totality of

the gods and is best translated "deity" rather than "God."[47]
The Egyptians were continually addressing their gods in
turn as god alone, beside whom there is no other, but there
is nothing of monotheism in this, as we have already
noted,[48] and scholars are now quite agreed on this, even
those who used to see in it an evidence of monotheism.[49]

If it had not been for Amenophis IV toward the end of
the Eighteenth Dynasty, Egypt apparently would not have
approached any nearer a thoroughgoing monotheism than
did Sumer, or Babylonia, or Assyria. However, the great
religious reform connected with Amenophis was in large
part simply the crystallization of previous tendencies toward
monotheism.[50] In fact, the movement seems to have come
to a head while Amenophis III was still alive and some
scholars are fully persuaded that he was more responsible
for the Aten religion than was his son. The crucial period
in the development of the cult was in the early years of the
reign of Amenophis IV and for most of these years his father
was evidently coregent with him and must have been
largely responsible for the policies adopted.[51] There is also

[47] see, e.g., A. Lods, *Revue d'histoire et de philosophie religieuses*, XIV
(1934), 197-204; *The Prophets and the Rise of Judaism* (Eng. trans., 1937),
pp. 74-76.
[48] See note 38 above.
[49] See, e.g., E. A. W. Budge, *The Book of the Dead, The Papyrus of
Ani* (1895), pp. cxxviii f., in contrast with *Tutānkhāmen* (1923), pp.
140 ff.
[50] See, e.g., K. Sethe, *Beiträge zur Geschichte Amenophis' IV* (1921);
A. W. Shorter, *An Introduction to Egyptian Religion* (1931), pp. 92 ff.
That Aten was addressed as god some considerable time before Amenophis
IV is clear from an inscription of his grandfather, Tuthmosis IV, published by A. W. Shorter, *Journal of Egyptian Archaeology*, XVII (1931),
23 ff.
[51] Cf. H. Frankfort and J. D. S. Pendlebury, *The City of Akhetaten*, II
(1933), 102-108; T. E. Peet, in *Kings and Queens of Ancient Egypt* (1924),
p. 88; S. R. K. Glanville, *Great Ones of Ancient Egypt* (1929), p. 122.
Note, e.g., the granite bowl discovered in Akhetaten inscribed with the

reason to believe that the Rē priesthood of Heliopolis may have given the religion some support as the one way left to them to undermine the growing power of the Amun priesthood of Thebes.[52] In fact, the movement itself was probably more political in its beginning than religious—an effort to liberate the Pharaoh from the autocratic power of the Amun priesthood, which was rapidly dominating the state. It was doubtless for this reason that the cult chose a name for its god that had not previously been a divine name, but merely a name for the physical sun disk in which the sun-god lived, the name "Aten."[53] The movement began as a reform, but with Amenophis IV it ended in a break with the past. The old magic spells disappeared and with them the old mortuary god Osiris, who had always meant so much to the Egyptians and had a place in all the old cults. The new religion as it finally developed permitted no image of Aten; instead his presence was symbolized by the sun disk, from which there extended a series of long diverging rays, each ending in a human hand which frequently held out the hieroglyphic sign for "life." The new god was not to be the sum total of all the gods nor the old national god under a new name. He was to be something more than the state god of Egypt; he was to be the one god of the whole world

---

later form of the name of the Aten, the name of Amenophis III, and the name of the city, Akhetaten; Frankfort and Pendlebury, op. cit., p. 102. This would seem to show that Akhetaten was founded before Amenophis III died and that he resided there in his later years. This is also the evidence of the stela published by F. Ll. Griffith, *Journal of Egyptian Archaeology*, XII (1926), 1 f., provided the stela was made during the lifetime of Amenophis and not after his death, as Griffith believes.

[52] That the relations between Amenophis IV and the Rē cult were not wholly unfriendly is evident from the fact that he gave names to his two youngest daughters in which Rē was an element and he himself continued to use the old royal title, "the son of Rē," even in his hymns to Aten; see E. A. W. Budge, *Tutānkhàmen* (1923), pp. 92, 116.

[53] See, e.g., Shorter, op. cit., p. 92.

beside whom there was really no other, a jealous, intolerant god. In token of this Amenophis changed his name to Akhenaten.[54] He broke with the powerful priesthood of Amun and the old religion, as his father had done only in part. He left the old capital and built for himself and his god a new capital which he called Akhetaten, "the horizon of Aten." He even went so far as to attempt to expunge the name of Amun everywhere from the monuments, and the names of other gods were sporadically obliterated by his more fanatical followers. The older Egyptologists have undoubtedly exaggerated Akhenaten's place in the development of monotheism, but we can probably agree with Peet[55] that what he aimed at was true monotheism, and yet it is probably not too much to say with Breasted[56] that he was the first monotheist in all history. He at least approximated it more closely than any other in the ancient East, and to him some scholars would credit the origin of Hebrew monotheism, claiming to find it in the religion of Moses.

Among critical scholars today there is none who claims monotheism for anyone earlier than Moses,[57] but there are some who do claim it for Moses, and of these W. F. Albright is unquestionably the most outstanding. His argument

[54] The meaning of this name is uncertain; perhaps "he who is beneficial to Aten"; so G. Steindorff and K. C. Seele, *When Egypt Ruled the East* (1942), p. 206.

[55] In *Cambridge Ancient History*, II (1931), 206. There is some ground for the belief that Akhenaten attempted a reconciliation with the Amun cult toward the end of his reign when Smenkhkare was coregent with him; see S. R. K. Glanville, in *Great Ones of Ancient Egypt* (1929), pp. 128 ff. In that case he could not have been much of a monotheist.

[56] In *Cambridge Ancient History*, II (1931), 127 f.; so also Shorter, *op. cit.*, p. 97.

[57] As a matter of fact, the Old Testament says explicitly that the early Hebrews were polytheists; see, e.g., Gen. 35:2 ff.; Josh. 24:2 f., 14; Judg. 3:6.

is a lengthy one,[58] but not at all convincing. In one place he says,[59] "The only time in the history of the ancient Near East when we find monotheism in the leading cultural centers, Egypt and Babylonia, is about the fourteenth century B.C.; it is also then that we find the closest approach to monotheism in Syria and Asia Minor. Since it is now an historical commonplace that we find similar ideas emerging simultaneously in different parts of a given cultural continuum, we should expect to find Israelite monotheism somehow emerging about that time"—viz., in the time of Moses, according to Albright. The argument is most unconvincing, and the statement can be challenged at a number of points. There was no great, onrushing movement toward monotheism in the Near East in the fourteenth century, such as Albright affirms. There is no evidence that Syria and Asia Minor were more monotheistic then than at any other period. The texts from Asia Minor do not show this, nor do the Ras Shamra texts, to which Albright apparently has reference. El may have been a great High God to the people of Ugarit (ancient Ras Shamra), but along with him were hosts of other deities, many of them little less important than he. We have already noted that the Babylonians and Assyrians never became real monotheists, and they were no more monotheistic in the fourteenth century than they were later. As a matter of fact they were less so, because the texts over the following centuries show an ever-growing

[58] See particularly *From the Stone Age to Christianity: Monotheism and the Historical Process* (1940). Albright's thesis has been submitted to a searching criticism by the present writer, *Journal of Biblical Literature*, LXI (1942), 21-43; *The Review of Religion*, IV (1940), 298-303; *Journal of the American Oriental Society*, LXI (1941), 64-66; cf. also M. Burrows, *Jewish Quarterly Review* (new series), XXXIII (1943), 474-478.

[59] *The American Scholar*, VII (1938), 186; so also in his *Archaeology of Palestine and the Bible* (1932), p. 163.

tendency to emphasize one god to the exclusion of the others (monolatry), or through the absorption of the others (henotheism),[60] so that the most monotheistic of the texts date considerably after the fourteenth century. The only real monotheist in the ancient Near East was Akhenaten of Egypt (and some scholars question this), and he had no great following. What following he got was obtained by force; his movement was as much political as religious, and he made so little impression upon his own people that his religion was stamped out as a vicious heresy immediately following his death after a brief reign of only seventeen years. Instead of helping the cause of monotheism Akhenaten killed it by bringing the Egyptian movement toward monotheism to a head too soon, by making too great a break with the old religion, by resorting to force to establish his religion, and by dying too soon, leaving no efficient successor to carry on his work. If Akhenaten was not able to convert his own people in his lifetime, it is surely unthinkable that he was able after his death to impress an alien like Moses, particularly when Moses lived, as Albright agrees, in the period of bitter reaction against Akhenaten.

However, even though Moses and his people were surrounded on every side by the most monotheistic of peoples, it would not follow at all that they would become monotheistic themselves, nor is there a necessary presumption to that effect. In contrast with the tiny flicker of monotheism which momentarily developed in Egypt in the time of Akhenaten is the dominating role of the resurrection idea throughout her whole history, and yet this idea, which had everything in favor of its adoption, made no impression what-

[60] The two terms, "monolatry" and "henotheism," are much confused by writers on religion and the present writer has been no exception. Max Müller was the inventor of the latter term and protested vigorously against its use in the sense of "monolatry."

soever on the Hebrews or any others of the ancient Near East. It is one of the enigmas of history that the Hebrews were so little affected by the religion of Egypt, when both history and archaeology show such intimate contacts between the two. Albright protests that "the history of religion in Israel was not a microcosmic reflection of the evolution of religion in world-history; it was just as homogeneous and as much an organic entity as the history of religion in Egypt, in Babylonia, or in ancient Rome,"[61] and yet he would derive Israel's monotheism from a hypothetical world movement instead of having it grow out of its own roots in Israel, in and out of its own environment, influenced no doubt by world thought, but largely independent of it—a monotheism that became the religion not of a single man or a few religionists, but of a whole people, and a monotheism that was strictly monotheistic, as the others, with the possible exception of Akhenaten's, were not. Albright protests against giving a unitarian definition to the word "monotheism," but the only acceptable use of the word is in its dictionary sense, and it is Albright and his kind, rather than his opponents, as he affirms, who are "highly misleading" when they read into a word a meaning that it cannot and should not bear.

We heartily endorse Albright's dictum that "the history of Yahwism in Israel, north and south, becomes unintelligible unless we accept the clear evidence of Israelite tradition";[62] but Israelite tradition nowhere says or indicates that Moses was a monotheist—not even in Albright's sense of the word. Since we have no autobiography of Moses, it is impossible to say with certainty what he did or did not believe. At best the Old Testament account can only be credited with

[61] *The American Scholar*, VII (1938), 187.
[62] *Ibid.*, p. 187.

general and not with detailed accuracy, and in that account the most explicit statement on the subject attributed to Moses is the first command in the Decalogue. There is no certainty of course that this command originated with Moses or that it was known in his day, but we can probably grant Albright's contention that it is in general accord with the movement that bears his name. However, the most that we can claim for Moses in it is monolatry. Neither here nor anywhere else does he deny the existence of gods other than Yahweh, nor does he assert the sole existence of Yahweh, and not having done that, he cannot be called a monotheist. Even Professor E. O. James, who is an anthropologist as well as an Old Testament scholar, with decided leanings toward the theory of primitive monotheism, has to acknowledge that the command asserts nothing more than monolatry and not pure monotheism,[63] and so conservative a churchman as the late Bishop Gore has to concede that it neither proves nor disproves either monolatry or monotheism.[64] The Lutheran Church is one of our most conservative denominations and yet one of its theological professors, Harold L. Creager, writes concerning the First Command in its official organ, *The Lutheran Church Quarterly*:[65] "In neither case [of two possible translations, "in addition to" and "in preference to"], of course, is there any teaching here of monotheism, but only of henotheism.[66] The possibility of worshipping other gods, either along with Jehovah or as entirely displacing him, is distinctly contemplated." Identical are the views of other leading conserva-

[63] In *A New Commentary on Holy Scripture,* ed. Charles Gore *et al.* (1928), p. 673*a*; cf. also S. L. Brown, *ibid.,* p. 84*a*.

[64] *Ibid.,* p. 84*a*, note.

[65] Vol. VII (1934), 279.

[66] Creager here uses "henotheism" when he should have used "monolatry."

tive scholars.[67] Albright translates the command as follows: "Thou shalt not prefer other gods to me."[68] This rendering, he asserts, agrees with the plain meaning of ʿal pānāi in several other passages; e.g., Gen. 16:12; 50:1; II Kings 13:14; Deut. 21:16. But in these passages the only one that can possibly have the meaning for which he argues is the last, and even here another possible rendering of the expression in question is "to the disadvantage of" and this has as good support as "in preference to." The expression is one that appears rather often in the Old Testament, but unfortunately with a great variety of meanings; e.g., "over," "in front of," "in the presence of," "on an equality with," "alongside of," "to the disadvantage of," "in preference to," "in addition to," "in defiance of," "during the lifetime of." In most occurrences the particular meaning intended is indicated with more or less certainty by the context, but in the case of the First Command the context is altogether too slight to indicate explicitly what meaning was intended. The whole command reads literally, "Since I, Yahweh, am your God who brought you out of the land of Egypt, out of a state of slavery, there must not be to you any other gods against my face," and no meaning that anyone has yet suggested for the last phrase indicates anything other than monolatry. Even if we follow Albright's rendering, the words can mean only that there are other gods beside Yahweh, but the Hebrews are to prefer none of these to him because it was he who showed himself to be their particular God by rescuing them from bondage in Egypt. Albright stands quite alone in his contention that there is any evidence here for monotheism.

[67] See, e.g., B. D. Eerdmans, *The Religion of Israel* (1947), pp. 27, 37; J. Hoschander, *The Priests and Prophets* (1938), pp. 39 ff.
[68] *From the Stone Age to Christianity* (1940), p. 331, n. 29.

Another statement attributed to Moses, but questionably so, is Deut. 6:4, which is usually translated, "Hear, O Israel, Yahweh our God, Yahweh is one," whatever that may mean. If it makes any sense at all, it seems to mean that there was only one Yahweh and not many, as there were of the Baals. According to the conservative Jewish scholar, Jacob Hoschander,[69] the words "express the Unity of the Lord as far as Israel was concerned, and do not imply the doctrine of an absolute Monotheism, which denies the very existence of all other gods." Against the popular rendering both grammar and syntax require the translation, "Hear, O Israel; Yahweh is our God, Yahweh alone,"[70] but even so there is again nothing to suggest anything more than monolatry. This is fully confirmed by other statements which the Old Testament attributes to Moses; e.g., Deut. 4:19: "Beware, when you lift your eyes to the heavens and see all the host of the heavens, the sun, the moon, and the stars, that you do not let yourself be allured into paying homage to them and serving them, whom Yahweh, your God, has allotted to all the peoples everywhere under the heavens." Albright tries to avoid the plain implications of this passage by affirming that it says only that the heavenly bodies have been assigned by Yahweh to all nations alike,[71] but he has to acknowledge that the usual interpretation is possible. It is surely the *only* possible one. From the early rabbinical commentators down to the present day the plain meaning of the passage has been taken to be that Yahweh allotted the gods to the various nations, and that is confirmed by the unequivocal terms of Deut. 29:25, which Albright completely ignores: "They [the Hebrews] went

[69] *Op. cit.*, p. 41.
[70] Cf. A. B. Ehrlich, *Randglossen zur hebräischen Bibel*, II (1909), 270.
[71] *Op. cit.*, p. 245.

and served alien gods and paid homage to them, gods of whom they had no experience and whom he [Yahweh] did not allot to them." In these two passages Yahweh is represented as a great High God assigning to the different peoples their deities,[72] but this is far removed from monotheism. Most polytheistic peoples have great High Gods; the Sumerians had two, An and Enlil, and likewise the people of Ugarit, El and Baal.

Nowhere in his writings does Albright mention the tradition that connects the bronze serpent of the wilderness with Moses. It is by no means certain that this tradition has any basis in fact,[73] but it is as well attested as other traditions connected with Moses that Albright accepts. The story (Num. 21:4b-9) belongs to the JE document and is further supported by the reference in II Kings 18:4. The striking fact about the story and the other stories connecting Moses with the serpent[74] is that they reflect as dynamistic a conception as any cited by Albright for the most primitive form of religion,[75] and that assuredly does not favor a monotheistic religion for Moses. Neither does the statement in II Kings 18:4 that the bronze serpent made by Moses was worshiped right down to the time of Hezekiah. If Moses was the monotheist that Albright makes him out to be, tradition would assuredly never have connected him with the bronze serpent.

In summarizing his arguments for the appearance of

---

[72] Cf. the first line of the Tilmun Myth of the Sumerians, quoted by T. Jacobsen, in *The Intellectual Adventure of Ancient Man* (1946), p. 159: "When you [the gods Enki and Ninhursaga] were dividing the virgin earth (with your fellow gods)."

[73] The story is usually interpreted as aetiological, but Albright himself has shown that the aetiological argument can easily be overdone; *op. cit.,* pp. 38 f., 209 f., 293, 316.

[74] See p. 132 above.

[75] *Op. cit.,* pp. 124 ff.

monotheism with Moses, Albright says,[76] "If the term 'monotheist' means one who teaches the existence of only one
God, the creator of everything, the source of justice, who
is equally powerful in Egypt, in the desert, and in Palestine,
who has no sexuality and no mythology, who is human in
form but cannot be seen by human eye and cannot be represented in any form—then the founder of Yahwism was certainly a monotheist." Of these several items only one or
two have any real bearing on the question of monotheism.
All the polytheistic peoples of the ancient Near East had
cosmic gods[77] and thought of their chief god as creator of
everything, equally powerful for his own people in all
lands, human in form, and rarely, if ever, seen by human
eye.[78] It is true that in the records as preserved to us Yahweh
has no sexuality and little or no mythology.[79] This is likewise true of the early Chinese gods and is accordingly no
evidence for monotheism. It is very debatable whether
Moses taught that Yahweh could not be represented in any
form.[80] He may have done so, but even that would not
make him a monotheist. Until the coming of Buddhism into
their land the Chinese had no images of their gods, nor did
the early Aryans of India, and there is reason to believe that
the Assyrians had no image of their chief god Ashur. This

[76] *Op. cit.*, p. 207.

[77] So also Albright, *op. cit.*, pp. 124 ff.; see especially p. 143: "The cosmic
gods of Mesopotamia were naïvely and unquestionably believed to rule
the entire world, each in his own designated sphere or function." Why
this conception of deity should be "naïve" in Mesopotamia, but monotheistic in Israel, is not clear.

[78] See also M. Burrows, *Jewish Quarterly Review* (new series) XXXIII
(1943), 477 f.

[79] There is good reason to believe that Yahweh had both originally and
that these features came to be suppressed in our records, leaving only
vestiges and reminiscences here and there, which are becoming more and
more apparent with our increasing knowledge of Canaanite mythology as
revealed in the Ras Shamra texts.

[80] See, e.g., W. A. Irwin, *The Crozer Quarterly*, XIX (1942), 292-301.

leaves only one item, the contention that Moses taught the existence of only one God, and there is no evidence of this. It is purely a subjective inference[81] without historical basis, because we do not have enough verifiable information about Moses to know exactly what he did teach.

Albright argues[82] that the stories of Moses, transmitted orally for four centuries or more before being put into fixed form, are at least as historically reliable as the accounts of Zoroaster and Gautama, which were transmitted much longer by oral tradition, and in this he is perfectly right. As a matter of fact, however, we have little dependable information about either Zoroaster or Gautama. Indeed we have so little about Zoroaster that we cannot even date him with any certainty, and the data for his religion are so obscure and so conflicting that no two specialists agree in their interpretation of the evidence, as Albright himself recognizes.[83] There was a time when we had complete and detailed biographies of every great religious leader: Moses,

[81] As proof that the reconstruction of the life and teachings of Moses must be very largely subjective, it is sufficient to note that Albright, op. cit., pp. 202, 205, attributes the prohibition of images and the Sabbath law to Moses, whereas R. H. Pfeiffer, Introduction to the Old Testament (1941), p. 231, says emphatically "It can positively be asserted that he [Moses] was concerned neither with images nor with the Sabbath."

[82] Op. cit., p. 192. Albright dates our earliest sources for the life of Moses, the documents J and E, between 925 and 750 B.C. He differs from current opinion in making the documents two recensions of a single original epic narrative, which view is a strange mixture of modern critical opinion and old-time orthodoxy because it rests on the old belief that the Hebrews were a unit from the beginning and remained a unit until the death of Solomon, going down into Egypt and coming out of Egypt as a single body, invading and conquering Palestine as a single body under a single head, and remaining a single body until the secession of Israel from Judah. Albright does not say explicitly that this is his view, but there are hints of it here and there and his interpretation of J and E requires it. It is a view of early Hebrew history that has long since been discarded by critical opinion and is true neither to the biblical nor to the extrabiblical records, as we have tried to show in Chapter I.

[83] Op. cit., p. 276.

Jesus, Zoroaster, Gautama, Laotze, Confucius, Muhammad, and the others. Modern historical criticism, however, has reduced these biographies to very small proportions, and that of Moses has shared the fate of all the others. If modern historians cannot agree (as they cannot) about the life and teachings of men so recent in history as Lincoln and Washington,[84] concerning whom we have such abundant contemporary records, and hence cannot speak with certainty about them, it is surely most presumptuous on our part to say that we can speak with certainty about Moses. There is much of truth in what Albright has to say about tradition,[85] but it can never have the accuracy that he accords it, and in this we are not hypercritical, as Albright asserts; we are simply realistic. Even contemporary written records are always biased and hence not absolutely accurate, as modern historians are discovering in the case of Lincoln and Washington and hosts of others. In the last analysis the best approach to an understanding of what Moses actually taught must be the psychological one. We do know something of the milieu in which Moses lived and we are pretty well agreed about that milieu—that toward the end of the second millennium B.C., somewhere in the southern Negeb, he gathered about himself a number of wandering tribes and consolidated them into a religious and political confederacy and thus laid the foundations for the nation and its religion. But monotheism to be monotheism must transcend national limitations; it must be supernational and

[84] Each succeeding biographer accuses his predecessors of inaccuracies. See, e.g., Bernard Knollenberg's severe indictment of earlier histories of Washington as inexcusably biased and quite unreliable as to both facts and interpretation in his *Washington and the Revolution: A Reappraisal* (1940). Cf. also S. G. Fisher, "The Legendary and Myth-making Process in Histories of the American Revolution," *Proceedings of the American Philosophical Society*, LI (1912), 53-76.
[85] *Op. cit.*, pp. 33 ff.

universal. The difference between Moses and Paul was that Paul was an internationalist. By no possible stretch of the imagination can it be said that the outlook of Moses was international. That would have been utterly impossible for him in the environment in which he found himself. He did the one thing that the situation demanded and the one thing to which his followers were in a position to respond. He organized them into a confederacy or amphictyony, and he made the god Yahweh the God of the amphictyony and in his name he made a covenant with the people that Yahweh was to be their confederate god and they were to be his people. This was monolatry and not monotheism. It was the selection of one god out of many for exclusive worship by a particular group as a group, and such theological particularism, as always, was the inevitable growth and accompaniment of a political particularism. As Principal W. C. Graham has well said,[86] "Modes of theological thought never establish themselves as disembodied ideologies. They develop along with and inside of corresponding institutional structures." This point cannot be too strongly emphasized, and yet Albright has completely ignored it. A world concept politically, a world view is the necessary prerequisite to the idea of a world god. In the time of Moses the Hebrews were just learning to take their first steps in the direction of nationalism and were still a long way off from internationalism. They could not possibly reach up to a world concept or a world god.[87] It may be said with considerable assurance that Moses sowed the seeds of monotheism, but the real fruitage did not come until centuries later because it could not. An idea cannot be born in a day; it comes only "in the fullness of time."

[86] *The American Scholar*, VII (1938), 423.
[87] See, e.g., J. Morgenstern, *Amos Studies*, I (1941), 407 ff., who shows that this concept with the Hebrews does not date earlier than Amos.

The new thing that came with Moses was not the worship of Yahweh to the exclusion of all other gods, but the united allegiance of a number of tribes to Yahweh as their confederate god, Yahweh being to the confederacy as a whole what the tribal god was to the tribe. This is monolatry and is quite like the monolatry that we noted in Babylonia, Assyria, Egypt, and elsewhere in the ancient world, and Albright is definitely wrong when he asserts that "no religion even remotely comparable to it appeared, and Mosaism remained absolutely unique."[88] Even by the time of David Yahweh had become nothing other than the national god of the united Hebrew state in exactly the same way as Rē became the national god of Egypt, or Marduk of Babylonia, or Ashur of Assyria, or Chemosh of Moab, or Milcom of Ammon, or a host of other gods that could be mentioned. Neither Moses nor David nor any other early Hebrew conceived of Yahweh as being the god of any other people than the Hebrew people. The early tribes had thought of Yahweh as the great High God, but now he was brought down from heaven to earth to become a state god, and so his people came to conceive of him as confined territorially to the land that they occupied.[89] Hence, when David took refuge with the Philistines to escape the jealous persecution of Saul, he felt that he could not take Yahweh with him into Philistine territory but must there worship the Philistine gods (I Sam. 26:19 f.). With greater imagination Naaman of Syria in the time of Elisha conceived the idea of taking two mule loads of Palestinian dirt with him so that he could take Yahweh with him to his homeland (II Kings 5:17).[90]

[88] *The Archaeology of Palestine and the Bible* (1932), pp. 168 f.
[89] Cf. J. Pedersen, *Israel: Its Life and Culture*, III-IV (1947), 650 ff.
[90] Note that in II Kings 5:15 Naaman is reported to have asserted that "there is no God in all the earth, except in Israel"—the kind of flattery that is so characteristic of the ancient world.

Even in the land that the Hebrews occupied Yahweh was by no manner of means the only god recognized and worshiped. He was the state god and for him Solomon built a state temple in Jerusalem, but that did not prevent Solomon from worshiping and building temples to other gods (see, e.g., I Kings 11:3 ff.). Over and over again the later prophets condemn their own and earlier generations for the worship of gods other than Yahweh. Hebrew personal names with god elements other than Yahweh prove beyond all question the worship of many gods, as likewise do the excavations in Palestine. The cult that became particularly popular, especially in the more agricultural north, was the fertility cult, and nothing is found in such abundance by the excavator as the paraphernalia of this cult. It was the most natural thing in the world that the Hebrews, as they settled on the land, should have adopted the gods of the land. In fact it was absolutely necessary that they should do so, if they were going to live on the land at all and enjoy its fruits. The gods of the land would have taken offense if they had been ignored, even as Yahweh did in a later period when the deportees brought into Israel by the Assyrians ignored him (II Kings 17:25 ff.). As gods of the land the local deities controlled its productivity. Yahweh, it was true, was the supreme god by right of conquest, but his department was the larger one of the state and not the affairs of ordinary, everyday agricultural and commercial life.[91] In a word, the early Hebrews, in so far as we are able to discover, were no more monotheistic than any other ancient people in the same stage of development.

And yet there was a force making for monotheism with the Hebrews that was not found elsewhere, and that was the new type of prophet that developed in the time of

[91] See note 34 above.

Samuel, the *nābî'* type as against the earlier seer, the *rô'ēh*
and *hôzēh*. The latter type was found all over the ancient
world, but the *nābî'* type in many of its aspects seems to
have been peculiar to the Hebrews.[92] It was characterized
by a spirit of intolerance, such as we find, for example, in
Deut. 11:16: "Take care lest you become so tolerant [*lit.*,
lest your mind become so open] that you turn aside and
serve other gods and pay homage to them."[93] This was an
attitude that was unusual in the ancient world and was
found elsewhere only with Akhenaten, and it did not come
from him to the Hebrews. It had its own independent origin,
growing out of its own peculiar circumstances, the oppression of the Hebrews by the Philistines. Like Muhammad,
the early Hebrew prophets, the *nĕbî'îm*, made the propaga-
tion of their religion and the establishment of the Hebrew
state an identical project, and so they went up and down
the land preaching the politico-religious crusade against the
Philistines that we have already noted.[94] So intensely devoted
were they to Yahweh and his cult that they resented the
intrusion of alien gods and stigmatized their worship as
disloyalty to Yahweh and the Hebrew nation. Thus they
became intolerant of all other cults, and that note of intolerance thus gained was never completely lost. When it was
on the point of disappearing with the professionalization
of prophecy, the rebirth of prophecy that came in the person of Elijah and his successors revived it with renewed
vigor. Prophecy with the Hebrews was a protest or protestant movement—a protest against alien cults and against the

[92] Of interest in this connection is the fact that *nābî'*, although derived
from a root not found in Hebrew, is itself found nowhere else except
in Arabic where it has been borrowed from Hebrew.

[93] For the justification of this translation see the present writer, *Journal
of Biblical Literature*, LXVII (1948), 235 f.

[94] See p. 157 above.

settled life on the land that was so largely responsible for the adoption of those cults. To the prophets and kindred orders, like the Nazirites and Rechabites, the olden time with its simple nomadic life and its simple monolatrous religion was the best time. Agricultural life, commercial ties, and treaty relations with other peoples[95] had brought in other cults to divide the religious loyalty of the people, and that they resented.

This would seem to give support to Albright's contention that the prophets were in no sense innovators, but simply revivers of the old Mosaic religion; that they had nothing whatever to do with initiating monotheism or anything else in Yahwism; they simply revived the old.[96] This surely is a low estimate of the prophets, but it is in line with Albright's view that Mosaism did not change in fundamentals from the time of Moses to the time of Christ.[97] What the prophets did, according to him, was to strip popular Yahwism of its Canaanite accretions and restore it to its pristine purity. He compares the work of the prophets to the Protestant Reformation in Christianity and the Wahhabi movement in Islam.[98] It is true that the Protestant reformers thought that they were restoring the original form of Christianity, even as 'Abd al-Wahhab thought that he was restoring the original religion of Muhammad, but every historian knows that neither the one nor the other did anything of the sort. They simply established what they *thought* was the original religion. It is true, as Albright notes,[99] that most of the nations of the Near East

---

[95] From the beginning the prophets were vigorously opposed to entangling alliances; see, e.g., in the later period, Hos. 5:13; 7:11; 8:8-10; 12:1; Is. 18:1 f.; 20:1-6; 30:1-5; 31:1 ff.

[96] *From the Stone Age to Christianity* (1940), pp. 86, 230 ff.

[97] *Op. cit.*, p. 309.

[98] *Op. cit.*, p. 86.

[99] *Op. cit.*, pp. 241 ff.

in the time of the later prophets were looking back with nostalgia to their more glorious past and were trying to revive it by imitating such things as the ancient script and language (which was nothing but sympathetic magic), but again we have to note that their efforts to recover the past were without success because of their deficient knowledge of the past. In a way the Book of Deuteronomy represents a similar effort on the part of the Hebrews; it may indeed have been "a conscious effort to recapture both the letter and the spirit of Mosaism which, the Deuteronomists believed, had been neglected or forgotten by the Israelites of the Monarchy," as Albright believes,[100] but even he hardly dares assert that they actually did recapture the letter and spirit of Mosaism, for he goes on to say that Deuteronomy clearly follows the *direction and development* already marked out by J and E, and a little later he speaks of the "cult of Yahweh as reconstructed for the Mosaic age by the Deuteronomic school." The Deuteronomists may have tried to recapture the original Mosaism, but after all it could only have been their idealized picture of the past that they produced. All peoples everywhere and in all times have idealized their past, and so did the Hebrew people. There is no question but what the prophets thought and professed that they were reviving the old religion,[101] but it was only their idealized reconstruction of that religion. This is apparent, among other things, from their claim that the ancient religion of Moses was without sacrificial rites of any kind (e.g., Amos 5:25; Is. 1:12; Jer. 7:21 ff.; Is. 43:23 f.). But one of the claims that Albright makes for Moses is that much of the sacrificial system must go back to him.[102] If the

[100] *Op. cit.*, p. 244.

[101] Cf. J. M. P. Smith, "The Conservatism of Early Prophecy," *American Journal of Theology*, XXIII (1919), 290-299.

[102] *Op. cit.*, pp. 192 f., 203 f.

prophets idealized the Mosaic religion with respect to its ritual, we have every reason to believe that they idealized it in other respects as well, and this is what scholars have long since maintained. More or less unconsciously the prophets read back into the past what they wanted for their own time, bolstering up their own ideas of what ought to be with the sanctity and authority that always belong to the past—a form of argument that is as old as man. Luther may possibly have thought that he was no innovator, but such he was, nevertheless, and so were the Hebrew prophets. Each made his contribution to the continuing stream of Hebrew religion and this stands out clearly as one reads the writings in chronological order. Indeed one cannot read Albright's own account of them, each in turn, without feeling the onward movement of the religion.

To the Hebrew prophets Yahweh was a jealous god who insisted upon having his people all to himself. As Elijah put it, if Yahweh was to be the people's god, they must follow him; if it was to be the Baal, then they should follow him: "How long will you go limping on two opposite contentions; if Yahweh is God, follow him, but if the Baal, follow him" (I Kings 18:21). The choice must be between the two; it could not include both, as was the case with other peoples. Yahweh was not like Marduk or Ashur or Rē or the usual run of ancient god, who was always ready to admit another cult along with his own so long as his own rights were not infringed. Even between Amun and Aten there was no great hostility until Akhenaten proceeded to displace Amun by Aten. With conquests and alliances and the adoption of new occupations the regular practice of the ancient world was to admit the gods of the conquered or allied states or the new occupations into their pantheon, but as subordinate gods to the state god, exactly as the conquered or allied states became subject states to their own; but the Hebrew prophets would brook no such admission. They insisted upon preserving the monolatry of the old nomadic days and would have one state god for the state, as previously the tribe for its simple life had had one tribal god. This was not monotheism, but an extension of earlier tribal monolatry to the state, and it reached its culmination finally in the revolution of Jehu, who not only made Yahweh the state god of Israel, but definitely attempted to suppress all the other cults, as related in II Kings 10. This account may not be true in all its details, but there is no question but that Jehu made a really serious attempt to stamp out the old Baal religion—a religious persecution that was unparalleled in the ancient world. After the eclipse of Yahwism in the time of Jeroboam I it was once again established as the official religion of the north, and the north was now independent of the south. For the first time in history we have here two distinct and independent, in fact two hostile, peoples worshiping one and the same god as state god, and in this a long step had been taken in the direction of making Yahweh an international and so a universal god,[103] and that further step was taken by the eighth-century prophets.

With other religions we noted a tendency to monotheism as the theologians came to interpret the various gods as simply forms or manifestations of the one chief god. It was monotheism by syncretism, if indeed it can be called monotheism at all. Strictly speaking it was not monotheism, because no effort was made to suppress any of the minor or local cults or priesthoods, or any of the local features of the cults. The several cults continued as always, with no change except

---

[103] Cf. J. M. P. Smith, "The Effect of the Disruption on the Hebrew Thought of God," *American Journal of Semitic Languages*, XXXII (1916), 261 ff. Smith, however, following the usual interpretation of Jeroboam I's revolt, predicates the phenomenon for the time of Jeroboam rather than for that of Jehu where it rightfully belongs.

the identification of the local god with the state god. The movement was pantheistic and henotheistic, but not reformatory. Not so was the propaganda of the Hebrew prophets. Thoroughgoing as Jehu's revolution had been, they were not satisfied with it, because he continued the cult of the golden calves, reinterpreting them simply as images of Yahweh. Here was syncretism somewhat after the order of the ancient world and the sort of thing that the common people could understand, because they had long since been giving their children names reflecting this syncretism, names like Baaliah (בעליה), "Baal is Yah," and Egelyo (עגליו), "The calf is Yaw."[104] But this was not acceptable to the later prophets and they condemned it, because it was to them simply the old bull cult under a new name; and because the images harked back to the old cults, they would have none of them and they came to condemn idolatry in all its forms and all the licentious practices that went with it. Hence, unlike Elisha, Hosea had no word of praise for Jehu, but condemnation only (1:4), and in 13:1 f. he says:

> Whenever Ephraim spoke there used to be awe;
> He was a prince in Israel.
> Then he incurred guilt through the Baal and died;
> And now they keep on sinning,
> In that they have made for themselves molten images
> Out of their silver, by their skill, idols,
> Wholly the work of craftsmen.
> "To such," they say, "sacrifice!"
> Men kissing calves!

And again in 8:5 ff.:

> Hateful is your calf, O Samaria;
> My anger blazes against them [i.e., its makers].

[104] This is the usual interpretation of the name, but M. Noth, *Die israelitischen Personennamen* (1928), pp. 150 ff., argues that the meaning is "Calf of Yaw."

> How long will they be incapable of innocence?
> For it is the creation of Israel,
> Since a craftsman made it,
> And it is not god.
> Verily, Samaria's calf
> Shall become splinters;
> For it was wind they sowed,
> And a whirlwind they shall reap.

Similar polemics are found in Hos. 4:17 f.; 12:12; 13:2; and Amos 4:4, and likewise in II Kings 20:29 ff., the prophetic writer of which approved of much that Jehu did, but condemned him for his preservation of the golden calves. To prevent the contamination of Yahwism by the idolatry and licentious rites of the local cults the prophets were led in time to oppose worship of any kind at the high places, because its inevitable effect upon the people was to produce a syncretism of the local cults with Yahwism, and that the prophets resisted. With might and main from the time of Amos onward they fought the practice, until eventually they obtained its absolute prohibition in the Book of Deuteronomy, and the Yahweh religion was centralized in one national sanctuary by Josiah, shorn of all heathen associations, or so it was supposed (II Kings 23:3-24:27).

Like the earlier prophets, Hosea saw that it was the agricultural life that had weaned the people away from Yahweh to the fertility cult of the bull-god, the Baal, but unlike them he saw the futility of preaching a god that was simply an austere desert god. If Yahweh was to be accepted, he must be presented as a god whom the people needed, a god to meet their requirements, in short a fertility-god.[105] So Hosea took over the idea of marriage with deity, which was such a

---

[105] Cf. the statement of one whose identity escapes me now: "Hosea had the genius to see how futile it was to preach an austere desert god to an agricultural people."

prominent feature of the popular religion, ethicized it, and gave a new interpretation of the old covenant idea, making it now a marriage rite with Yahweh. Since the agricultural life had led to the corruption of Baalism, he would wrench the people from the soil and return them to their earlier Bedouin life of the desert; then in the desert they would return to Yahweh as in the olden days, and Yahweh would once more betroth them to him and bring them back to their own land. The soil would again be tilled, bountiful harvests would result, and the people would learn at last that it was Yahweh and not the Baals who gave the grain and wine and oil: "And it shall come to pass on that day," it is the oracle of Yahweh, "that you will call me 'My husband,' and you will no longer call me 'My Baal.' For I will put away the names of the Baals from her [Israel's] mouth, and they shall no longer be invoked by their name" (Hos. 2:16 f.).[106] Thus Hosea disengaged the life of agriculture from the perils that threatened the religion and succeeded in making an alliance between civilization and the religion of Israel, and he succeeded also in commending Yahweh to his people, divorced from all licentious practices, idolatry, and magic rites. It was syncretism of a sort, more properly eclecticism. Hosea took the meat, but left the shell. He took what was vital in the popular cults, appropriated it for Yahweh, and surcharged it with spiritual meaning.

The establishment of Yahweh as the god of two distinct nations like Judah and Israel, and the recognition that he could use an alien people like the Assyrians as an instrument of punishment against his own people when they failed him, eventually led the prophets to see in Yahweh a god of the world, a god universal. So far as we can discover Amos was

---

[106] The same idea was taken up by the later prophets; see, e.g., Jer. 2:2; 3:1 ff.; Ez. 16:8 ff.; 23:4; Is. 54:5; 62:4 ff.; Mal. 2:14.

the first to regard Yahweh as the god of peoples other than the Hebrews, but he nowhere denies the existence of other gods nor does he say anywhere that Yahweh alone is god in the world. Neither does Hosea, nor Micah, nor First Isaiah, nor Zephaniah. More and more, however, the prophets were underrating the alien gods, and this despite the fact that as Assyria grew strong public opinion rated its gods higher and higher, until Ahaz was moved to introduce their worship on a small scale (II Kings 16:10 ff.), and Manasseh on a large scale (II Kings 21:1 ff.). To save Yahweh from the oblivion of his people the prophets had to liberate Yahweh from his people and make him the god of the world, who for his own beneficent purpose exalts, now this people, now that people, to the end that all may know him and obey him. To Isaiah, accordingly, the rival gods were but 'ĕlîlîm, worthless creatures, vain and unavailing (Is. 2:8, 18, 20; 10:10 f.; 19:1, 3; 31:7). This was theoretical monotheism, which very quickly blossomed into the practical, thoroughgoing monotheism of Jeremiah[107] and Second Isaiah, who declared in most emphatic terms that Yahweh alone was God and all the so-called gods had no real existence at all; they were merely figments of the imagination, the creation of man himself (see, e.g., Jer. 5:7; 10:2 ff.; 16:20; Is. 41:21 ff.; 44:9 ff.). This was monotheism of a kind that none among the neighboring nations ever attained, with the possible exception of Akhenaten of Egypt. But Hebrew monotheism was surely not derived from him. Similarity or even identity of ideas does not necessarily imply borrowing. Faced with similar problems under similar conditions, it is only natural that men should make similar responses, no matter what the age or what the

[107] The conservative Jewish scholar, Jacob Hoschander, is not fully persuaded that Jeremiah was a rigid monotheist, maintaining that Second Isaiah was the first real monotheist in history; *The Priests and Prophets* (1938), pp. 48 ff.

nationality. Hebrew monotheism grew up in its own way with the Hebrew prophets, in and out of its own environment, influenced no doubt by world thought, but largely independent of it. It was the crystallization of an earlier Hebrew movement, even as that of Akhenaten was of an earlier Egyptian movement, and there is nothing to indicate that the one grew out of the other.

It was not until the time of Jeremiah and Second Isaiah that a thoroughgoing monotheism was possible with the Hebrews. Imperialism was in the air, and "monotheism is but imperialism in religion."[108] There had been a succession of world empires—first the Assyrian, then the Babylonian, and now the Persian. Was there likewise a succession of World Gods? Or was there one World God directing the course of world history? It was left to Second Isaiah to answer this and he did so in no uncertain terms, particularly in chapters 41 to 48.[109] Over and over again he ridicules the idea that there can be more gods than one and for the first time in history we have a man preaching the religious solidarity of mankind, as much interested in the well-being of other peoples as in his own.[110] And yet the one god of the world is the Hebrew God Yahweh, but in Second Isaiah Yahweh loses in large part his earlier character as the national god of Israel and becomes instead the Universal God,[111] and in his effort to express that more adequately Second Isaiah often uses a term for deity that has no national connotation whatsoever, the pronoun הוא, literally "He," "the One who is"[112]

[108] J. H. Breasted, *The Development of Religion and Thought in Ancient Egypt* (1912), p. 315.

[109] See C. C. Torrey, *The Second Isaiah* (1928), pp. 67-76.

[110] See Torrey, *op. cit.*, pp. 111-134.

[111] Convincingly demonstrated by S. H. Blank, *Hebrew Union College Annual*, XV (1940), 1-46. Cf. also H. G. May, *Journal of Bible and Religion*, XVI (1948), 100-107.

[112] See J. Morgenstern, *Journal of Biblical Literature*, LXII (1943),

The Hebrew prophets began as champions of Yahweh. That led them to oppose all alien cults, and bit by bit that led them to the position that Yahweh alone was God. With them monolatry blossomed into monotheism, nationalism into universalism, and religion became a matter of the heart and of righteous living rather than mere ritualistic practice. With them developed a new interpretation of god, a new interpretation of man, and a new interpretation of religion. With them origins ceased and the fruitage of ages of intensest religious experience was given to mankind in those mighty oracles which still remain the wonder and admiration of the world.

269-281. Even though we discount the contentions of Blank and Morgenstern and make Second Isaiah "an essentially nationalistic prophet" with N. H. Snaith, in *Studies in Old Testament Prophecy*, ed. H. H. Rowley (1950), pp. 191 ff., it still leaves Second Isaiah with a monotheism not much different from our own, because the God of most moderns is a Muslim God, or a Christian God, or even a Catholic or a Protestant God; and two World Wars have shown us that with most peoples God is still a German God, or a French God, or an English God—scarcely a universal God, but one narrowly nationalistic.

SUBJECT INDEX

Aaronites, priests of the bull cult, 137, 140; rivals of the Levites, 126 n., 133, 147; reinstated by Jeroboam I, 137, 165 f.

Abraham (Abram), the first Hebrew, 1, 7, 17; date of, 14 f.

Ahab, as patron of Baalism, 168; relation to Yahwism, 169; conflict with Elijah, 170 ff.

Ahijah, relations with Jeroboam I, 163 ff.

Akhenaten (see Amenophis IV)

Amenophis IV (Akhenaten), religious reform of, 202 ff., 206, 207, 227

Amos, as prophet, 174 ff., 178 f., 224, 225 f.

Amphictyony (see Confederacy)

Amraphel, 14

Ancestor worship, with the Hebrews, 86 ff.

Animatism (see Naturism)

Animism, with the Hebrews, 87 ff.

ʿApiru, in relation to the Hebrews (Habiru), 11 ff., 15, 25, 31, 33 f., 35. See also Hebrews

Asher, tribe of, 30, 42, 111

Aten cult, 202 ff.

Baal (see Bull-god)

Baalism (see Bull cult)

Babylonian Code (see Hammurabi Code)

Benjamin, tribe of, 14, 43

Bethel, as god, 85, 166 n.

Biblical records, character of, 2 f., 22 ff., 27 f., 43 f., 82 f., 125 ff., 163 f.

Bilalama Code (see Eshnunna laws)

Book of the Covenant, 28, 37, 56, 58, 66, 69, 72

Bull cult, of northern origin, 136 ff., 161; eclipse under David, 136, 137, 147, 160; reinstated by Jeroboam I, 137, 160 ff., 166 ff.; influenced Yahwism, 136, 160, 171 f., 223. See also Aaronites

Bull-god, called Baal, 134 f., 224 f.; connected with the north, 134 ff., 138 ff.; connected with Aaron, 135 ff.; identical with Adad (Hadad), 141 f. See also Bull cult

Canaanites, in relation to the Hebrews, 22, 26

Canaanite law, influenced Hebrew law, 69 ff., 81

Confederacy (Amphictyony), of the northern tribes under Joshua, 25 ff., 140; of the southern tribes under Moses, 36, 38 ff., 116 f., 215

Dan, tribe of, 30, 42, 111

David, as patron of Yahwism, 117, 136, 146 f., 160, 168, 216

Deborah, Song to, 99, 143 f.

Decalogues, Hebrew, 37 f., 57 f.

Documentary hypothesis, ix f., xii, 56

Egyptian laws, 53

Elijah, as prophet, 170 ff., 174, 218, 221

Elisha, as prophet, 171 ff., 174, 223

Ephraim, tribe of, 43

Eshnunna laws (Bilalama Code), 52 f.

Exodus, date of, 15, 34 ff., 43 f.

Ezekiel, as prophet, 177, 178, 179

Fertility cult, 141 f., 164, 166 f., 217, 224. See also Bull cult

Gad, tribe of, 30, 43, 111

Gilead, tribe of, 43

AUTHOR INDEX

Albright, W. F., 5, 7, 11, 13, 14, 15, 18, 19, 23, 24, 25, 26, 29, 32, 39, 72, 73, 74, 84, 90, 99, 100, 103, 105, 106, 107, 109, 110, 115, 124, 129, 130, 133, 135, 141, 142, 143, 144, 150, 157, 161, 162, 165, 168, 183, 188, 198, 204, 205, 206, 207, 208, 209, 210, 211, 212, 214, 215, 219, 220
Alleman, H. C., 144
Alm, R. von der, 93
Alt, A., 5, 72
Astley, H. J. D., 190

Badawi, A. M., 12
Barton, G. A., 96, 111, 164, 196
Baudissin, Graf W. von, 133
Bauer, H., 97, 187
Bauer, Th., 103, 104
Bentzen, A., x, 37, 57, 58, 73, 75, 148, 154, 177, 181
Bergman, A., 23
Blank, S. H., 227, 228
Bloomfield, M., 189
Böhl, F. M. Th., 7
Boissier, A., 52
Bowman, R. A., 109
Breasted, J. H., 29, 35, 181, 204, 227
Briggs, C. A., 57
Brooks, B. A., 141
Brown, S. L., 208
Budde, K., 159
Budge, Sir E. A. W., 170, 202, 203
Burney, C. F., 23, 29, 42, 45, 111, 122, 126, 127, 131
Burrows, E., 192
Burrows, M., 16, 48, 65, 205, 212

Cazalles, H., 58
Chadwick, H. M., ix, 29
Chadwick, N. K., ix, 29
Charles, R. H., 126

Chiera, E., 8, 13
Contenau, G., 51
Cook, S. A., 83, 102, 127, 133, 146, 184, 190
Cornelius, F., 14
Creager, H. L., 157, 208
Cross, F. M., Jr., 144

Daiches, S., 104
Danell, G. A., 46
Daube, D., 57
David, M., 72, 81
Deimel, A., 49, 111, 122
Delitzsch, F., 102 f., 188
Dhorme, E., 7, 8, 14, 32, 86
Dillmann, A., 133
Dossin, G., 3, 14
Dougherty, R. P., 104
Driver, G. R., 50, 51, 103, 104, 106
Driver, S. R., 44, 126
Dussaud, R., 14, 73, 141, 186

Ebeling, E., 195, 198
Edelkoort, A. H., 179
Eerdmans, B. D., 209
Eilers, W., 55
Eissfeldt, O., 141
Ehrlich, A. B., 59, 80, 95, 100, 138, 165, 210
Engberg, R. M., 5, 99, 142, 143
Engnell, I., 179
Erman, A., 94, 120

Falkenstein, A., 192
Feiler, W., 4
Ferm, V., 73
Finegan, J., 48
Fisher, S. G., 214
Flack, E. E., 144
Flight, J. W., 113
Forrer, E., 9, 13
Fowler, W. W., 121

233

SCRIPTURE INDEX

237

I KINGS 1, 160; 1:9, 132; 4:5, 122; 6:1, 43; 8:5, 62 ff., 159; 8:11, 101; 9:25, 159; 9:26, 35; 11:1-10, 160; 11:3 ff., 217; 11:29-39, 163; 12:1, 47; 12:1 ff., 27; 12:17, 164; 12:26 ff., 161; 12:28, 162; 12:28-33, 137; 12:29, 166; 12:30, 165; 12:31, 165; 12:31 ff., 165; 12:32 f., 167; 12:33, 159, 166; 13:1 ff., 166; 13:7 f., 173; 13:33, 165; 13:33b, 165; 13:34, 165; 14:2 ff., 173; 14:7-16, 164; 14:9, 165; 14:14, 100; 14:15, 166; 14:16, 165; 14:20, 165; 15:26, 30, 34, 165; 16:26, 165; 16:31 ff., 169; 16:32 f., 168; 17:21, 88; 18:4, 169; 18:18, 170; 18:19, 142, 170, 171, 173; 18:21, 221; 18:26-29, 155; 18:26 ff., 172; 18:30 ff., 122; 18:46, 152; 19:10, 14, 170; 19:18, 169; 20:13, 22, 28, 35-42, 157; 20:38, 172; 20:41, 172; 21, 16; 22:5 ff., 175; 22:6, 173; 22:6, 10-12, 157; 22:11, 178; 22:14, 175; 22:52, 165

II KINGS 1:2, 168; 2:3, 173; 2:3, 5, 149; 2:5, 7, 15, 173; 2:9, 15 f., 152; 2:11, 91; 2:12, 157; 3:3, 165; 3:11-20, 157; 3:13, 171; 3:15, 152, 172; 4:38, 149, 173; 5:1 ff., 129; 5:15, 216; 5:16, 173; 5:17, 216; 5:26 f., 173; 6:1-7, 173; 6:8-23, 157; 8:7 ff., 129; 8:8 ff., 173; 8:18, 168; 9:11, 152; 10, 222; 10:15-28, 95; 10:18 ff., 171; 10:29 ff., 171; 10:29, 31, 165; 11:18, 169; 13:2, 6, 165; 13:14, 157, 209; 13:14-19, 157; 14:24, 165; 14:25, 157; 15:9, 18, 24, 28, 165; 16:10 ff., 226; 16:10-16, 161; 17:13, 150; 17:21 f., 165; 17:25 ff., 217; 18:4, 123, 132, 211; 20:29 ff., 224; 21:1 ff., 226; 22:12-15, 179; 23:3-24:27, 224; 23:4, 142; 23:5, 165; 23:15, 165, 166; 23:24, 90

I CHRONICLES 1-8, 30; 1:18 f., 7; 2 ff., 114; 2:55, 114; 5:1 f., 47; 6:3, 31; 6:13, 18, 160; 6:22 f., 37, 32 f.; 6:28, 33, 146; 9:22, 150; 18:10, 178; 21:9, 150; 23:13, 31; 25:1, 172; 25:5, 150; 26:4, 124; 26:16, 124; 26:28, 150; 29:29, 150

II CHRONICLES 9:29, 150; 11:13-16, 164; 11:14, 165; 11:15, 161; 12:15, 150; 13:8, 161; 13:9, 165; 16:7, 10, 150; 16:14, 89; 18:1, 168; 19:2, 150; 21:6, 168; 21:19, 89; 24:20, 152; 29:25, 30, 150; 33:18 f., 150; 35:15, 150

EZRA 2:38, 33; 3:12, 100; 4:8-6:18, 185; 7:12-26, 185; 8:33, 33

NEHEMIAH 2:13, 132; 5:5, 84; 8:17, 113; 9:38, 122

ESTHER 9:1, 110

JOB 36:26-37:13, 101; 38:1, 101; 40:6, 101; 41:25, 84

PSALMS 7:12 f., 101; 11:6, 101; 18:6-15, 101; 18:13 f., 101; 29, 143; 29:3-10, 101; 29:3 ff., 101; 36:6, 84; 48:7, 101; 50:3, 101; 65:5-13, 101; 68:4, 101; 68:7 f., 100; 68:7-17, 33, 101; 68:8, 100; 81:5, 113; 81:7, 101; 83:15, 101; 93:1-4, 101; 97:3-5, 101; 99:7, 101; 104:1-13, 32, 101; 104:7, 101; 104:24 f., 100; 106:28, 89; 118:14, 106; 132:2, 5, 140; 147:15-18, 101

PROVERBS 3:27, 84

ECCLESIASTES 3:21, 88; 4:2, 110; 12:7, 88

SONG OF SONGS 5:16, 100

ISAIAH 1:11-17, 180; 1:12, 220; 1:20, 151; 1:24, 140; 2:8, 18, 20, 226; 4:5, 101; 6, 178, 179; 6:2, 6, 132; 7:14, 106; 8:3, 106; 8:19, 89; 9:6, 106; 10:10 f., 226; 12:2, 106; 14:29, 132; 18:1 f., 219; 19:1, 101; 19:1, 3, 226; 20:1-6, 178, 219; 22:12, 90; 23:13, 100; 26:9, 88; 28:7, 180; 28:7 f., 172; 29:10, 150; 30:1-5, 150, 219; 30:6, 132; 30:10, 150; 30:30, 101; 31:1 ff., 219; 31:7,

GALLAUDET UNIVERSITY
933M49h 1960
Hebrew origin   gal,stx

3 2884 001 569 515